About This Course

This OER course has been designed for students in Julie Lindh's PSY200 – Lifespan Psychology course at Fulton-Montgomery Community College (SUNY).

Except where expressly noted otherwise, the contents of this course are based on materials published in the Open Course Library by Linda Overstreet. These materials were originally published freely under a Creative Commons Attribution
License (you can review the license at http://creativecommons.org/licenses/by/3.0/). The original version of the materials as published as Psyc 200 Lifespan Development may be accessed for free at http://opencourselibrary.org/econ-201/.

Julie Lindh

Module 1: Lifespan Psychology

Introduction to Life Span, Growth and Development

Learning Objectives

At the end of this lesson, you should be able to:

Explain the study of human development.
Define physical, cognitive, and psychosocial development.
Differentiate periods of human development.
Analyze your own location in the life span.
Judge the most and least preferable age groups with which to work.
Contrast social classes with respect to life chances.
Explain the meaning of social cohort.
Critique stage theory models of human development.
Define culture and ethnocentrism and describe ways that culture impacts development.
Explain the reasons scientific methods are more objective than personal knowledge.
Contrast qualitative and quantitative approaches to research.
Compare research methods noting the advantages and disadvantages of each.
Differentiate between independent and dependent variables.

Welcome to life span, growth and development. This is the study of how and why people change or remain the same over time.

This course is commonly referred to as the "womb to tomb" course because it is the story of our journeys from conception to death. Human development is the study of how we change over time. Although this course is often offered in psychology, this is a very interdisciplinary course. Psychologists, nutritionists, sociologists, anthropologists, educators, and health care professionals all contribute to our knowledge of the life span.

We will look at how we change physically over time from early development through aging and death. We examine cognitive change, or how our ability to think and remember changes over time. We look at how our concerns and psychological state is influenced by age and finally, how our social relationships change throughout life. There are several goals of those involved in this discipline:

1. **Describing change**-many of the studies we will examine simply involve the first step in investigation, which is description. Arnold Gesell's study on infant motor skills, for example.

2. **Explaining changes** is another goal. Theories provide explanations for why we change over time. For example, Erikson offers an explanation about why our two-year-old is temperamental.

Think about how you were 5, 10, or even 15 years ago. In what ways have you changed? In what ways have you remained the same? You have probably changed physically; perhaps you've grown taller and become heavier. But you may have also experienced changes in the way you think and solve problems. Cognitive change is noticeable when we compare how 6 year olds, 16 year olds, and 46 year olds think and reason, for example. Their thoughts about others and the world are probably quite different. Consider friendship for instance. The 6 year old may think that a friend is someone with whom you can play and have fun. A 16 year old may seek friends who can help them gain status or popularity. And the 46 year old may have acquaintances, but rely more on family members to do things with and confide in. You may have also experienced psychosocial change. This refers emotions and psychological concerns as well as social relationships. Psychologist Erik Erikson suggests that we struggle with issues of independence, trust, and intimacy at various points in our lives. (We will explore this thoroughly throughout the course.)

Our journeys through life are more than biological; they are shaped by culture, history, economic and political realities as much as they are influenced by physical change. This is a very interesting and practical course because it is about us and those with whom we live and work. One of the best ways to gain perspective on our own lives is to compare our experiences with that of others. By periodically making cross-cultural and historical comparisons and by presenting a variety of views on issues such as healthcare, aging, education, gender and family roles, I hope to give you many eyes with which to see your own development. This occurs frequently in the classroom as students from a variety of cultural backgrounds discuss their interpretations of developmental tasks and concerns. I hope to recreate this rich experience as much as possible in this text. So, for example, we will discuss current concerns about the nutrition of children in the United States (for a middle-class boy of 11 years who is 130 pounds overweight and suffering with Pediatric Type II diabetes) as well as malnutrition experienced by children in Ethiopia as a result of drought. Being self-conscious can enhance our ability to think critically about the systems we live in and open our eyes to new courses of action to benefit the quality of life. And knowing about other people and their circumstances can help us live and work with them more effectively. An appreciation of diversity enhances the social skills needed in nursing, education, or any other field.

New Assumptions and Understandings

I took my first graduate course in life span over 20 years ago. Much time was spent on the period of childhood, less on adolescence, and very little attention was given to adulthood. The message was clear: once you are 25, your development is essentially completed. Our academic knowledge of the life span has changed and although there is still less research on adulthood than on childhood, adulthood is gaining increasing attention. This is particularly true now that the large cohort known as the baby boomers are beginning to enter late adulthood. There is so much we need to find out about love, housing, health, nutrition, exercise, social, and emotional development with this large group. (Visit your local bookstore or search the internet and you will find many new titles in the self-help and psychology sections that address this population.)

I was also introduced to the theories of Freud, Erikson, and Piaget, the classic stage theorists whose models depict development as occurring in a series of predictable stages. Stage theories had a certain appeal to an American culture experiencing dramatic change in the early part of the 20th century. But that sense of security was not without its costs; those who did not develop in predictable ways were often thought of as delayed or abnormal. And Freudian interpretations of problems in childhood development, such as autism, held that such difficulties were in response to poor parenting. Imagine the despair experienced by mothers accused of causing their child's autism by being cold and unloving. It was not until the 1960s that more medical explanations of autism began to replace Freudian assumptions.

Freud and Piaget present a series of stages that essentially end during adolescence. For Freud, we enter the genital stage in which much of our motivation is focused on sex and reproduction and this stage continues through adulthood. Piaget's fourth stage, formal operational thought, begins in adolescence and continues through adulthood. Again, neither of these theories highlights developmental changes during adulthood. Erikson, however, presents eight developmental stages that encompass the entire lifespan. For that reason, Erikson is known as the "father" of developmental psychology and his psychosocial theory will form the foundation for much of our discussion of psychosocial development.

Today we are more aware of the variations in development and the impact that culture and the environment have on shaping our lives. We no longer assume that those who develop in predictable ways are normal and those who do not are abnormal. And the assumption that early childhood experiences dictate our future is also being called into question. Rather, we have come to appreciate that growth and change continues throughout life and experience continues to have an impact on who we are and how we relate to others. And we recognize that adulthood is a dynamic period of life marked by continued cognitive, social, and psychological development.

Who Studies Human Development?

Many academic disciplines contribute to the study of life span and this course is offered in some schools as psychology; in other schools it is taught under sociology or human development. This multidisciplinary course is made up of contributions from researchers in the areas of health care, anthropology, nutrition, child development, biology, gerontology, psychology, and sociology among others. Consequently, the stories provided are rich and well-rounded and the theories and findings can be part of a collaborative effort to understand human lives.

Many Contexts

People are best understood in context. What is meant by the word "context"? It means that we are influenced by when and where we live and our actions, beliefs, and values are a response to circumstances surrounding us. Sternberg describes a type of intelligence known as "contextual" intelligence as the ability to understand what is called for in a situation (Sternberg, 1996). The key here is to understand that behaviors, motivations, emotions, and choices are all part of a bigger picture. Our concerns are such because of who we are socially, where we live, and when we live; they are part of a social climate and set of realities that surround us. Our social locations include cohort, social class, gender, race, ethnicity, and age. Let's explore two of these: cohort and social class.

REFERENCES

Aries, P. (1962). Centuries of childhood. A social history of family life. New York: Vintage.

Davis, N. (1999). Youth crisis: Growing up in the high risk society. Westport, CN: Praeger.

Debt juggling. The new middle class addiction. (2005, March/April). The Sunday Times Review. Retrieved from www.timesonline.co.uk/article/o..2092-1551813.00.html

DeNavas-Walt, C., & Cleveland, R. W. (2002). Money income in the United States: 2001. Current population reports. (P60-218) (United States, U. S. Census Bureau). U. S. Government Printing Office.

Gilbert, D. (2003). The American class structure in an age of growing inequality. (6th ed.). Belmont, CA: Wadsworth.

Gilbert, D., & Kahl, J. A. (1998). The American class structure. (5th ed.). Belmont, CA: Wadsworth.

Glazer, B. G., & Strauss, A. L. (1967). The discovery of grounded theory: Strategies for qualitative research. New York: Aldine.

Kohn, M. L. (1977). Class and conformity: A study in values. (2nd ed.). Homewood, IL: Dorsey.

Mawathe, A. (2006, March/April). Period misery for Kenya schoolgirls. BBC News. Retrieved August 10, 2006, from http://news.bbc.co.uk/hi/africa/4816558.stm

Seccombe, K., & Warner, R. L. (2004). Marriages and families: Relationships in social context. Belmont, CA: Wadsworth.

Sternberg, R. J. (1996). Sucessful intelligence. New York: Simon and Shuster.

The secret life of the credit card. (2004). PBS: Public Broadcasting Service. Retrieved May 02, 2011, from http://www.pbs.org/cgi-registry/generic/trivia.cgi

Thornton, S. (2005, June/July). Karl Popper (Stanford Encyclopedia of Philosophy/Summer 2005 Edition). Stanford Encyclopedia of Philosophy. Retrieved May 02, 2011, from http://plato.stanford.edu/archives/sum2005/entries/popper

United States, U. S. Census Bureau, Housing and Household Economics Statistics Division. (2005). Poverty Thresholds 2005. Retrieved August 10, 2006, from http://www.census.gov/hhes/www/poverty/threshld/thresh05.html

Weitz, R. (2007). The sociology of health, illness, and health care: A critical approach, (4th ed.). Belmont, CA: Thomson.

CC licensed content, Shared previously

- Psyc 200 Lifespan Psychology. **Authored by**: Laura Overstreet. **Located at**: http://opencourselibrary.org/econ-201/. **License**: *CC BY: Attribution*
- Family picture. **Authored by**: Wazzle. **Provided by**: Wikimedia. **Located at**: https://commons.wikimedia.org/wiki/File:African_Family.jpg. **License**: *CC BY: Attribution*

The Cohort Effect

One important context that is sometimes mistaken for age is the cohort effect. A cohort is a group of people who are born at roughly the same period in a particular society. Cohorts share histories and contexts for living. Members of a cohort have experienced the same historic events and cultural climates which have an impact on the values, priorities, and goals that may guide their lives.

Boys collecting old tires for rubber during WWII.

Consider a young boy's concerns as he grows up in the United States during World War II. What his family buys is limited by their small budget and by a governmental program set up to ration food and other materials that are in short supply because of the war. He is eager rather than resentful about being thrifty and sees his actions as meaningful contributions to the good of others. As he grows up and has a family of his own, he is motivated by images of success tied to his past experience: a successful man is one who can provide for his family financially, who has a wife who stays at home and cares for the children, and children who are respectful but enjoy the luxury of days filled with school and play without having to consider the burdens of society's struggles. He marries soon after completing high school, has four children, works hard to support his family and is able to do so during the prosperous postwar economics of the 1950s in America. But economic conditions change in the mid-1960s and through the 1970s. His wife begins to work to help the family financially and to overcome her boredom with being a stay-at-home mother. The children are teenagers in a very different social climate: one of social unrest, liberation, and challenging the status quo. They are not sheltered from the concerns of society; they see television broadcasts in their own living room of the war in Vietnam and they fear the draft. And they are part of a middle-class youth culture that is very visible and vocal. His employment as an engineer eventually becomes difficult as a result of downsizing in the defense industry. His marriage of 25 years ends in divorce. This is not a unique personal history, rather it is a story shared by many members of his cohort. Historic contexts shape our life choices and motivations as well as our eventual assessments of success or failure during the course of our existence.

Consider your cohort. Can you identify it? Does it have a name and if so, what does the name imply? To what extent does your cohort shape your values, thoughts, and aspirations? (Some cohort labels popularized in the media for generations in the United States include Baby Boomers, Generation X, and Generation M.)

Socioeconomic Status

Another context that influences our lives is our social standing, socioeconomic status, or social class. Socioeconomic status is a way to identify families and households based on their shared levels of education, income, and occupation. While there is certainly individual variation, members of a social class tend to share similar lifestyles, patterns of consumption, parenting styles, stressors, religious preferences, and other aspects of daily life. (Consider, for example, some terms that have been used in marketing to refer to different consumer groups: the "truck and trailer" or the "pool and poodle" group referring to working class and upper middle-class groups.) All of us born into a class system or are socially located and may move up or down depending on a combination of both socially and individually created limits and opportunities. Below is a model of the class system identified in the United States (Gilbert 2003; Gilbert and Kahl, 1998), a description of these social classes, and a partial listing of the impact that social class can have on individual and family life (Seccombe and Warner, 2004).

Model of Social Class Based on Socioeconomic Status

Upper Class: This group makes up about 1 percent of the population in the United States. They own substantial wealth and after-tax annual family income of between $200,000 to $750,000 (DeNavas-Walt and Cleveland, 2002). The upper class is subdivided into "upper-upper" and "lower-upper" categories based on how money and wealth was acquired. The "upper-upper class" (0.5%) has money from investments or inheritance and tend to be stewards of the family fortune. This "old money" brings a sense of polish and sophistication now shared by those with "new money". The newly rich (0.5%) have made their fortunes as personalities in sports and media or as entrepreneurs. Members of the newly rich tend to flaunt their wealth; a practice looked upon with disdain by old money. One of my former students reported her experience as a flight attendant working first class on a trip from New York to Los Angeles. One of her passengers had a name that would be familiar to many Americans as a family with old money. Seated several rows behind him was a couple from the newly rich and she wore a long fur coat, they became drunk on champagne and were quite loud during the flights. The plane had landed, and as the flight attendant was helping her upper-upper class guest on with his coat and he looked over his shoulder at the couple and sneered, "New money." (So consider this: if you ever win the lottery, you may risk being shunned by "old money"!)

Upper Middle Class: About 14 percent of the population in the United States is considered upper middle class. Income levels are more often between $100,000 and $200,000 annually and hold professional degrees that involve education beyond a four-year bachelor's degree. One of the distinctions made between the middle class overall and members of the working class is that members of the middle class have occupations in which they are paid for their education and expertise. These white-collar workers (a term that originally referred to the distinction between what office workers wore to work as opposed to factory workers designated as "blue collar" workers) hold professional positions such as physicians or attorneys and as professionals enjoy a good deal of freedom and control over their occupations. They determine the regulations of their work through professional organizations (such as the American Medical Association). Having a sense of autonomy or control is a key factor in experiencing job satisfaction and personal happiness and ultimately health and well-being (Weitz, 2007).

Middle Class: Another 30 percent of the population is considered middle class. These individuals work in lower-paying, less autonomous white-collar jobs such as teaching and nursing or as lower-level managers. Members of the middle class may hold 2 or 4 year degrees, but often from less prestigious, state-supported schools. Their income typically ranges between $25,000 and $75,000 annually. They own less property and have less discretionary income than members of the upper-middle and upper class and yet they may share the values and standards held by the upper-middle class. Yet, acquiring larger homes, newer vehicles, and pursing travel, paying for health care and dental expenses often means taking on substantial debt. This problem is not unique to the United States, however. Consider this excerpt from a British newspaper describing today's "impoverished professionals" in which a couple goes to dinner before a movie and realizes that they have no cash. So out come the 9 credit cards.

> I've brought all the cards . . .trouble is, I can't remember which ones are up to their limit . . .Go to a cash machine? Forget it. Both our current accounts have been frozen. Welcome to the world of middle-class debt . . . On paper, my husband and I are what is known in polite parlance as "comfortably off". In reality, we have no money. Anything that comes in goes immediately on debt repayment . . . That and paying the nanny so we can both go out to work and earn more money for more debt repayment. An Impoverished Professional, I call myself. And there are plenty of us out there.

The average amount of credit card debt in American households is $8,000 and out of 144 million Americans who carry an "all purpose" credit card, only 55 million pay their entire balance off each month. The industry refers to these people as "deadbeats" and prefers the almost 90 million customers who extend their payment over months. These "revolvers" create nearly $30 billion in profits for the industry. (Frontline, 2004). Carrying debt can be extremely stressful and have a negative effect on health and social well-being. The consequences of such debt are still being explored.

The Working Class: Thirty percent of Americans are considered members of the working class. The working class is comprised of those working in occupations such as retail, clerical or factory jobs. Their jobs are typically routine and more heavily supervised than those of the middle class and require less formal education than do white-collar jobs. Members of the working class are subject to plant closings, lower pay, and more frequent lay-offs, and may rely on fewer workers contributing to the family income. Fewer earners and less job stability impacts not only family income, it also impacts the likelihood of having adequate health care. Being employed does not insure adequate healthcare; in fact, sixty-nine percent of the 45 million Americans who lack any medical insurance live in households where there is at least one full-time employee (Kaiser Commission on Medicaid and the Uninsured, 2004). Americans who are self-employed or working in companies with fewer than 200 employees are less likely to have health insurance benefits than those who work in companies with 200 or more employees (Weitz, 2007). And the cost of obtaining even minimal health insurance as an individual is often prohibitive.

Social class differences go beyond financial concerns, however. In a classic study on parenting styles and social class, Melvin Kohn (1977) found that working class parents emphasized obedience, honesty, and conformity in their children while middle-class parents valued independence, initiative, and self-reliance. These differences are attributed to the expectations made of parents as workers; blue-collar workers are rewarded for conformity while white-collar workers are rewarded for initiative.

The Working Poor: Twenty percent of Americans are categorized as the working poor. These people live near the poverty level and hold seasonal or temporary jobs as unskilled laborers. This includes migrant farm workers, temporary employees in service industries such as restaurants or in retail typically for minimum wage. The poor and working poor experience many of the same problems that can have an impact on development. We will examine this list after describing the next social class.

The Underclass: Approximately five percent of Americans are part of the underclass described as temporary workers, part-time workers, those who are chronically unemployed or underemployed (Gilbert, 2003). They may receive some governmental assistance and tend to be looked down upon by other members of society. Since 2008, we have seen national unemployment rates in the United States hovering around 10 percent due to changes in the economy and being unemployed is less stigmatized but still very stressful. Many of the underclass are children or are disabled. It is estimated that there are about 3.5 million homeless people in the United States and 1.5 of them are children (Urban Institute, 2000).

Application

Find out more about homelessness at www.nationalhomeless.org. Life on the streets can be extremely dangerous involving addiction, deceit, violence, sexual assault, and prostitution or "survival sex" which refers to exchanging food for shelter (Davis, 1999).

Other Consequences of Poverty: Poverty level is an income amount established by the Social Security Administration that is based on a formula called the "thrifty food plan" that allows one-third of income for food. Those living at or near poverty level may find it extremely difficult to sustain a household with this amount of income. Buying the least expensive, most filling foods typically means buying foods high in fat, starch and sugar. Living in poorer housing with the fear of eviction or poor plumbing and disruptive neighbors can also be stressful.

Poverty is associated with poorer health and a lower life expectancy due to poorer diet, less healthcare, greater stress, working in more dangerous occupations, higher infant mortality rates, poorer prenatal care, greater iron deficiencies, greater difficulty in school, and many other problems. Members of the middle class may fear losing status, but the poor may have greater concerns over losing housing. And while those in the middle class are more likely to use shopping or travel as a way to cope with stressors, the poor are more likely to eat or smoke in response to stress (Seccombe and Warner, 2004).

Examples

- Use THIS TOOL to calculate your social class position based on four commonly used indicators of socioeconomic status in the United States:
- Explore many other chances and choices in life that are impacted by social class by clicking HERE and reviewing the stories given on the left of the screen.

Culture

Culture is often referred to as a blueprint or guideline shared by a group of people that specifies how to live. It includes ideas about what is right and wrong, what to strive for, what to eat, how to speak, what is valued, as well as what kinds of emotions are called for in certain situations. Culture teaches us how to live in a society and allows us to advance because each new generation can benefit from the solutions found and passed down from previous generations.

Culture is learned from parents, schools, churches, media, friends and others throughout a lifetime. The kinds of traditions and values that evolve in a particular culture serve to help members function in their own society and to value their own society. We tend to believe that our own culture's practices and expectations are the right ones. (This belief that our own culture is superior is called **ethnocentrism** and is a normal by-product of growing up in a culture. It becomes a roadblock, however, when it inhibits understanding of cultural practices from other societies.) Cultural relativity is an appreciation for cultural differences and the understanding that cultural practices are best understood from the standpoint of that particular culture.

Culture is an extremely important context for human development and understanding development requires being able to identify which features of development are culturally based. This understanding is somewhat new and still being explored. So much of what developmental theorists have described in the past has been culturally bound and difficult to apply to various cultural contexts. The reader should keep this in mind and realize that there is still much that is unknown when comparing development across cultures. (For example, consider Erikson's assumption that teenagers struggle with identity assumes that all teenagers live in a society in which they have many options and must make an individual choice about their future. In many parts of the world, one's identity is determined by family status or society's dictates. In other words, there is no choice to make.)

Even the most biological of events can be viewed in cultural contexts that vary extremely. Consider two very different cultural responses to menstruation in young girls. In the United States, girls in public school often receive information on menstruation in around 5th grade. The extent to which they are also taught about sexual intercourse, reproduction, or sexually transmitted infections depends on the policy of the school district guided by state and local community standards and sentiments. But menstruation is addressed and girls receive information and a kit containing feminine hygiene products, brochures, and other items. For example, menstruation is interpreted as an event that can affect the mood of a young girl and temporarily render her difficult, hostile, or simply hard to be around. But, she is encouraged to have a "happy" period with this product and is also encouraged to wish her friends a happy period as well through a product-sponsored website (www.beinggirl.com/happy).

Kenyan boys and girls performing a traditional dance.

Contrast this with the concern that a lack of sanitary "towels" or feminine napkins causes many girls across Africa to miss more than a month of school each year during menstruation. Education is essential in these countries for moving ahead and the lack of sanitary towels places these girls at a tremendous educational disadvantage. The one-dollar price tag on towels is prohibitive in countries such as Kenya where most families earn about 54 cents per day. The lack of towels also results in unsanitary practices such as the use of blankets or old cloths to manage the menstrual flow. In some parts of Africa, reusable or washable sanitary towels are used, but in countries such as Kenya where there is little water, this would not be a solution. And in instances where towels were donated and given out without educating girls on how to use them, girls have folded them up and used them as tampons, a practice that can lead to serious infection (Mawathe, 2006). (Find out more about this at the Girl Child Network at http://www.girlchildnetwork.org/sanitary-towels-campaign-programme.html).

CC licensed content, Shared previously

- Psyc 200 Lifespan Psychology. **Authored by**: Laura Overstreet. **Located at**: http://opencourselibrary.org/econ-201/. **License**: *CC BY: Attribution*

Periods of Development

Think about the life span and make a list of what you would consider the periods of development. How many stages are on your list? Perhaps you have three: childhood, adulthood, and old age. Or maybe four: infancy, childhood, adolescence, and adulthood. Developmentalists break the life span into nine stages as follows:

- Prenatal Development
- Infancy and Toddlerhood
- Early Childhood
- Middle Childhood
- Adolescence
- Early Adulthood
- Middle Adulthood
- Late Adulthood
- Death and Dying

This list reflects unique aspects of the various stages of childhood and adulthood that will be explored in this book. So while both an 8 month old and an 8 year old are considered children, they have very different motor abilities, social relationships, and cognitive skills. Their nutritional needs are different and their primary psychological concerns are also distinctive. The same is true of an 18 year old and an 80 year old, both considered adults. We will discover the distinctions between being 28 or 48 as well. But first, here is a brief overview of the stages.

Prenatal Development

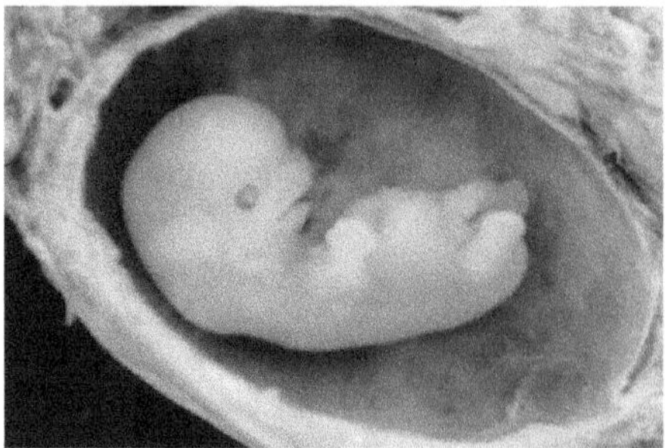

Conception occurs and development begins. All of the major structures of the body are forming and the health of the mother is of primary concern. Understanding nutrition, teratogens (or environmental factors that can lead to birth defects), and labor and delivery are primary concerns.

Infancy and Toddlerhood

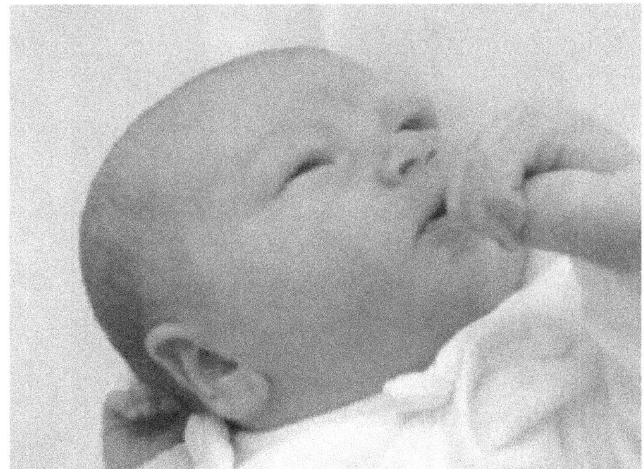

Newborn photo courtesy Fenja2

The first year and a half to two years of life are ones of dramatic growth and change. A newborn, with a keen sense of hearing but very poor vision is transformed into a walking, talking toddler within a relatively short period of time. Caregivers are also transformed from someone who manages feeding and sleep schedules to a constantly moving guide and safety inspector for a mobile, energetic child.

Early Childhood

Photo Courtesy Walter de Maria

Early childhood is also referred to as the preschool years consisting of the years which follow toddlerhood and precede formal schooling. As a three to five-year-old, the child is busy learning language, is gaining a sense of self and greater independence, and is beginning to learn the workings of the physical world. This knowledge does not come quickly, however, and preschoolers may have initially have interesting conceptions of size, time, space and distance such as fearing that they may go down the drain if they sit at the front of the bathtub or by demonstrating how long something will take by holding out their two index fingers several inches apart. A toddler's fierce determination to do something may give way to a four-year-old's sense of guilt for doing something that brings the disapproval of others.

Middle Childhood

Photo Courtesy Pink Sip

The ages of six through eleven comprise middle childhood and much of what children experience at this age is connected to their involvement in the early grades of school. Now the world becomes one of learning and testing new academic skills and by assessing one's abilities and accomplishments by making comparisons between self and others. Schools compare students and make these comparisons public through team sports, test scores, and other forms of recognition. Growth rates slow down and children are able to refine their motor skills at this point in life. And children begin to learn about social relationships beyond the family through interaction with friends and fellow students.

Adolescence

Photo Courtesy Overstreet

Adolescence is a period of dramatic physical change marked by an overall physical growth spurt and sexual maturation, known as puberty. It is also a time of cognitive change as the adolescent begins to think of new possibilities and to consider abstract concepts such as love, fear, and freedom. Ironically, adolescents have a sense of invincibility that puts them at greater risk of dying from accidents or contracting sexually transmitted infections that can have lifelong consequences.

Early Adulthood

Photo Courtesy Josh Gray

The twenties and thirties are often thought of as early adulthood. (Students who are in their mid 30s tend to love to hear that they are a young adult!). It is a time when we are at our physiological peak but are most at risk for involvement in violent crimes and substance abuse. It is a time of focusing on the future and putting a lot of energy into making choices that will help one earn the status of a full adult in the eyes of others. Love and work are primary concerns at this stage of life.

Middle Adulthood

The late thirties through the mid-sixties is referred to as middle adulthood. This is a period in which aging, that began earlier, becomes more noticeable and a period at which many people are at their peak of productivity in love and work. It may be a period of gaining expertise in certain fields and being able to understand problems and find solutions with greater efficiency than before. It can also be a time of becoming more realistic about possibilities in life previously considered; of recognizing the difference between what is possible and what is likely. This is also the age group hardest hit by the AIDS epidemic in Africa resulting in a substantial decrease in the number of workers in those economies (Weitz, 2007).

Late Adulthood

Photo Courtesy Overstreet

This period of the life span has increased in the last 100 years, particularly in industrialized countries. Late adulthood is sometimes subdivided into two or three categories such as the "young old" and "old old" or the "young old", "old old", and "oldest old". We will follow the former categorization and make the distinction between the "young old" who are people between 65 and 79 and the "old old" or those who are 80 and older. One of the primary differences between these groups is that the young old are very similar to midlife adults; still working, still relatively healthy, and still interested in being productive and active. The "old old" remain productive and active and the majority continues to live independently, but risks of the diseases of old age such as arteriosclerosis, cancer, and cerebral vascular disease increases substantially for this age group. Issues of housing, healthcare, and extending active life expectancy are only a few of the topics of concern for this age group. A better way to appreciate the diversity of people in late adulthood is to go beyond chronological age and examine whether a person is experiencing optimal aging (like the gentleman pictured above who is in very good health for his age and continues to have an active, stimulating life), normal aging (in which the changes are similar to most of those of the same age), or impaired aging (referring to someone who has more physical challenge and disease than others of the same age).

Death and Dying

This topic is seldom given the amount of coverage it deserves. Of course, there is a certain discomfort in thinking about death but there is also a certain confidence and acceptance that can come from studying death and dying. We will be examining the physical, psychological and social aspects of death, exploring grief or bereavement, and addressing ways in which helping professionals work in death and dying. And we will discuss cultural variations in mourning, burial, and grief.

CC licensed content, Shared previously

- Embryo at 8 weeks. **Located at**: https://commons.wikimedia.org/wiki/File:Human_Embryo_-_Approximately_8_weeks_estimated_gestational_age.jpg. **License**: *CC BY: Attribution*
- Psyc 200 Lifespan Psychology. **Authored by**: Laura Overstreet. **Located at**: http://opencourselibrary.org/econ-201/. **License**: *CC BY: Attribution*

Research Methods

How do we know what we know?

An important part of learning any science is having a basic knowledge of the techniques used in gathering information. The hallmark of scientific investigation is that of following a set of procedures designed to keep questioning or skepticism alive while describing, explaining, or testing any phenomenon. Not long ago a friend said to me that he did not trust academicians or researchers because they always seem to change their story. That, however, is exactly what science is all about; it involves continuously renewing our understanding of the subjects in question and an ongoing investigation of how and why events occur. Science is a vehicle for going on a never-ending journey. In the area of development, we have seen changes in recommendations for nutrition, in explanations of psychological states as people age, and in parenting advice. So think of learning about human development as a lifelong endeavor.

Personal Knowledge

How do we know what we know? Take a moment to write down two things that you know about childhood...Okay. Now, how do you know? Chances are you know these things based on your own history (experiential reality) or based on what others have told you or cultural ideas (agreement reality) (Seccombe and Warner, 2004). There are several problems with personal inquiry. Read the following sentence aloud:

> Paris in the
> the spring

Are you sure that is what it said? Read it again:

> Paris in the
> the spring

If you read it differently the second time (adding the second "the") you just experienced one of the problems with personal inquiry; that is, the tendency to see what we believe. Our assumptions very often guide our perceptions, consequently, when we believe something, we tend to see it even if it is not there. This problem may just be a result of cognitive 'blinders' or it may be part of a more conscious attempt to support our own views. Confirmation bias is the tendency to look for evidence that we are right and in so doing, we ignore contradictory evidence. Popper suggests that the distinction between that which is scientific and that which is unscientific is that science is falsifiable; scientific inquiry involves attempts to reject or refute a theory or set of assumptions (Thornton, 2005). Theory that cannot be falsified is not scientific. And much of what we do in personal inquiry involves drawing conclusions based on what we have personally experienced or validating our own experience by discussing what we think is true with others who share the same views.

Science offers a more systematic way to make comparisons guard against bias. One technique used to avoid sampling bias is to select participants for a study in a random way. This means using a technique to insure that all members have an equal chance of being selected. Simple random sampling may involve using a set of random numbers as a guide in determining who is to be selected. For example, if we have a list of 400 people and wish to randomly select a smaller group or sample to be studied, we use a list of random numbers and select the case that corresponds with that number (Case 39, 3, 217 etc.). This is preferable to asking only those individuals with whom we are familiar to participate in a study; if we conveniently chose only people we know, we know nothing about those who had no opportunity to be selected. There are many more elaborate techniques that can be used to obtain samples that represent the composition of the population we are studying. But even though a randomly selected representative sample is preferable, it is not always used because of costs and other limitations. (As a consumer of research, however, you should know how the sample was obtained and keep this in mind when interpreting results.)

Scientific Methods

One method of scientific investigation involves the following steps:

- Determining a research question
- Reviewing previous studies addressing the topic in question (known as a literature review)
- Determining a method of gathering information
- Conducting the study
- Interpreting results
- Drawing conclusions; stating limitations of the study and suggestions for future research
- Making your findings available to others (both to share information and to have your work scrutinized by others)

Your findings can then be used by others as they explore the area of interest and through this process a literature or knowledge base is established. This model of scientific investigation presents research as a linear process guided by a specific research question. And it typically involves quantifying or using statistics to understand and report what has been studied. Many academic journals publish reports on studies conducted in this manner and a good way to become more familiar with these steps is to look at journal articles which will be written in sections that follow these steps. For example, after a section entitled "Statement of the Problem", you might find a second section entitled, "Literature Review". Other headings will reflect the stages of research mentioned above.

Another model of research referred to as qualitative research may involve steps such as these:

- Begin with a broad area of interest
- Gain entrance into a group to be researched
- Gather field notes about the setting, the people, the structure, the activities or other areas of interest
- Ask open ended, broad "grand tour" types of questions when interviewing subjects
- Modify research questions as study continues
- Note patterns or consistencies
- Explore new areas deemed important by the people being observed
- Report findings

In this type of research, theoretical ideas are "grounded" in the experiences of the participants. The researcher is the student and the people in the setting are the teachers as they inform the researcher of their world (Glazer &

Strauss, 1967). Researchers are to be aware of their own biases and assumptions, acknowledge them and bracket them in efforts to keep them from limiting accuracy in reporting. Sometimes qualitative studies are used initially to explore a topic and more quantitative studies are used to test or explain what was first described.

Types of Studies

Not all studies are designed to reach the same goal. **Descriptive studies** focus on describing an occurrence. Some examples of descriptive questions include:

- "How much time do parents spend with children?"
- "How many times per week do couples have intercourse?"
- "When is marital satisfaction greatest?"

Explanatory studies are efforts to answer the question "why" such as:

- "Why have rates of divorce leveled off?"
- "Why are teen pregnancy rates down?"

Evaluation research is designed to assess the effectiveness of policies or programs. For instance, a research might be designed to study the effectiveness of safety programs implemented in schools for installing car seats or fitting bicycle helmets. Do children wear their helmets? Do parents use car seats properly? If not, why not?
CC licensed content, Shared previously

- Psyc 200 Lifespan Psychology. **Authored by**: Laura Overstreet. **Located at**: http://opencourselibrary.org/econ-201/. **License**: *CC BY: Attribution*
- question mark. **Authored by**: Alexas_Fotos. **Located at**: https://pixabay.com/en/question-mark-tissue-structure-1098294/. **License**: *CC0: No Rights Reserved*

Module 2: Developmental Theories

Introduction to Developmental Theories

Learning Objectives

At the end of this lesson, you will be able to:

Define theory.
Describe Freud's theory of psychosexual development.
Identify the parts of the self in Freud's model.
List five defense mechanisms.
Describe five defense mechanisms.
Appraise the strengths and weaknesses of Freud's theory.
List Erikson's eight stages of psychosocial development.
Apply Erikson's stages to examples of people in various stages of the lifespan.
Appraise the strengths and weaknesses of Erikson's theory of psychosocial development.
Compare and contrast Freud and Erikson's theories of human development.
Describe the principles of classical conditioning.
Identify unconditioned stimulus, conditioned stimulus, unconditioned response, and conditioned response in classical conditioning.
Describe the principles of operant conditioning.
Identify positive and negative reinforcement, and primary and secondary reinforcement.
Contrast reinforcement and punishment.
Contrast classical and operant conditioning and the kinds of behaviors learned in each.
Describe social learning theory.
Describe Piaget's theory of cognitive development.
Define schema, assimilation, accommodation, and cognitive equilibrium.
List Piaget's stages of cognitive development.
Describe Piaget's stages of cognitive development.
Critique Piaget's theory of cognitive development.
Describe Vygotsky's sociocultural theory of cognitive development.
Explain what is meant by the zone of proximal development.
Explain guided participation.
Describe scaffolding.
Compare Piaget and Vygotsky's models of cognitive development.
Describe Bronfenbrenner's ecological systems model.

What is a theory?

Students sometimes feel intimidated by theory; even the phrase, "Now we are going to look at some theories..." is met with blank stares and other indications that the audience is now lost. But theories are valuable tools for understanding human behavior; if fact they are proposed explanations for the "how" and "whys" of development. Have you ever wondered, "Why is my 3 year old so inquisitive?" or "Why are some fifth graders rejected by their classmates?" Theories can help explain these and other occurrences. Developmental theories offer explanations about how we develop, why we change over time and the kinds of influences that impact development.

A theory guides and helps us interpret research findings as well. It provides the researcher with a blueprint or model to be used to help piece together various studies. Think of theories are guidelines much like directions that come with an appliance or other object that required assembly. The instructions can help one piece together smaller parts more easily than if trial and error are used.

Theories can be developed using induction in which a number of single cases are observed and after patterns or similarities are noted, the theorist develops ideas based on these examples. Established theories are then tested through research; however, not all theories are equally suited to scientific investigation. Some theories are difficult to test but are still useful in stimulating debate or providing concepts that have practical application. Keep in mind that theories are not facts; they are guidelines for investigation and practice, and they gain credibility through research that fails to disprove them.

REFERENCES

Bandura, A. (1977). Social learning theory. New York: General Learning Press.

Bandura, A. (1986). Social foundations of thought and action; A social-cognitive theory. Upper Saddle River, NJ: Prentice Hall.

Bandura, A, Ross, D. &. Ross S. (1963). Imitation of film-mediated aggressive models. Journal of Abnormal and social Psychology 66:3-11.

Bronfenbrenner, U. (1979). The ecology of human development: Experiments by nature and design. Cambridge, MA: Harvard University Press.

Erikson, E. H. (1950). Childhood and society. New York: Norton.

Erikson, E. H. (1968). Identity, youth, and crisis. New York: Norton.

O'Grady, D. & Metz, J. (1987). Resilience in children at high risk for psychological disorder. Journal of Pediatric Psychology 12(1):3-23.

Piaget, J. (1929). The child's conception of the world. NY: Harcourt, Brace Jovanovich.

Psychodynamic Theory

Sigmund Freud.

We begin with the often controversial figure, Sigmund Freud. Freud has been a very influential figure in the area of development; his view of development and psychopathology dominated the field of psychiatry until the growth of behaviorism in the 1950s. His assumptions that personality forms during the first few years of life and that the ways in which parents or other caregivers interact with children have a long-lasting impact on children's emotional states have guided parents, educators, clinicians, and policy-makers for many years. We have only recently begun to recognize that early childhood experiences do not always result in certain personality traits or emotional states. There is a growing body of literature addressing resiliency in children who come from harsh backgrounds and yet develop without damaging emotional scars (O'Grady and Metz, 1987). Freud has stimulated an enormous amount of research and generated many ideas. Agreeing with Freud's theory in its entirety is hardly necessary for appreciating the contribution he has made to the field of development.

Background

Sigmund Freud (1856-1939) was a Viennese M. D. who was trained in neurology and asked to work with patients suffering from hysteria, a conditioned marked my uncontrollable emotional outbursts, fears and anxiety that had puzzled physicians for centuries. He was also asked to work with women who suffered from physical symptoms and forms of paralysis which had no organic causes. During that time, many people believed that certain individuals were genetically inferior and thus more susceptible to mental illness. Women were thought to be genetically inferior and thus prone to illnesses such as hysteria (which had previously been attributed to a detached womb which was traveling around in the body).

However, after World War I, many soldiers came home with problems similar to hysteria. This called into questions the idea of genetic inferiority as a cause of mental illness. Freud began working with hysterical patients and discovered that when they began to talk about some of their life experiences, particularly those that took place in early childhood, their symptoms disappeared. This led him to suggest the first purely psychological explanation for physical problems and mental illness. What he proposed was that unconscious motives and desires, fears and anxieties drive our actions. When upsetting memories or thoughts begin to find their way into our consciousness, we develop defenses to shield us from these painful realities. These **defense mechanisms** include denying a reality, repressing or pushing away painful thoughts, rationalization or finding a seemingly logical explanation for circumstances, projecting or attributing our feelings to someone else, or outwardly opposing something we inwardly desire (called reaction formation). Freud believed that many mental illnesses are a result of a person's inability to accept reality. **Freud emphasized the importance of early childhood experiences in shaping our personality and behavior**. In our natural state, we are biological beings. We are driven primarily by instincts. During childhood, however, we begin to become social beings as we learn how to manage our instincts and transform them into socially acceptable behaviors. The type of parenting the child receives has a very power impact on the child's personality development. We will explore this idea further in our discussion of psychosexual development.

Theory of the Mind

Freud believed that most of our mental processes, motivations and desires are outside of our awareness. Our consciousness, that of which we are aware, represents only the tip of the iceberg that comprises our mental state. The preconscious represents that which can easily be called into the conscious mind. During development, our motivations and desires are gradually pushed into the unconscious because raw desires are often unacceptable in society.

Theory of the Self

As adults, our personality or self consists of three main parts: the **id**, the **ego** and the **superego**. The ID is the part of the self with which we are born. It consists of the biologically-driven self and includes our instincts and drives. It is the part of us that wants immediate gratification. Later in life, it comes to house our deepest, often unacceptable desires such as sex and aggression. It operates under the pleasure principle which means that the criteria for determining whether something is good or bad is whether it feels good or bad. An infant is all ID.The ego is the part of the self that develops as we learn that there are limits on what is acceptable to do and that often, we must wait to have our needs satisfied. This part of the self is realistic and reasonable. It knows how to make compromises. It operates under the reality principle or the recognition that sometimes need gratification must be postponed for practical reasons. It acts as a mediator between the Id and the Superego and is viewed as the healthiest part of the self.

Defense mechanisms emerge to help a person distort reality so that the truth is less painful. Defense mechanisms include repression which means to push the painful thoughts out of consciousness (in other words, think about something else). Denial is basically not accepting the truth or lying to the self. Thoughts such as "it won't happen to me" or "you're not leaving" or "I don't have a problem with alcohol" are examples. Regression refers to going back to a time when the world felt like a safer place, perhaps reverting to one's childhood. This is less common than the first two defense mechanisms. Sublimation involves transforming unacceptable urges into more socially acceptable behaviors. For example, a teenager who experiences strong sexual urges uses exercise to redirect those urges into more socially acceptable behavior. Displacement involves taking out frustrations on to a safer target. A person who is angry at a boss may take out their frustration at others when driving home or at a spouse upon arrival. Projection is a defense mechanism in which a person attributes their unacceptable thoughts onto others. If someone is frightened, for example, he or she accuses someone else of being afraid. Finally, reaction formation is a defense mechanism in which a person outwardly opposes something they inwardly desire, but that they find unacceptable. An example of this might be homophobia or a strong hatred and fear of homosexuality. This is a partial listing of defense mechanisms suggested by Freud. If the ego is strong, the individual is realistic and accepting of reality and remains more logical, objective, and reasonable. Building ego strength is a major goal of psychoanalysis (Freudian psychotherapy). So for Freud, having a big ego is a good thing because it does not refer to being arrogant, it refers to being able to accept reality.

The superego is the part of the self that develops as we learn the rules, standards, and values of society. This part of the self takes into account the moral guidelines that are a part of our culture. It is a rule-governed part of the self that operates under a sense of guilt (guilt is a social emotion-it is a feeling that others think less of you or believe you to be wrong). If a person violates the superego, he or she feels guilty. The superego is useful but can be too strong; in this case, a person might feel overly anxious and guilty about circumstances over which they had no control. Such a person may experience high levels of stress and inhibition that keeps them from living well. The id is inborn, but the ego and superego develop during the course of our early interactions with others. These interactions occur against a backdrop of learning to resolve early biological and social challenges and play a key role in our personality development.

Psychosexual Stages

Freud's psychosexual stages of development are presented below. At any of these stages, the child might become "stuck" or fixated if a caregiver either overly indulges or neglects the child's needs. A fixated adult will continue to try and resolve this later in life. Examples of fixation are given after the presentation of each stage.

For about the first year of life, the infant is in the **oral stage** of psychosexual development. The infant meets needs primarily through oral gratification. A baby wishes to suck or chew on any object that comes close to the mouth. Babies explore the world through the mouth and find comfort and stimulation as well. Psychologically, the infant is all Id. The infant seeks immediate gratification of needs such as comfort, warmth, food, and stimulation. If the caregiver meets oral needs consistently, the child will move away from this stage and progress further. However, if the caregiver is inconsistent or neglectful, the person may stay stuck in the oral stage. As an adult, the person might not feel good unless involved in some oral activity such as eating, drinking, smoking, nail-biting, or compulsive talking. These actions bring comfort and security when the person feels insecure, afraid, or bored.

During the **anal stage** which coincides with toddlerhood or mobility and potty-training, the child is taught that some urges must be contained and some actions postponed. There are rules about certain functions and when and where they are to be carried out. The child is learning a sense of self-control. The ego is being developed. If the caregiver is extremely controlling about potty training (stands over the child waiting for the smallest indication that the child might need to go to the potty and immediately scoops the child up and places him on the potty chair, for example), the child may grow up fearing losing control. He may becoming fixated in this stage or "anal retentive"-fearful of letting go. Such a person might be extremely neat and clean, organized, reliable, and controlling of others. If the caregiver neglects to teach the child to control urges, he may grow up to be "anal expulsive" or an adult who is messy, irresponsible, and disorganized.

The **Phallic stage** occurs during the preschool years (ages 3-5) when the child has a new biological challenge to face. Freud believed that the child becomes sexually attracted to his or her opposite sexed parent. Boys experience the "Oedipal Complex" in which they become sexually attracted to their mothers but realize that Father is in the way. He is much more powerful. For awhile, the boy fears that if he pursues his mother, father may castrate him (castration anxiety). So rather than risking losing his penis, he gives up his affections for his mother and instead learns to become more like his father, imitating his actions and mannerisms and thereby learns the role of males in his society. From this experience, the boy learns a sense of masculinity. He also learns what society thinks he should do and experiences guilt if he does not comply. In this way, the superego develops. If he does not resolve this successfully, he may become a "phallic male" or a man who constantly tries to prove his masculinity (about which he is insecure) by seducing women and beating up men! A little girl experiences the "Electra Complex" in which she develops an attraction for her father but realizes that she cannot compete with mother and so gives up that affection and learns to become more like her mother. This is not without some regret, however. Freud believed that the girl feels inferior because she does not have a penis (experiences "penis envy"). But she must resign herself to the fact that she is female and will just have to learn her inferior role in society as a female. However, if she does not resolve this conflict successfully, she may have a weak sense of femininity and grow up to be a "castrating female" who tries to compete with men in the workplace or in other areas of life.

During middle childhood (6-11), the child enters the **latent stage** focusing his or her attention outside the family and toward friendships. The biological drives are temporarily quieted (latent) and the child can direct attention to a larger world of friends. If the child is able to make friends, he or she will gain a sense of confidence. If not, the child may continue to be a loner or shy away from others, even as an adult.

The final stage of psychosexual development is referred to as the **genital stage**. From adolescence throughout adulthood a person is preoccupied with sex and reproduction. The adolescent experiences rising hormone levels and the sex drive and hunger drives become very strong. Ideally, the adolescent will rely on the ego to help think logically through these urges without taking actions that might be damaging. An adolescent might learn to redirect their sexual urges into safer activity such as running, for example. Quieting the Id with the Superego can lead to feeling overly self-conscious and guilty about these urges. Hopefully, it is the ego that is strengthened during this stage and the adolescent uses reason to manage urges.

Strengths and Weaknesses of Freud's Theory

Freud's theory has been heavily criticized for several reasons. One is that it is very difficult to test scientifically. How can parenting in infancy be traced to personality in adulthood? Are there other variables that might better explain development? The theory is also considered to be sexist in suggesting that women who do not accept an inferior position in society are somehow psychologically flawed. Freud focuses on the darker side of human nature and suggests that much of what determines our actions is unknown to us. So why do we study Freud? As mentioned above, despite the criticisms, Freud's assumptions about the importance of early childhood experiences in shaping our psychological selves have found their way into child development, education, and parenting practices. Freud's theory has heuristic value in providing a framework from which elaborate and modify subsequent theories of development. Many later theories, particularly behaviorism and humanism, were challenges to Freud's views.

CC licensed content, Shared previously

- Psyc 200 Lifespan Psychology. **Authored by**: Laura Overstreet. **Located at**: http://opencourselibrary.org/econ-201/. **License**: *CC BY: Attribution*

Public domain content

- Freud Image. **Authored by**: Max Halberstadt. **Located at**: https://en.wikipedia.org/wiki/Sigmund_Freud#/media/File:Sigmund_Freud_LIFE.jpg. **License**: *Public Domain: No Known Copyright*

Psychosocial Theory

Now, let's turn to a less controversial psychodynamic theorist, the father of developmental psychology, Erik Erikson.

The Ego Rules

Erik Erikson (1902-1994) was a student of Freud's and expanded on his theory of psychosexual development by emphasizing the importance of culture in parenting practices and motivations and adding three stages of adult development (Erikson, 1950; 1968). He believed that we are aware of what motivates us throughout life and the ego has greater importance in guiding our actions than does the Id. We make conscious choices in life and these choices focus on meeting certain social and cultural needs rather than purely biological ones. Humans are motivated, for instance, by the need to feel that the world is a trustworthy place, that we are capable individuals, that we can make a contribution to society, and that we have lived a meaningful life. These are all psychosocial problems. Erikson divided the life span into eight stages. In each stage, we have a major psychosocial task to accomplish or crisis to overcome. Erikson believed that our personality continues to take shape throughout our life span as we face these challenges in living. We will discuss each of these stages in length as we explore each period of the life span, but here is a brief overview:

Psychosocial Stages

Trust vs. mistrust (0-1): the infant must have basic needs met in a consistent way in order to feel that the world is a trustworthy place

Autonomy vs. shame and doubt (1-2): mobile toddlers have newfound freedom they like to exercise and by being allowed to do so, they learn some basic independence

Initiative vs. Guilt (3-5): preschoolers like to initiate activities and emphasize doing things "all by myself"

Industry vs. inferiority (6-11): school aged children focus on accomplishments and begin making comparisons between themselves and their classmates
Identity vs. role confusion (adolescence): teenagers are trying to gain a sense of identity as they experiment with various roles, beliefs, and ideas
Intimacy vs. Isolation (young adulthood): in our 20s and 30s we are making some of our first long-term commitments in intimate relationships
Generativity vs. stagnation (middle adulthood): the 40s through the early 60s we focus on being productive at work and home and are motivated by wanting to feel that we've made a contribution to society
Integrity vs. Despair (late adulthood): we look back on our lives and hope to like what we see-that we have lived well and have a sense of integrity because we lived according to our beliefs.

These eight stages form a foundation for discussions on emotional and social development during the life span. Keep in mind, however, that these stages or crises can occur more than once. For instance, a person may struggle with a lack of trust beyond infancy under certain circumstances. Erikson's theory has been criticized for focusing so heavily on stages and assuming that the completion of one stage is prerequisite for the next crisis of development. His theory also focuses on the social expectations that are found in certain cultures, but not in all. For instance, the idea that adolescence is a time of searching for identity might translate well in the middle-class culture of the United States, but not as well in cultures where the transition into adulthood coincides with puberty through rites of passage and where adult roles offer fewer choices.

CC licensed content, Shared previously

- Psyc 200 Lifespan Psychology. **Authored by**: Laura Overstreet. **Located at**: http://opencourselibrary.org/econ-201/. **License**: *CC BY: Attribution*

Public domain content

- Erik Erikson. **Located at**: https://en.wikipedia.org/wiki/Erik_Erikson#/media/File:Erik_Erikson.png. **License**: *Public Domain: No Known Copyright*

Exploring Behavior

How do we act?

Learning theories focus on how we respond to events or stimuli rather than emphasizing what motivates our actions. These theories provide an explanation of how experience can change what we are capable of doing or feeling.

Classical Conditioning and Emotional Responses

Classical Conditioning theory helps us to understand how our responses to one situation become attached to new situations. For example, a smell might remind us of a time when we were a kid (elementary school cafeterias smell like milk and mildew!). If you went to a new cafeteria with the same smell, it might evoke feelings you had when you were in school. Or a song on the radio might remind you of a memorable evening you spent with your first true love. Or, if you hear your entire name (John Wilmington Brewer, for instance) called as you walk across the stage to get your diploma and it makes you tense because it reminds you of how your father used to use your full name when he was mad at you, you've been classically conditioned!

Classical conditioning explains how we develop many of our emotional responses to people or events or our "gut level" reactions to situations. New situations may bring about an old response because the two have become connected. Attachments form in this way. Addictions are affected by classical conditioning, as anyone who's tried to quit smoking can tell you. When you try to quit, everything that was associated with smoking makes you crave a cigarette.

Pavlov

Ivan Pavlov

Ivan Pavlov (1880-1937) was a Russian physiologist interested in studying digestion. As he recorded the amount of salivation his laboratory dogs produced as they ate, he noticed that they actually began to salivate before the food arrived as the researcher walked down the hall and toward the cage. "This," he thought, "is not natural!" One would expect a dog to automatically salivate when food hit their palate, but BEFORE the food comes? Of course, what had happened was . . . you tell me. That's right! The dogs knew that the food was coming because they had learned to associate the footsteps with the food. The key word here is "learned". A learned response is called a "conditioned" response. Pavlov began to experiment with this "psychic" reflex. He began to ring a bell, for instance, prior to introducing the food. Sure enough, after making this connection several times, the dogs could be made to salivate to the sound of a bell. Once the bell had become an event to which the dogs had learned to salivate, it was called a conditioned stimulus. The act of salivating to a bell was a response that had also been learned, now termed in Pavlov's jargon, a conditioned response. Notice that the response, salivation, is the same whether it is conditioned or unconditioned (unlearned or natural). What changed is the stimulus to which the dog salivates. One is natural (unconditioned) and one is learned (conditioned). Well, enough of Pavlov's dogs. Who cares? Let's think about how classical conditioning is used on us. One of the most widespread applications of classical conditioning principles

Watson and Behaviorism

Watson believed that most of our fears and other emotional responses are classically conditioned. He had gained a good deal of popularity in the 1920s with his expert advice on parenting offered to the public. He believed that parents could be taught to help shape their children's behavior and tried to demonstrate the power of classical conditioning with his famous experiment with an 18 month old boy named "Little Albert". Watson sat Albert down and introduced a variety of seemingly scary objects to him: a burning piece of newspaper, a white rat, etc. But Albert remained curious and reached for all of these things. Watson knew that one of our only inborn fears is the fear of loud noises so he proceeded to make a loud noise each time he introduced one of Albert's favorites, a white rat. After hearing the loud noise several times paired with the rat, Albert soon came to fear the rat and began to cry when it was introduced. Watson filmed this experiment for posterity and used it to demonstrate that he could help parents achieve any outcomes they desired, if they would only follow his advice. Watson wrote columns in newspapers and in magazines and gained a lot of popularity among parents eager to apply science to household order. Parenting advice was not the legacy Watson left us, however. Where he really made his impact was in advertising. After Watson left academia, he went into the world of business and showed companies how to tie something that brings about a natural positive feeling to their products to enhance sales. Thus the union of sex and advertising! So, let's use a much more interesting example than Pavlov's dogs to check and see if you understand the difference between conditioned and unconditioned stimuli and responses. In the experiment with Little Albert, identify the unconditioned stimulus, the unconditioned response, and, after conditioning, the conditioned stimulus and the conditioned response.

Operant Conditioning and Repeating Actions

Operant Conditioning is another learning theory that emphasizes a more conscious type of learning than that of classical conditioning. A person (or animal) does something (operates something) to see what effect it might bring. Simply said, operant conditioning describes how we repeat behaviors because they pay off for us. It is based on a principle authored by a psychologist named Thorndike (1874-1949) called the law of effect. The law of effect suggest that we will repeat an action if it is followed by a good effect.

Skinner and Reinforcement

B.F. Skinner (1904-199 expanded on Thorndike's principle and outlined the principles of operant conditioning. Skinner believed that we learn best when our actions are reinforced. For example, a child who cleans his room and is reinforced (rewarded) with a big hug and words of praise is more likely to clean it again than a child whose deed goes unnoticed.Skinner believed that almost anything could be reinforcing. A reinforcer is anything following a behavior that makes it more likely to occur again. It can be something intrinsically rewarding (called intrinsic or primary reinforcers), such as food or praise, or it can be something that is rewarding because it can be exchanged for what one really wants (such as using money to buy a cookie). Such reinforcers are referred to as secondary reinforcers or extrinsic reinforcers.

Positive and negative reinforcement

B. F. Skinner (1950)

Sometimes, adding something to the situation is reinforcing as in the cases we described above with cookies, praise and money. Positive reinforcement involves adding something to the situation in order to encourage a behavior. Other times, taking something away from a situation can be reinforcing. For example, the loud, annoying buzzer on your alarm clock encourages you to get up so that you can turn it off and get rid of the noise. Children whine in order to get their parents to do something and often, parents give in just to stop the whining. In these instances, negative reinforcement has been used.

Operant conditioning tends to work best if you focus on trying to encourage a behavior or move a person into the direction you want them to go rather than telling them what not to do. Reinforcers are used to encourage a behavior; punishers are used to stop behavior. A punisher is anything that follows an act and decreases the chance it will reoccur. But often a punished behavior doesn't really go away. It is just suppressed and may reoccur whenever the threat of punishment is removed. For example, a child may not cuss around you because you've washed his mouth out with soap, but he may cuss around his friends. Or a motorist may only slow down when the trooper is on the side of the freeway. Another problem with punishment is that when a person focuses on punishment, they may find it hard to see what the other does right or well. And punishment is stigmatizing; when punished, some start to see themselves as bad and give up trying to change.

Reinforcement can occur in a predictable way, such as after every desired action is performed, or intermittently, after the behavior is performed a number of times or the first time it is performed after a certain amount of time. The schedule of reinforcement has an impact on how long a behavior continues after reinforcement is discontinued. So a parent who has rewarded a child's actions each time may find that the child gives up very quickly if a reward is not immediately forthcoming. A lover who is warmly regarded now and then may continue to seek out his or her partner's attention long after the partner has tried to break up. Think about the kinds of behaviors you may have learned through classical and operant conditioning. You may have learned many things in this way. But sometimes we learn very complex behaviors quickly and without direct reinforcement. Bandura explains how.

Social Learning Theory

Albert Bandura is a leading contributor to social learning theory. He calls our attention to the ways in which many of our actions are not learned through conditioning; rather, they are learned by watching others (1977). Young children frequently learn behaviors through imitation. Sometimes, particularly when we do not know what else to do, we learn by modeling or copying the behavior of others. An employee on his or her first day of a new job might eagerly look at how others are acting and try to act the same way to fit in more quickly. Adolescents struggling with their identity rely heavily on their peers to act as role-models. Newly married couples often rely on roles they may have learned from their parents and begin to act in ways they did not while dating and then wonder why their relationship has changed. Sometimes we do things because we've seen it pay off for someone else. They were operantly conditioned, but we engage in the behavior because we hope it will pay off for us as well. This is referred to as vicarious reinforcement (Bandura, Ross and Ross, 1963).

Do parents socialize children or do children

socialize parents?

Bandura (1986) suggests that there is interplay between the environment and the individual. We are not just the product of our surroundings, rather we influence our surroundings. There is interplay between our personality and the way we interpret events and how they influence us. This concept is called reciprocal determinism. An example of this might be the interplay between parents and children. Parents not only influence their child's environment, perhaps intentionally through the use of reinforcement, etc., but children influence parents as well. Parents may respond differently with their first child than with their fourth. Perhaps they try to be the perfect parents with their firstborn, but by the time their last child comes along they have very different expectations both of themselves and their child. Our environment creates us and we create our environment. Other social influences: TV or not TV? Bandura (et als. 1963) began a series of studies to look at the impact of television, particularly commercials, have on the behavior of children. Are children more likely to act out aggressively when they see this behavior modeled? What if they see it being reinforced? Bandura began by conducting an experiment in which he showed children a film of a woman hitting an inflatable clown or "bobo" doll. Then the children were allowed in the room where they found the doll and immediately began to hit it. This was without any reinforcement whatsoever. Later they viewed a woman hitting a real clown and sure enough, when allowed in the room, they too began to hit the clown! Not only that, but they found new ways to behave aggressively. It's as if they learned an aggressive role.

Children view far more television today than in the 1960s; so much, in fact, that they have been referred to as Generation M (media). Based on a study of a national representative sample of over 7,000 8-18 year olds, the Kaiser Foundation reports that children spend just over 8 hours a day involved with media outside of schoolwork. This includes almost 4 hours of television viewing and over an hour on the computer. Two-thirds have television in their room and those children watch an average of 1.27 hours more of television per day than those do not have television in their bedroom (Kaiser Family Foundation, 2005). The prevalence of violence, sexual content, and messages promoting foods high in fat and sugar in the media are certainly cause for concern and the subjects of ongoing research and policy review. Many children spend even more time on the computer viewing content from the internet. And the amount of time spent connected to the internet continues to increase with the use of smart phones that essentially serve as mini-computers. What are the implications of this?

CC licensed content, Shared previously

- Psyc 200 Lifespan Psychology. **Authored by**: Laura Overstreet. **Located at**: http://opencourselibrary.org/econ-201/. **License**: *CC BY: Attribution*

All rights reserved content

- Pigeon Turn. **Authored by**: BFSkinner Foundation. **Located at**: http://youtu.be/TtfQlkGwE2U. **License**: *Other*. **License Terms**: Standard YouTube license
- The Brain: A Secret History - Emotions; Bandura Bobo Doll Experiment. **Authored by**: DebateFilms. **Located at**: http://youtu.be/zerCK0lRjp8. **License**: *Other*. **License Terms**: Standard YouTube license

Exploring Cognition

What do we think?

Cognitive theories focus on how our mental processes or cognitions change over time. We will examine the ideas of two cognitive theorists: Jean Piaget and Lev Vygotsky.

Piaget: Changes in thought with maturation

Jean Piaget.

Jean Piaget (1896-1980) is one of the most influential cognitive theorists in development inspired to explore children's ability to think and reason by watching his own children's development. He was one of the first to recognize and map out the ways in which children's intelligence differs from that of adults. He became interested in this area when he was asked to test the IQ of children and began to notice that there was a pattern in their wrong answers! He believed that children's intellectual skills change over time that that maturation rather than training brings about that change. Children of differing ages interpret the world differently.

Making sense of the world

Piaget believed that we are continuously trying to maintain cognitive equilibrium or a balance or cohesiveness in what we see and what we know. Children have much more of a challenge in maintaining this balance because they are constantly being confronted with new situations, new words, new objects, etc. When faced with something new, a child may either fit it into an existing framework (**schema**) and match it with something known (**assimilation**) such as calling all animals with four legs "doggies" because he or she knows the word doggie, or expand the framework of knowledge to accommodate the new situation (**accommodation**) by learning a new word to more accurately name the animal. This is the underlying dynamic in our own cognition. Even as adults we continue to try and "make sense" of new situations by determining whether they fit into our old way of thinking or whether we need to modify our thoughts.

Stages of Cognitive Development

Piaget outlined four major stages of cognitive development. Let me briefly mention them here. We will discuss them in detail throughout the course.For about the first two years of life, the child experiences the world primarily through their senses and motor skills. Piaget referred to this type of intelligence as sensorimotor intelligence. During the preschool years, the child begins to master the use of symbols or words and is able to think of the world symbolically but not yet logically. This stage is the preoperational stage of development. The concrete operational stage in middle childhood is marked by an ability to use logic in understanding the physical world. In the final stage, the formal operational stage the adolescent learns to think abstractly and to use logic in both concrete and abstract ways.

Criticisms of Piaget's Theory

Piaget has been criticized for overemphasizing the role that physical maturation plays in cognitive development and in underestimating the role that culture and interaction (or experience) plays in cognitive development. Looking across cultures reveals considerable variation in what children are able to do at various ages. Piaget may have underestimated what children are capable of given the right circumstances.

Vygotsky: Changes in thought with guidance

Lev Vygotsky (1896-1934) was a Russian psychologist who wrote in the early 1900s but whose work was discovered in the United States in the 1960s but became more widely known in the 1980s. Vygotsky differed with Piaget in that he believed that a person not only has a set of abilities, but also a set of potential abilities that can be realized if given the proper guidance from others. His **sociocultural theory** emphasizes the importance of culture and interaction in the development of cognitive abilities. He believed that through guided participation known as scaffolding, with a teacher or capable peer, a child can learn cognitive skills within a certain range known as the zone of proximal development. Have you ever taught a child to perform a task? Maybe it was brushing their teeth or preparing food. Chances are you spoke to them and described what you were doing while you demonstrated the skill and let them work along with you all through the process. You gave them assistance when they seemed to need it, but once they knew what to do-you stood back and let them go. This is scaffolding and can be seen demonstrated throughout the world. This approach to teaching has also been adopted by educators. Rather than assessing students on what they are doing, they should be understood in terms of what they are capable of doing with the proper guidance. You can see how Vygotsky would be very popular with modern day educators. We will discuss Vygotsky in greater depth in upcoming lessons.

Putting it all together: Ecological Systems Model

Urie Brofenbrenner (1917-2005) provides a model of human development that addresses its many influences. Brofenbrenner recognized that human interaction is influenced by larger social forces and that an understanding of those forces is essential for understanding an individual. The individual is impacted by **microsystems** such as parents or siblings; those who have direct, significant contact with the person. The input of those is modified by the cognitive and biological state of the individual as well. And these influence the person's actions which in turn influence systems operating on him or her. The **mesosystem** includes larger organizational structures such as school, the family, or religion. These institutions impact the microsystems just described. For example, the religious teachings and traditions may guide the child's family's actions or create a climate that makes the family feel stigmatized and this indirectly impacts the child's view of self and others. The philosophy of the school system, daily routine, assessment methods, and other characteristics can affect the child's self-image, growth, sense of accomplishment, and schedule thereby impacting the child, physically, cognitively, and emotionally. These mesosystems both influence and are influenced by the larger contexts of community referred to as the exosystem. A community's values, history, and economy can impact the organizational structures it houses. And the community is influenced by **macrosystems** which are cultural elements such as global economic conditions, war, technological trends, values, philosophies, and a society's responses to the global community. In sum, a child's experiences are shaped by larger forces such as the family, schools, and religion, and culture. All of this occurs in an historical context or chronosystem. Bronfenbrenner's model helps us combine each of the other theories described above and gives us a perspective that brings it all together.

Research Designs

We have just been looking at models of the research process and goals of research. The following is a comparison of research methods or techniques used to describe, explain, or evaluate. Each of these designs has strengths and weaknesses and is sometimes used in combination with other designs within a single study.

Observational studies involve watching and recording the actions of participants. This may take place in the natural setting, such as observing children at play at a park, or behind a one-way glass while children are at play in a laboratory playroom. The researcher may follow a check list and record the frequency and duration of events (perhaps how many conflicts occur among 2 year olds) or may observe and record as much as possible about an event as a participant (such as attending an Alcoholics Anonymous meeting and recording the slogans on the walls, the structure of the meeting, the expressions commonly used, etc.). The researcher may be a participant or a non-participant. What would be the strengths of being a participant? What would be the weaknesses? Consider the strengths and weaknesses of not participating. In general, observational studies have the strength of allowing the researcher to see how people behave rather than relying on self-report. What people do and what they say they do are often very different. A major weakness of observational studies is that they do not allow the researcher to explain causal relationships. Yet, observational studies are useful and widely used when studying children. Children tend to change their behavior when they know they are being watched (known as the **Hawthorne effect**) and may not survey well.

Experiments are designed to test **hypotheses** (or specific statements about the relationship between **variables**) in a controlled setting in efforts to explain how certain factors or events produce outcomes. A variable is anything that changes in value. Concepts are **operationalized** or transformed into variables in research which means that the researcher must specify exactly what is going to be measured in the study. For example, if we are interested in studying marital satisfaction, we have to specify what marital satisfaction really means or what we are going to use as an indicator of marital satisfaction. What is something measurable that would indicate some level of marital satisfaction? Would it be the amount of time couples spend together each day? Or eye contact during a discussion about money? Or maybe a subject's score on a marital satisfaction scale. Each of these is measurable but these may not be equally valid or accurate indicators of marital satisfaction. What do you think? These are the kinds of considerations researchers must make when working through the design.

Three conditions must be met in order to establish cause and effect. Experimental designs are useful in meeting these conditions.

The **independent and dependent variables must be related**. In other words, when one is altered, the other changes in response. (The independent variable is something altered or introduced by the researcher. The dependent variable is the outcome or the factor affected by the introduction of the independent variable. For example, if we are looking at the impact of exercise on stress levels, the independent variable would be exercise; the dependent variable would be stress.)

The cause must come before the effect. Experiments involve measuring subjects on the dependent variable before exposing them to the independent variable (establishing a baseline). So we would measure the subjects' level of stress before introducing exercise and then again after the exercise to see if there has been a change in stress levels. (Observational and survey research does not always allow us to look at the timing of these events which makes understanding causality problematic with these designs.)

The cause must be isolated. The researcher must ensure that no outside, perhaps unknown variables are actually causing the effect we see. The experimental design helps make this possible. In an experiment, we would make sure that our subjects' diets were held constant throughout the exercise program. Otherwise, diet might really be creating the change in stress level rather than exercise.

A basic experimental design involves beginning with a sample (or subset of a population) and randomly assigning subjects to one of two groups: the **experimental group or the control group**. The experimental group is the group that is going to be exposed to an independent variable or condition the researcher is introducing as a potential cause of an event. The control group is going to be used for comparison and is going to have the same experience as the experimental group but will not be exposed to the independent variable. After exposing the experimental group to the independent variable, the two groups are measured again to see if a change has occurred. If so, we are in a better position to suggest that the **independent variable** caused the change in the **dependent variable**. The basic experimental model looks like this:

Sample is randomly assigned to one of the groups below:	Measure DV	Introduce IV	Measure DV
Experimental Group	X	X	X
Control Group	X	–	X

The major advantage of the experimental design is that of helping to establish cause and effect relationships. A disadvantage of this design is the difficulty of translating much of what concerns us about human behavior into a laboratory setting. I hope this brief description of experimental design helps you appreciate both the difficulty and the rigor of conducting an experiment.

Case studies involve exploring a single case or situation in great detail. Information may be gathered with the use of observation, interviews, testing, or other methods to uncover as much as possible about a person or situation. Case studies are helpful when investigating unusual situations such as brain trauma or children reared in isolation. And they often used by clinicians who conduct case studies as part of their normal practice when gathering information about a client or patient coming in for treatment. Case studies can be used to explore areas about which little is known and can provide rich detail about situations or conditions. However, the findings from case studies cannot be **generalized** or applied to larger populations; this is because cases are not randomly selected and no control group is used for comparison. (Read "The Man Who Mistook His Wife for a Hat" by Dr. Oliver Sacks as a good example of the case study approach.)

Surveys are familiar to most people because they are so widely used. Surveys enhance accessibility to subjects because they can be conducted in person, over the phone, through the mail, or online. A survey involves asking a standard set of questions to a group of subjects. In a highly structured survey, subjects are forced to choose from a response set such as "strongly disagree, disagree, undecided, agree, strongly agree"; or "0, 1-5, 6-10, etc." Surveys are commonly used by sociologists, marketing researchers, political scientists, therapists, and others to gather information on many independent and dependent variables in a relatively short period of time. Surveys typically yield surface information on a wide variety of factors, but may not allow for in-depth understanding of human behavior. Of course, surveys can be designed in a number of ways. They may include **forced choice** questions and **semi-structured questions** in which the researcher allows the respondent to describe or give details about certain events. One of the most difficult aspects of designing a good survey is wording questions in an unbiased way and asking the right questions so that respondents can give a clear response rather that choosing "undecided" each time. Knowing that 30% of respondents are undecided is of little use! So a lot of time and effort should be placed on the construction of survey items. One of the benefits of having forced choice items is that each response is coded so that the results can be quickly entered and analyzed using statistical software. Analysis takes much longer when respondents give lengthy responses that must be analyzed in a different way. Surveys are useful in examining stated values, attitudes, opinions, and reporting on practices. However, they are based on **self-report** or what people say they do rather than on observation and this can limit accuracy.

Secondary/Content analysis involves analyzing information that has already been collected or examining documents or media to uncover attitudes, practices or preferences. There are a number of data sets available to those who wish to conduct this type of research. For example, the U. S. Census Data is available and widely used to look at trends and changes taking place in the United States (go to http://www.census.gov/ and check it out).

There are a number of other agencies that collect data on family life, sexuality, and many other areas of interest in human development (go to http://www.norc.uchicago.edu/ or http://www.kff.org/ and see what you find.). The researcher conducting secondary analysis does not have to recruit subjects but does need to know the quality of the information collected in the original study.

Content analysis involves looking at media such as old texts, pictures, commercials, lyrics or other materials to explore patterns or themes in culture. An example of content analysis is the classic history of childhood by Aries (1962) called "Centuries of Childhood" or the analysis of television commercials for sexual or violent content. Passages in text or programs that air can be randomly selected for analysis as well. Again, one advantage of analyzing work such as this is that the researcher does not have to go through the time and expense of finding respondents, but the researcher cannot know how accurately the media reflects the actions and sentiments of the population.

Developmental designs are techniques used in life span research (and other areas as well). These techniques try to examine how age, cohort, gender, and social class impact development. **Cross-sectional** research involves beginning with a sample that represents a cross-section of the population. Respondents who vary in age, gender, ethnicity, and social class might be asked to complete a survey about television program preferences or attitudes toward the use of the Internet. The attitudes of males and females could then be compared as could attitudes based on age. In cross-sectional research, respondents are measured only once. This method is much less expensive than longitudinal research but does not allow the researcher to distinguish between the impact of age and the cohort effect. Different attitudes about the Internet, for example, might not be altered by a person's biological age as much as their life experiences as members of a cohort.

Longitudinal research involves beginning with a group of people who may be of the same age and background, and measuring them repeatedly over a long period of time. One of the benefits of this type of research is that people can be followed through time and be compared with them when they were younger. A problem with this type of research is that it is very expensive and subjects may drop out over time. (The film 49 Up is a example of following individuals over time. You see how people change physically, emotionally, and socially through time.) What would be the drawbacks of being in a longitudinal study? What about 49 Up? Would you want to be filmed every 7 years? What would be the advantages and disadvantages? Can you imagine why some would continue and others drop out of the project?

Cross-sequential research involves combining aspects of the previous two techniques; beginning with a cross-sectional sample and measuring them through time. This is the perfect model for looking at age, gender, social class, and ethnicity. But it the drawbacks of high costs and attrition are here as well.
CC licensed content, Shared previously

- Psyc 200 Lifespan Psychology. **Authored by**: Laura Overstreet. **Located at**: http://opencourselibrary.org/econ-201/. **License**: *CC BY: Attribution*
- magnifying glass. **Authored by**: nachar. **Located at**: https://pixabay.com/en/magnifying-glass-magnifier-glass-189254/. **License**: *CC0: No Rights Reserved*

Assignment 1

1. Read this article: When new motherhood hurts–the hidden shame of post-partum depression. (News)

(You may need to enter your *My*FM username and password to access article.)

2. Answer the following questions with at least 1 page double spaced:

a) Describe Postpartum Depression.

b) What factors affect whether a new mother seeks help for Postpartum Depression?

c) What factors influence a women's risk of developing Postpartum Depression?

Module 3: Prenatal Development

Introduction to Heredity, Prenatal Development, and Birth

Learning Objectives

At the end of this lesson, you will be able to

Define gene.
Define chromosome.
Define gamete.
Explain what determines the chromosomal sex of the child.
Question the assertion that human traits are genetic.
Compare monozygotic and dizygotic twins.
Differentiate between genetic disorders and chromosomal abnormalities.
Describe Trisomy 21.
Differentiate between the germinal, embryonic, and fetal periods of development.
Describe human development during the germinal, embryonic, and fetal periods.
Describe a normal delivery and complications of pregnancy and delivery.
Predict the risks to prenatal development posed by exposure to teratogens.
Interpret APGAR scores.
Discover problems of newborns

Heredity: The Epigenetic Framework

Nature or Nurture?

In this lesson, we will look at some of the ways in which heredity helps to shape the way we are. We will look at what happens genetically during conception and take a brief look some genetic abnormalities. Before going into these topics, however, it is important to emphasize the interplay between heredity and the environment. Why are you the way you are? As you consider some of your features (height, weight, personality, being diabetic, etc.), ask yourself whether these features are a result of heredity or environmental factors-or both. Chances are, you can see the ways in which both heredity and environmental factors (such as lifestyle, diet, and so on) have contributed to these features. For decades, scholars have carried on the "nature/nurture" debate. For any particular feature, those on the "nature" side would argue that heredity plays the most important role in bringing about that feature. Those on the "nurture" side would argue that one's environment is most significant in shaping the way we are. This debate continues in questions about what makes us masculine or feminine (Lippa, 2002), concerns about vision (Mutti, Kadnik and Adams, 1996), and many other developmental issues. (Check out www.googlescholar.com for over 20,000 entries for "current nature/nurture debates"!) Yet most scholars agree that there is a constant interplay between the two forces. It is difficult to isolate the root of any single behavior as a result solely of nature or nurture and most scholars believe that even determining the extent to which nature or nurture impacts a human feature is difficult to answer. In fact, almost all human features are polygenic (a result of many genes) and multifactorial (a result of many factors, both genetic and environmental). It's as if one's genetic make-up sets up a range of possibilities, which may or may not be realized depending upon one's environmental experiences. For instance, a person might be genetically predisposed to develop diabetes, but the person's lifestyle may help bring about the disease.

The Epigenetic Framework

Gottlieb (1998, 2000, 2002) suggests an analytic framework for the nature/nurture debate that recognizes the interplay between the environment, behavior, and genetic expression. This bidirectional interplay suggests that the environment can effect the expression of genes just as genetic predispositions can impact a person's potentials. And environmental circumstances can trigger symptoms of a genetic disorder. For example, a person who has sickle cell anemia, a recessive gene linked disorder, can experience a sickle cell crisis under conditions of oxygen deprivation. Someone predisposed genetically for type two diabetes can trigger the disease through poor diet and little exercise.

The Human Genome Project

The Human Genome Project is an internationally funded effort to map the locations of human genes and understand the role these genes play in development, health and illness. (Check out recent developments at www.genome.gov) Genes are segments of chromosomes (46 strands of a chemical substance called DNA that are contained in the nucleus of each normal human cell) that vary in length. There are an estimated 25,000 to 30,000 genes on each chromosome; a number far below the estimate of 100,000-150,000 held before the work of the Human Genome Project.

Understanding the role of genes in health and illness can bring about both harm and good (Weitz, 2007). A person who knows that they are at risk for developing a genetic disorder may be able to adopt lifestyle practices that minimize the risk and a person who discovers that they are not at risk may find comfort in knowing that they do not have to fear a particular disease. However, a person who finds out that they are at risk and there is nothing that can be done about it may experience years of fear and anxiety. And the availability of genetic testing may be more widespread than the availability of genetic counseling which can be very expensive. The possible stigma and discrimination that those with illness or at risk for illness must also be considered. In light of the high costs of health insurance, many companies are starting to offer benefits contingent on health assessments and lifestyle recommendations; and continued coverage depends on an employee following these recommendations. So a smoker may have to pay a higher premium than a non-smoker or a person who is overweight may be required to engage in a program of exercise and be monitored for improvement. What if a person finds out that they carry the gene for Huntington's disease (a neurological disorder that is ultimately fatal) which may surface when a person reaches their 40s? The impact this knowledge will have on health care still remains unknown. Who should know what is on your genome? Do you think this information should be shared between mates? What about employers? What would be the advantages and disadvantages?

Conception

Gametes

There are two types of sex cells or gametes involved in reproduction: the male gametes or sperm and female gametes or ova. The male gametes are produced in the testes in a process called spermatogenesis which begin at about 12 years of age. The female gametes or ova which are stored in the ovaries are present at birth but are immature. Each ovary contains about 250,000 (Rome 1998) but only about 400 of these will become mature eggs (Mackon and Fauser 2000). Beginning at puberty, one ovum ripens and is released about every 28 days, a process called oogenesis.

After the ovum or egg ripens and is released from the ovary, it is drawn

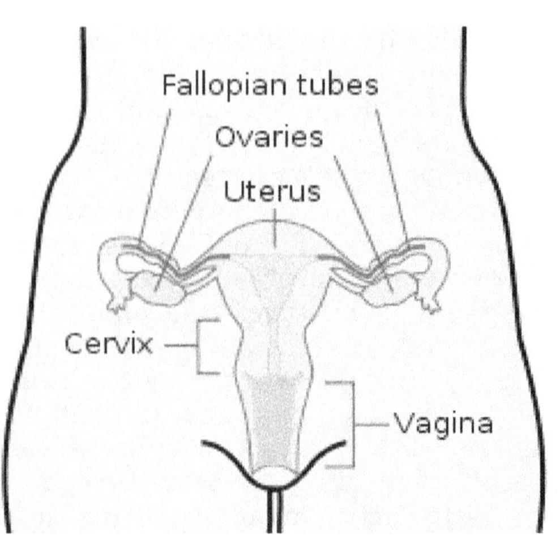

into the fallopian tube and in 3 to 4 days, reaches the uterus. It is *The Female Reproductive System* typically fertilized in the fallopian tube and continues its journey to the uterus. At ejaculation, millions of sperm are released into the vagina, but only a few reach the egg and typically, only one fertilizes the egg. Once a single sperm has entered the wall of the egg, the wall becomes hard and prevents other sperm from entering. After the sperm has entered the egg, the tail of the sperm breaks off and the head of the sperm, containing the genetic information from the father, unites with the nucleus of the egg. As a result, a new cell is formed. This cell, containing the combined genetic information from both parents, is referred to as a zygote.

Chromosomes contain genetic information from each parent. While other normal human cells have 46 chromosomes (or 23 pair), gametes contain 23 chromosomes. In a process called meiosis, segments of the chromosomes from each parent form pairs and genetic segments are exchanged as determined by chance. Because of the unpredictability of this exchange the likelihood of having offspring that are genetically identical (and not twins) is one in trillions (Gould and Keeton, 1997).

Determining the Sex of the Child

Twenty-two of those chromosomes from each parent are similar in length to a corresponding chromosome from the other parent. However, the remaining chromosome looks like an X or a Y. Half of the male's sperm contain a Y chromosome and half contain an X. All of the ova contain two X chromosomes. If the child receives the combination of XY, the child will be genetically male. If it receives the XX combination, the child will be genetically female.

Many potential parents have a clear preference for having a boy or a girl and would like to determine the sex of the child. Through the years, a number of tips have been offered for the potential parents to maximize their chances for having either a son or daughter as they prefer. For example, it has been suggested that sperm which carry a Y chromosome are more fragile than those carrying an X. So, if a couple desires a male child, they can take measures to maximize the chance that the Y sperm reaches the egg. This involves having intercourse 48 hours after ovulation, which helps the Y sperm have a shorter journey to reach the egg, douching to create a more alkaline environment in the vagina, and having the female reach orgasm first so that sperm are not pushed out of the vagina during orgasm. Today, however, there is new technology available that makes it possible to isolate sperm containing either an X or a Y, depending on the preference, and use that sperm to fertilize a mother's egg.

Monozygotic and Dizygotic Twins

Monozygotic twins occur when a single zygote or fertilized egg splits apart in the first two weeks of development. The result is the creation of two separate but genetically identical offspring. About one-third of twins are monozygotic twins. Are you an identical twin?

Sometimes, however, two eggs or ova are released and fertilized by two separate sperm. The result is dizygotic or fraternal twins. About two-thirds of twins are dizygotic. These two individuals share the same amount of genetic material as would any two children from the same mother and father. Older mothers are more likely to have dizygotic twins than are younger mothers and couples who use fertility drugs are also more likely to give birth to dizygotic twins. Consequently, there has been in increase in the number of fraternal twins in recent years (Bortolus et. al., 1999).

What are the other possibilities? Various degrees of sharing the placenta can occur depending on the timing of the separation and duplication of cells. This is known as placentiation. Here is a diagram that illustrates various types of twins.

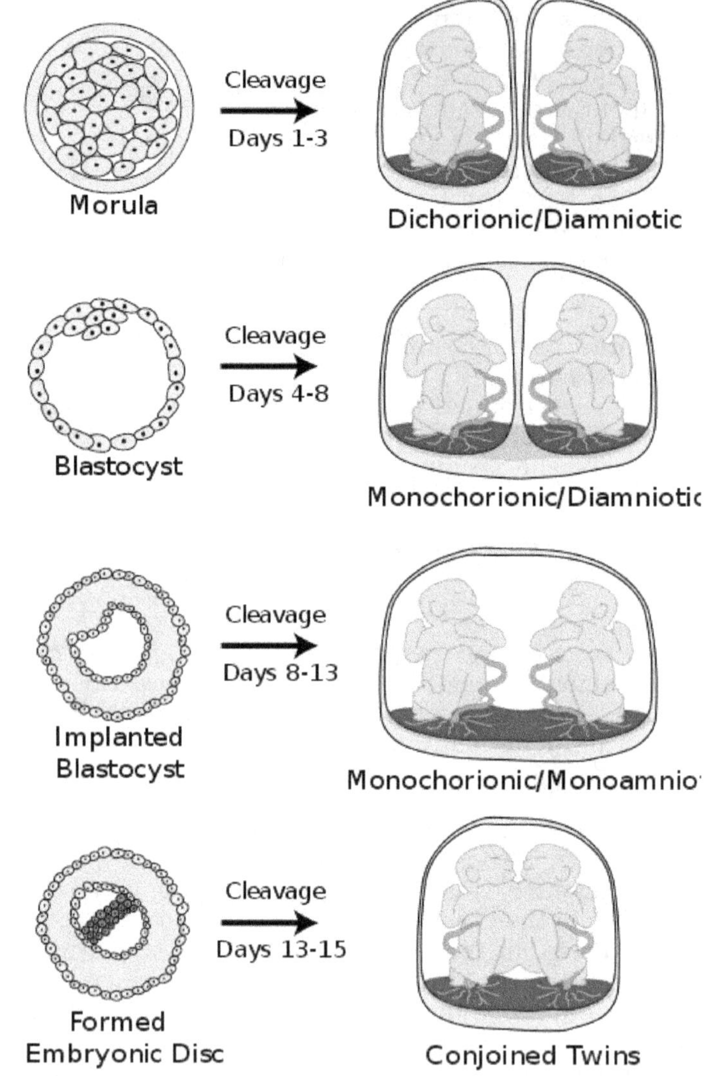

Author Kevin Dufenbach

Genotypes and Phenotypes (or why what you get is not always what you see)

The word genotype refers to the sum total of all the genes a person inherits. The word phenotype refers to the features that are actually expressed. Look in the mirror. What do you see, your genotype or your phenotype? What determines whether or not genes are expressed? Actually, this is quite complicated (Berger, 2005). Some features follow the additive pattern which means that many different genes contribute to a final outcome. Height and skin tone are examples. In other cases, a gene might either be turned on or off depending on the gene with which it is paired. Some genes are considered dominant because they will be expressed. Others, termed recessive, are only expressed in the absence of a dominant gene. Some characteristics which were once thought of as dominant-recessive, such as eye color, are now believed to be a result of the interaction between several genes (McKusick, 1998). Dominant traits include curly hair, facial dimples, normal vision, and dark hair. Recessive characteristics include red hair, pattern baldness, and nearsightedness. Sickle cell anemia is a recessive disease; Huntington disease is a dominant disease. Other traits are a result of partial dominance or co-dominance in which both genes are influential. For example, if a person inherits both recessive genes for sickle cell anemia, the disease will occur. But if a person has only one recessive gene for the disease, the person may experience effects of the disease only under circumstances of oxygen deprivation such as high altitudes or physical exertion (Berk, 2004).

Chromosomal Abnormalities and Genetic Disorders

A chromosomal abnormality occurs when there a child inherits too many or two few chromosomes. The most common cause of chromosomal abnormalities is the age of the mother. A 20 year old woman has a 1 in 800 chance of having a child with a common chromosomal abnormality. A woman of 44, however, has a one in 16 chance. It is believed that the problem occurs when the ovum is ripening prior to ovulation each month. As the mother ages, the ovum is more likely to suffer abnormalities at this time.

Some gametes do not divide evenly when they are forming. Therefore, some cells have more than 46 chromosomes. In fact, it is believed that close to half of all zygotes have an odd number of chromosomes. Most of these zygotes fail to develop and are spontaneously aborted by the body. If the abnormal number occurs on pair #21 or # 23, however, the individual may have certain physical or other abnormalities.

One of the most common chromosomal abnormalities is on pair 21. Trisomy 21 occurs when there are three rather than two chromosomes on #21. A person with Down syndrome experiences problems such as mental retardation and certain physical features such as having short fingers and toes, having folds of skin over the eyes, and a protruding tongue. Life expectancy of persons with Down syndrome has increased in recent years. Keep in mind that there is as much variation in people with Down Syndrome as in most populations and those differences need to be recognized and appreciated. Watch the following video clip about Down Syndrome from the National Down Syndrome Society:

https://www.youtube.com/watch?v=TIcbFrt4F_c

When the abnormality is on pair #23, the result is a sex-linked chromosomal abnormality. A person might have XXY, XYY, XXX, XO, or 45 or 47 chromosomes as a result. Two of the more common sex-linked chromosomal disorders are Turner's syndrome and Klinefelter's syndrome. Turner's syndrome occurs in 1 of every 2,500 live female births (Carroll, 2007) when an ovum which lacks a chromosome is fertilized by a sperm with an X chromosome. The resulting zygote has an XO composition. Fertilization by a Y sperm is not viable. Turner syndrome affects cognitive functioning and sexual maturation. The external genitalia appear normal, but breasts and ovaries do not develop fully and the woman does not menstruate. Turner's syndrome also results in short stature and other physical characteristics. Learn more at www.turnersyndrome.org/. Klinefelter's syndrome (XXY) occurs in 1 out of 700 live male births and results when an ovum containing an extra X chromosome is fertilized by a Y sperm. The Y chromosome stimulates the growth of male genitalia, but the additional X chromosome inhibits this development. An individual with Klinefelter's syndrome has some breast development, infertility (this is the most common cause of infertility in males), and has low levels of testosterone.

Most of the known genetic disorders are dominant gene-linked; however, the vast majority of dominant gene linked disorders are not serious disorders, or if they are, they may still not be debilitating. For example, the majority of those with Tourette's Syndrome suffer only minor tics from time to time and can easily control or cover up their symptoms. Huntington's Disease is a dominant gene linked disorder that affects the nervous system and is fatal but does not appear until midlife. Recessive gene disorders, such as cystic fibrosis and sickel-cell anemia, are less common but may actually claim more lives because they are less likely to be detected as people are unaware that they are carriers of the disease. If the genes inherited from each parent are the same, the child is homozygous for a particular trait and will inherit the trait. If, however, the child inherits a gene from one parent but not the other, the child is heterozygous, and interaction between the genes will in part determine whether or not that trait is expressed (Berk, 2004).

REFERENCES

Berger, K. S. (2005). The developing person through the life span (6th ed.). New York: Worth.

Berk, L. (2004). Development through the life span (3rd ed.). Boston: Allyn and Bacon.

Bortolus, R., Parazzini, F., Chatenoud, L., Benzi, G., Bianchi, M. M., & Marini, A. (1999). The epidemiology of multiple births. Human Reproduction Update, 5, 179-187.

Brazelton, T. B., & Nugent, J. K. (1995). Neonatal behavioral assessment scale. London: Mac Keith Press.

Carrell, D. T., Wilcox, A. L., Lowry, L., Peterson, C. M., Jones, K. P., & Erikson, L. (2003). Elevated sperm chromosome aneuploidy and apoptosis in patients with unexplained recurrent pregnancy loss. Obstetrics and Gynecology, 101(6), 1229-1235.

Carroll, J. L. (2007). Sexuality now: Embracing diversity (2nd ed.). Belmont, CA: Thomson.

Dietrich, K. N. (1999). Environmental toxicants and child development. In Tager-Flusberg (Ed.), Neurodevelopmental disorders (pp. 469-490). Boston: MIT Press.

FASD, NCBDDD, CDC. (2006, July/August). Centers for Disease Control and Prevention. Retrieved May 03, 2011, from http://www.cdc.gov/ncbddd/fas/fasask.htm

Galinsky, E. (1987). The six stages of parenthood. Reading, MA: Addison-Wesley Pub.

Gottlieb, G. (1998). Normally occurring environmental and behavioral influences on gene activity: From central dogma to probabilistic epigenesis. Psychological Review, 105, 792-802.

Gottlieb, G. (2000). Environmental and behavioral influences on gene activity. Current Directions in Psychological Science, 9, 93-97.

Gottlieb, G. (2002). Individual development and evolution: The genesis of novel behavior. New York: Oxford University Press.

Gould, J. L. (1997). Biological science. New York: Norton.

Lippa, R. A. (2002). Gender, nature, and nurture. Mahwah, NJ: L. Erlbaum.

MacDorman, M., Menacker, F., & Declercq, E. (2010, August 30). Trends and Characteristics of Home and Other out of Hospital Births in the United States, 1990-2006 (United States, Center for Disease Control). Retrieved December 22, 2010, from http://www.cdc.gov/nchs/data/nvsr/nvsr58;nvsr58_11.PDF

Mackon, N., & Fauser, B. (2000). Aspects of ovarian follicle development throughout life. Hormone Research, 52, 161-170.

McKusick, V. A. (1998). Mendelian inheritance in man: A catalog of human genes and genetic disorders. Baltimore, MD: Johns Hopkins University Press.

Moore, K. L., & Persaud, T. V. (1998). Before we are born (5th ed.). Philadelphia, PA: Saunders.

Mutti, D. O., Zadnik, K., & Adams, A. J. (n.d.). Myopia. The nature versus nurture debate goes on. Investigative Ophthalmology & Visual Science. Retrieved May 03, 2011, from http://www.iovs.org/cgi/reprint/37/6/952

Newell, M. (2005). Current issues in the prevention of mother-to-child transmission of HIV-1 infection. Transactions of the Royal Society of Tropical Medicine and Hygiene, 100(1), 1-5. doi: 10.1016/j.trstmh.2005.05.012

Rome, E. (1998). Anatomy and physiology of sexuality and reproduction. In The New Our Bodies, Ourselves (pp. 241-258). Carmichael, CA: Touchstone Books.

UNAIDS, World Health Organization. (2005). Adults and Children Estimated to Be Living with HIV as of the End of 2005. Retrieved August 13, 2006, from http://www.unaids.org?NetTools/Misc/DocInfo.aspx?LANG=en&href http://GVA-DOC-OWL/WEBcontent/Documents/pub/Topics/Epidemiology/Slides02/12-05/EpiCoreDec05Slide004_en.ppt

United States, Center for Disease Control. (n.d.). The Health Consequences of Smoking: 2004 Report of the Surgeon General. Retrieved August 14, 2004, from http://www.cdc.gov/tobacco/sqr/sqr_2004

United States, Center for Disease Control. (2006, July/August). Sexually Transmitted Diseases Treatment Guidelines. Retrieved August 14, 2006, from http://www.cdc.gov/std/treatment/2006/rr5511.pdf

United States, Center for Disease Control, Health and Human Services. (2010, October 5). Centers for Disease Control and Prevention. Retrieved May 03, 2011, from http://www.cdc.gov/nchs/faststats/birthwt.htm

United States, Center for Disease Control, National Center on Birth Defects and Developmental Disabilities.

(2004, October 29). Fast Facts about Medication Use during Pregnancy and While Breastfeeding. Retrieved August 10, 2006, from http://www.cdc.gov/ncbddd/fas/fasask.htm

World Health Organization. (2010, September 15). Maternal Deaths Worldwide Drop by a Third, WHO. Retrieved December 22, 2010, from http://www.who.int/mediacentre/news/releases/2010/maternal_mortality_20100915/en/index.html

CC licensed content, Shared previously

- Psyc 200 Lifespan Psychology. **Authored by**: Laura Overstreet. **Located at**: http://opencourselibrary.org/econ-201/. **License**: *CC BY: Attribution*
- Down Syndrome - Ability Awareness PSA Video. **Authored by**: rosaryfilms. **Located at**: https://www.youtube.com/watch?v=TIcbFrt4F_c. **License**: *CC BY: Attribution*

Prenatal Development

Periods of Prenatal Development

Now we turn our attention to prenatal development which is divided into three periods: the germinal period, the embryonic period, and the fetal period. Here is an overview of some of the changes that take place during each period.

The Germinal Period

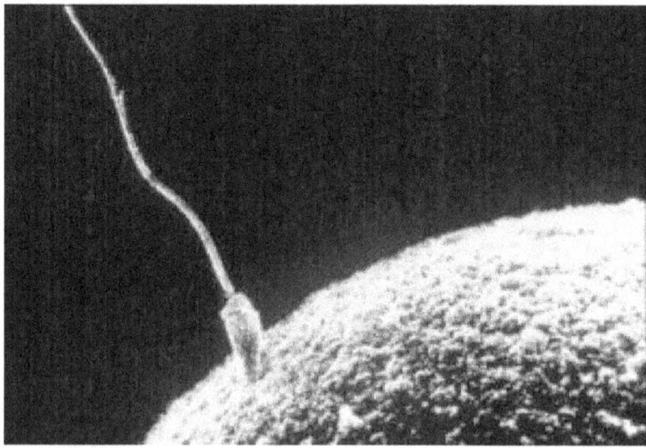

Sperm and Ovum at Conception

The germinal period (about 14 days in length) lasts from conception to implantation of the zygote (fertilized egg) in the lining of the uterus. During this time, the organism begins cell division and growth. After the fourth doubling, differentiation of the cells begins to occur as well. It's estimated that about 60 percent of natural conceptions fail to implant in the uterus. The rate is higher for in vitro conceptions.

The Embryonic Period

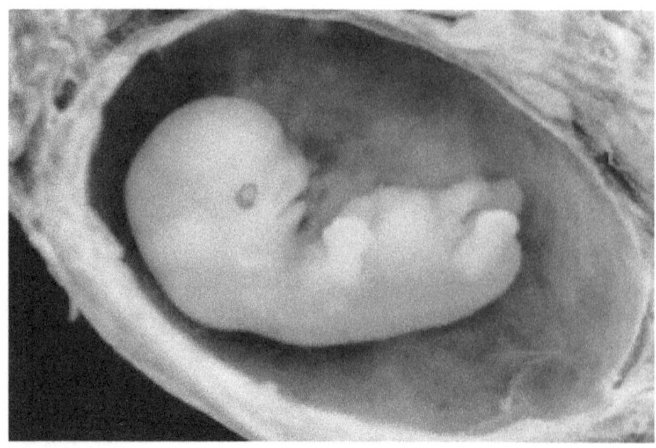

Photo by Lunar Caustic

This period begins once the organism is implanted in the uterine wall. It lasts from the third through the eighth week after conception. During this period, cells continue to differentiate and at 22 days after conception the neural tube forms which will become the brain and spinal column. Growth during prenatal development occurs in two major directions: from head to tail (cephalocaudal development) and from the midline outward (proximodistal development). This means that those structures nearest the head develop before those nearest the feet and those structures nearest the torso develop before those away from the center of the body (such as hands and fingers). The head develops in the fourth week and the precursor to the heart begins to pulse. In the early stages of the embryonic period, gills and a tail are apparent. But by the end of this stage, they disappear and the organism takes on a more human appearance. About 20 percent of organisms fail during the embryonic period, usually due to gross chromosomal abnormalities. As in the case of the germinal period, often the mother does not yet know that she is pregnant. It is during this stage that the major structures of the body are taking form making the embryonic period the time when the organism is most vulnerable to the greatest amount of damage if exposed to harmful substances. (We will look at this in the section on teratology below.) Potential mothers are not often aware of the risks they introduce to the developing child during this time. The embryo is approximately 1 inch in length and weighs about 4 grams at the end of this period. The embryo can move and respond to touch at this time.

The Fetal Period

From the ninth week until birth, the organism is referred to as a fetus. During this stage, the major structures are continuing to develop. By the 12th week, the fetus has all its body parts including external genitalia. In the following weeks, the fetus will develop hair, nails, teeth and the excretory and digestive systems will continue to develop. At the end of the 12th week, the fetus is about 3 inches long and weighs about 28 grams.

During the 4-6th months, the eyes become more sensitive to light and hearing de, hearing develops. Respiratory system continues to develop. Reflexes such as sucking, swallowing and hiccupping develop during the 5th month. Cycles of sleep and wakefulness are present at that time as well. The first chance of survival outside the womb, known as the age of viability is reached at about 22 and 26 weeks (Moore & Persaud, 1998). Many practitioners hesitate to resuscitation before 24 weeks. The majority of the neurons in the brain have developed by 24 weeks although they are still rudimentary and the glial or nurse cells that support neurons continue to grow. At 24 weeks the fetus can feel pain (Royal College of Obstetricians and Gynecologists, 1997).

Between the 7th and 9th months the fetus is primarily preparing for birth. It is exercising its muscles, its lungs begin to expand and contract. It is developing fat layers under the skin. The fetus gains about 5 pounds and 7 inches during this last trimester of pregnancy which includes a layer of fat gained during the 8th month. This layer of fat serves as insulation and helps the baby regulate body temperature after birth.
CC licensed content, Shared previously

Environmental Risks

Teratology

Good prenatal care is essential. The developing child is most at risk for some of the most severe problems during the first three months of development. Unfortunately, this is a time at which most mothers are unaware that they are pregnant. Today, we know many of the factors that can jeopardize the health of the developing child. The study of factors that contribute to birth defects is called teratology. Teratogens are factors that can contribute to birth defects which include some maternal diseases, pollutants, drugs and alcohol.

Factors influencing prenatal risks: There are several considerations in determining the type and amount of damage that might result from exposure to a particular teratogen (Berger, 2004). These include:

- The timing of the exposure: Structures in the body are vulnerable to the most severe damage when they are forming. If a substance is introduced during a particular structure's critical period (time of development), the damage to that structure may be greater. For example, the ears and arms reach their critical periods at about 6 weeks after conception. If a mother exposes the embryo to certain substances during this period, the arms and ears may be malformed.
- The amount of exposure: Some substances are not harmful unless the amounts reach a certain level. The critical level depends in part on the size and metabolism of the mother.
- Genetics: Genetic make-up also plays a role on the impact a particular teratogen might have on the child. This is suggested by fraternal twin studies who are exposed to the same prenatal environment, yet do not experience the same teratogenic effects. The genetic make-up of the mother can also have an effect; some mothers may be more resistant to teratogenic effects than others.
- Being male or female: Males are more likely to experience damage due to teratogens than are females. It is believed that the Y chromosome, which contains fewer genes than the X, may have an impact.

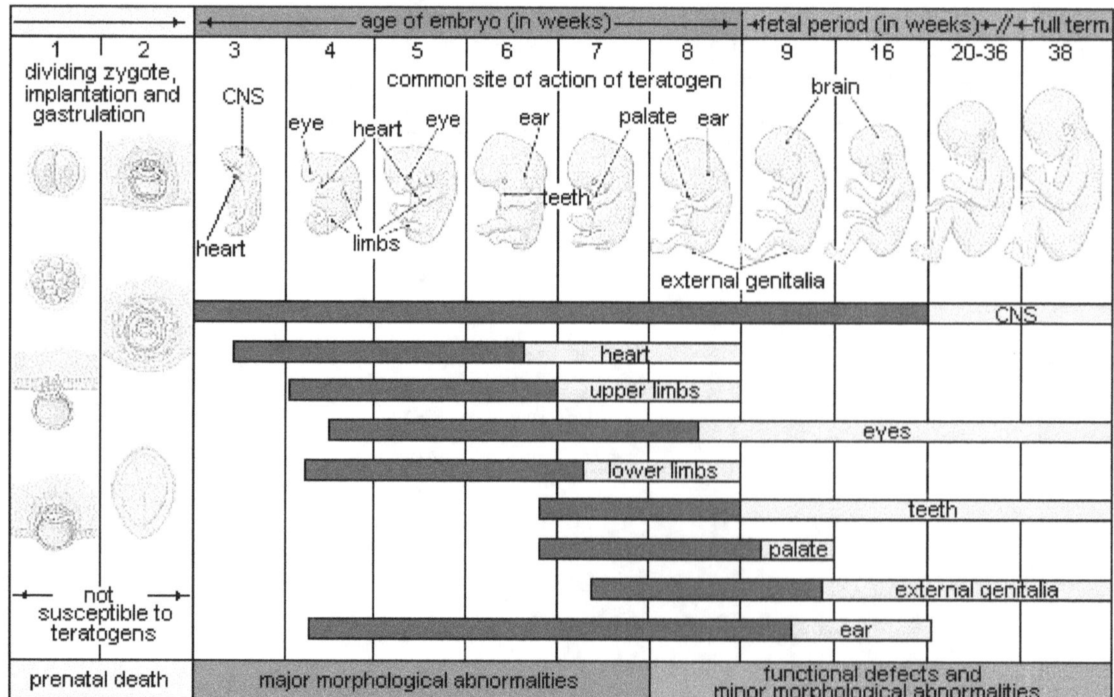

Critical Periods of Prenatal Development

A look at some teratogens

One of the most commonly used teratogens is alcohol and because half of all pregnancies in the United States are unplanned, it is recommended that women of child-bearing age take great caution against drinking alcohol when not using birth control or when pregnant (Surgeon General's Advisory on Alcohol Use During Pregnancy, 2005). Alcohol consumption, particularly during the second month of prenatal development but at any point during pregnancy may lead to neurocognitive and behavioral difficulties that can last a lifetime. Binge drinking (5 or more on a single occasion) or 7 or more drinks during a single week place a child at risk. In extreme cases, alcohol consumption can lead to fetal death but more frequently it can result in fetal alcohol spectrum disorders (FASD) (this terminology is now used when looking at the effects of exposure and replaces the term fetal alcohol syndrome. It is preferred because it recognizes that symptoms occur on a spectrum and that all individuals do not have the same characteristics.) Children with FASD share certain physical features such as flattened noses, small eye holes, and small heads, intellectual developmental delay, and behavioral problems. Those with FASD are more at risk for lifelong problems such as criminal behavior, psychiatric problems, and unemployment (CDC, 2006). The terms alcohol-related neurological disorder (ARND) and alcohol-related birth defects (ARBD) have replaced the term Fetal Alcohol Effects to refer to those with less extreme symptoms of FASD. ARBD include kidney, bone and heart problems.

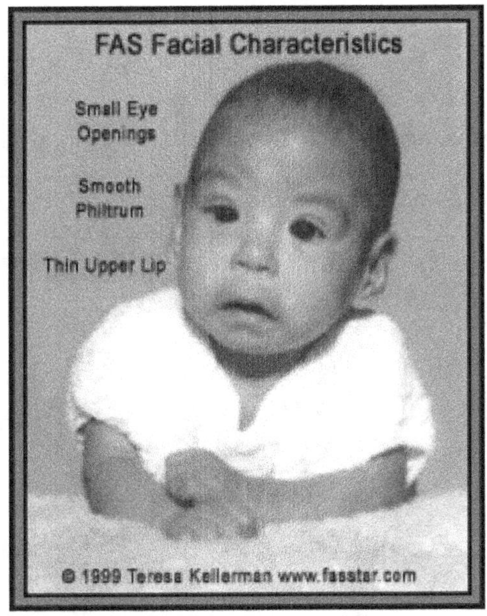

Tobacco is the second most widely used teratogen and the number of adolescent females who smoke is increasing. In fact, among adolescents, females are just as likely to smoke as are males. Tobacco use during pregnancy has been associated with low birth weight, placenta previa, preterm delivery, fetal growth restriction and sudden infant death syndrome (Center for Disease Control, 2004).

Illicit drugs as well as prescribed medications can have serious teratogenic effects. It is difficult to completely determine the effects of a particular illicit drug on a developing child because most mothers, who use, use more than one substance. However, several problems seem clear. The use of cocaine is connected with low birth weight, stillbirths and spontaneous abortion. Heavy marijuana use is associated with brain damage and mothers addicted to heroin often pass that addiction to their child. And many medications do not include adequate information on risks posed if taken during pregnancy (Center for Disease Control, 2004).

Pollutants

Some environmental pollutants of major concern include lead poisoning, which is connected with low birth weight and slowed neurological development. Children who live in older housing in which lead based paints have been used have been known to eat peeling paint chips thus being exposed to lead. The chemicals in certain herbicides are also potentially damaging. Radiation is another environmental hazard. If a mother is exposed to radiation, particularly during the first 3 months of pregnancy, the child may suffer some congenital deformities. There is also an increased risk of miscarriage and stillbirth. Mercury leads to physical deformities and mental retardation (Dietrich, 1999).

HIV

One of the most potentially devastating teratogens is HIV. In the United States, the fastest growing group of people with AIDS is women; globally half of all people infected with HIV are women (UNAIDS, 2005). It is estimated that between 630,000 to 820,000 children were newly infected with HIV worldwide in 2005. Most of this infection is from mother-to-child through the placenta or birth canal (Newell, 2005). There are some measures that can be taken to lower the chance the child will contract the disease (such as the use of antiretroviral drugs from 14 weeks after conception until birth, avoiding breastfeeding, and delivering the child by c-section), many women do not know they are HIV positive during pregnancy. Still others cannot afford the costly drugs used for treating AIDS. The transmission rate of HIV from mother to child has been reduced in the United States to between 100-200 infants annually. Go to http://www.cdc.gov/hiv/topics/perinatal/resources/factsheets/perinatal.htm to learn more.

Maternal Diseases

German measles (or rubella) have been associated with a number of maladies. If the mother contracts the disease during the first three months of pregnancy, damage can occur in the eyes, ears, heart or brain of the unborn child. Deafness is almost certain if the mother has German measles before the 11th week of prenatal development and can also cause brain damage. Gonorrhea, syphilis, and Chlamydia are sexually transmitted infections that can be passed to the fetus by an infected mother; mothers should be tested as early as possible to minimize the risk of spreading these infections (Center for Disease Control, 2006).

CC licensed content, Shared previously

Pregnancy

Complications of Pregnancy

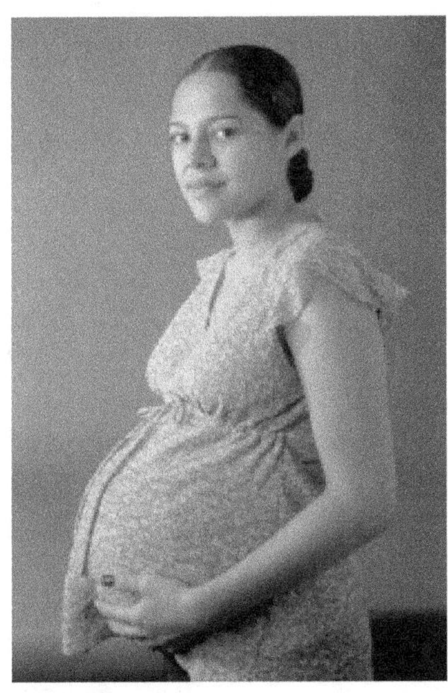

Minor complications: There are a number of common side effects of pregnancy. Not everyone experiences all of these nor to the same degree. And although they are considered "minor" this is not to say that these problems are potentially very uncomfortable. These side effects include nausea (particularly during the first 3-4 months of pregnancy as a result of higher levels of estrogen in the system), heartburn, gas, hemorrhoids, backache, leg cramps, insomnia, constipation, shortness of breath or varicose veins (as a result of carrying a heavy load on the abdomen). What is the cure? Delivery!

Major Complications: The following are some serious complications of pregnancy which can pose health risks to mother and child and that often require hospitalization. Ectopic pregnancy occurs when the zygote becomes attached to the fallopian tube before reaching the uterus. About 1 in 50 pregnancies in the United States are tubal pregnancies and this number has been increasing because of the higher rates of pelvic inflammatory disease and Chlamydia (Carroll, 2007). Abdominal pain, vaginal bleeding, nausea and fainting are symptoms of ectopic pregnancy. Toxemia or blood poisoning due to kidney malfunction is experienced by 6 to 7 percent of women during their last months of pregnancy. If untreated toxemia can lead to preeclampsia or swelling and hypertension or progress to eclampsia which is can involve coma or death.

Maternal Mortality: Approximately 1000 women die in childbirth around the world each day (World Health Organization, 2010). Rates are highest in Subsaharan Africa and South Asia although there has been a substantial decrease in these rates. The campaign to make childbirth safe for everyone has led to the development of clinics accessible to those living in more isolated areas and training more midwives to assist in childbirth.

Spontaneous abortion is experienced in an estimated 20-40 percent of undiagnosed pregnancies and in another 10 percent of diagnosed pregnancy. Usually the body aborts due to chromosomal abnormalities and this typically happened before the 12th week of pregnancy. Cramping and bleeding result and normal periods return after several months. Some women are more likely to have repeated miscarriages due to chromosomal, amniotic, or hormonal problems; but miscarriage can also be a result of defective sperm (Carroll et. al., 2003).

Problems of the Newborn

Low Birth weight

We have been discussing a number of teratogens associated with low birth weight such as cocaine, tobacco, etc. A child is considered low birth weight if he or she weighs less than 5.8 pounds (2500 grams). About 8.2 percent of babies born in the United States are of low birth weight (Center for Disease Control, 2010). A low birth weight baby has difficulty maintaining adequate body temperature because it lacks the fat that would otherwise provide insulation. Such a baby is also at more risk for infection. And 67 percent of these babies are also preterm which can make them more at risk for respiratory infection. Very low birth weight babies (2 pounds or less) have an increased risk of developing cerebral palsy. Many causes of low birth weight are preventable with proper prenatal care, however.

Premature Birth

A child might also have a low birth weight if it is born at less than 37 weeks gestation (which qualifies it as a preterm baby). Early birth can be triggered by anything that disrupts the mother's system. For instance, vaginal infections or gum disease can actually lead to premature birth because such infection causes the mother to release anti-inflammatory chemicals which, in turn, can trigger contractions. Smoking and the use of other teratogens can lead to preterm birth.

Anoxia

Anoxia is a temporary lack of oxygen to the brain. Difficulty during delivery may lead to anoxia which can result in brain damage or in severe cases, death. Babies who suffer both low birth weight and anoxia are more likely to suffer learning disabilities later in life as well.

CC licensed content, Shared previously

- Psyc 200 Lifespan Psychology. **Authored by**: Laura Overstreet. **Located at**: http://opencourselibrary.org/econ-201/. **License**: *CC BY: Attribution*

Childbirth

Approaches to Childbirth

Prepared childbirth refers to being not only physically in good condition to help provide a healthy environment for the baby to develop, but also helping a couple to prepare to accept their new roles as parents and to get information and training that will assist them for delivery and life with the baby as much as possible. The more a couple can learn about childbirth and the newborn, the better prepared they will be for the adjustment they must make to a new life. (Nothing can prepare a couple for this completely). Once a couple finds that they are to have a child, they begin to conjure up images of what they think the experience will involve. Once the child is born, they must reconcile those images with reality (Galinsky, 1987). Knowing more of what to expect does help them in forming more realistic images thus making the adjustment easier. Let's explore some of the methods of prepared childbirth.

The Dick-Read Method of Natural Childbirth

Grantley Dick-Read was an English obstetrician and pioneer of prepared childbirth in the 1930s. In his book Childbirth Without Fear, he suggests that the fear of childbirth increases tension and make the process of childbearing more painful. He believed that if mothers were educated, the fear and tension would be reduced and the need for medication could frequently be eliminated. The Dick-Read method emphasized the use of relaxation and proper breathing with contractions as well as family support and education. (For more current information on this method go to www.hypnobirthing.com) This method influenced the most commonly taught method in the U.S. today, the Lamaze Method.

The Lamaze Method

This method originated in Russia and was brought to the United States in the 1950s by Fernand Lamaze. The emphasis of this method is on teaching the woman to be in control in the process of delivery. It includes learning muscle relaxation, breathing though contractions, having a focal point (usually a picture to look at) during contractions and having a support person who goes through the training process with the mother and serves as a coach during delivery.

Birthing Centers/Birthing Rooms

The trend now is to have birthing rooms that are hospital rooms that look more like a suite in a hotel equipped with a bed that can be converted for delivery. These rooms are also equipped with a bed and monitoring systems for the newborn. However, many hospitals have only one or two of these rooms and availability can be a problem.

The LeBoyer Method

Other birthing options include the use of birthing chairs, which make use of gravity in assisting the woman giving birth and the Leboyer Method of "Gentle Birthing". This method involves giving birth in a quiet, dimly lit room and allowing the newborn to lie on the mother's stomach with the umbilical cord intact for sever minutes while being given a warm bath.

Home Birth and Nurse-Midwives

Historically in the United States, most babies were born under the care of lay midwives. In the 1920s, middle class women were increasingly using doctors to assist with childbirth but rural women were still being assisted by lay midwives. The nursing profession began educating nurse-midwives to assist these women. Nurse-midwives continued to assist most rural women with delivery until the 1970s and 1980s when their growth is thought to have posed a threat to the medical profession (Weitz, 2007). Since that time, nurse-midwives have found it more difficult to sustain practices with the high costs of malpractice insurance. (Many physicians have changed areas of specialization in response to these costs as well.) Women who are at low risk for birth complications can successfully deliver under the care of nurse-midwives but only 1 percent of births occur at home. Because one out of every 20 births involves a complication, most medical professionals recommend that delivery take place in a hospital. However, some couples choose to have their baby at home. About 1 percent of births occur out of a hospital in the United States. Two-thirds of these are homebirths and more than half of these are assisted by midwives. Midwives are trained and licensed to assist in delivery and are far less expensive than the cost of a hospital delivery. One-third of out-of-hospital births occur in freestanding clinics, birthing centers, or in physicians offices or other locations. In the United States, women who have had previous children, who are over 25 and who are white are more likely to have out-of-hospital births (MacDorman, et. als., 2010).

The Process of Delivery

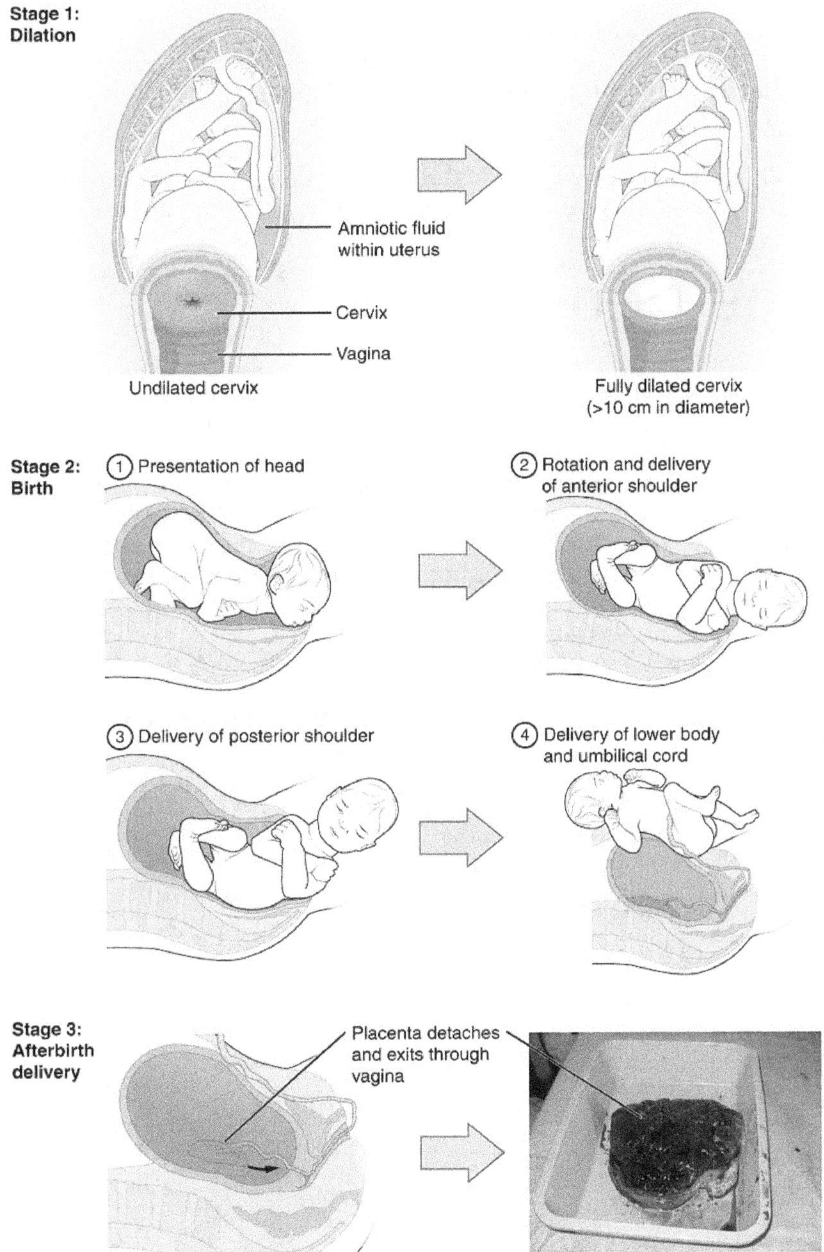

The stages of childbirth.

The First Stage of labor begins with uterine contractions that may initially last about 30 seconds and be spaced 15 to 20 minutes apart. These increase in duration and frequency to more than a minute in length and about 3 to 4 minutes apart. Typically, doctors advise that they be called when contractions are coming about every 5 minutes. Some women experience false labor or Braxton-Hicks contractions, especially with the first child. These may come and go. They tend to diminish when the mother begins walking around. Real labor pains tend to increase with walking. Labor may also be signaled by a bloody discharge being expelled from the cervix. In one out of 8 pregnancies, the amniotic sac or water in which the fetus is suspended may break before labor begins. In such cases, the physician may induce labor with the use of medication if it does not begin in order to reduce the risk of infection. Normally this sac does not rupture until the later stages of labor.

The first stage of labor is typically the longest. During this stage the cervix or opening to the uterus dilates to 10 centimeters or just under 4 inches. This may take around 12-16 hours for first children or about 6-9 hours for women who have previously given birth. It takes one woman in 9 over 24 hours to dilate completely. Labor may also begin with a discharge of blood or amniotic fluid. If the amniotic sack breaks, labor will be induced if necessary to reduce the risk of infection.

The second stage involves the passage of the baby through the birth canal. This stage takes about 10-40 minutes. Contractions usually come about every 2-3 minutes. The mother pushes and relaxes as directed by the medical staff. Normally the head is delivered first. The baby is then rotated so that one shoulder can come through and then the other shoulder. The rest of the baby quickly passes through. At this stage, an episiotomy may be performed to avoid tearing the tissue of the back of the vaginal opening. The baby's mouth and nose are suctioned out. The umbilical cord is clamped and cut.

The third stage is relatively painless. During this stage, the placenta or afterbirth is delivered. This typically within 20 minutes after delivery. If an episiotomy was performed it is stitched up during this stage.

Assessing the Neonate

There are several ways to assess the condition of the newborn. The most widely used tool is the Neonatal Behavioral Assessment Scale (NBAS) developed by T. Berry Brazelton. This tool has been used around the world to help parents get to know their infants and to make comparisons of infants in different cultures (Brazelton & Nugent, 1995). The baby's motor development, muscle tone, and stress response is assessed. The Apgar is conducted one minute and five minutes after birth. This is a very quick way to assess the newborn's overall condition. Five measures are assessed: the heart rate, respiration, muscle tone (quickly assessed by a skilled nurse when the baby is handed to them or by touching the baby's palm), reflex response (the Babinski reflex is tested), and color. A score of 0 to 2 is given on each feature examined. An Apgar of 5 or less is cause for concern. The second Apgar should indicate improvement with a higher score.
CC licensed content, Shared previously

Module 4: Infancy

Introduction to Infancy

Learning Objectives

At the end of this lesson, you will be able to

Summarize overall physical growth during infancy.
Describe the growth of the brain during infancy.
Contrast development of the senses in newborns.
Compare gross and fine motor skills and give examples of each.
Explain the merits of breastfeeding.
Discuss nutritional concerns of marasmus and kwashiorkor.
List and describe the six substages of sensorimotor intelligence.
Describe stages of language development during infancy.
Define babbling, holophrasic speech, and overregularization.
Contrast styles of attachment.
Discuss the importance of temperament and goodness of fit.
Describe self-awareness, stranger wariness, and separation anxiety.
Use Erikson's theory to characterize psychosocial development during infancy.

Introduction

Welcome to the story of development from infancy through toddlerhood; from birth until about two years of age. Researchers have given this part of the life span more attention than any other period, perhaps because changes during this time are so dramatic and so noticeable and perhaps because we have assumed that what happens during these years provides a foundation for one's life to come. However, it has been argued that the significance of development during these years has been overstated (Bruer, 1999). Nevertheless, this is a period of life that contemporary educators, healthcare providers, and parents have focused on most heavily. We will examine growth and nutrition during infancy, cognitive development during the first 2 years, and then turn our attention toward attachments formed in infancy.

REFERENCES

Berger, K. S. (2001). The developing person through the life span. New York: Worth.

Berger, K. S. (2005). The developing person through the life span (6th ed.). New York: Worth.

Berk, L. E. (n.d.). Development through the life span (4th ed.). Boston: Allyn and Bacon.

Bruer, J. T. (1999). The myth of the first three years: A new understanding of early brain development and lifelong learning. New York: Simon and Schuster.

Chess, S., & Thomas, A. (1996). Temperament: Theory and practice. New York: Brunner/Mazel.

Children's Welfare. (1998). Welfarem-L Digest, june 25. Retrieved August 10, 2006, from welfare-L@American.edu

Hart, S., & Carrington, H. (2002). Jealousy in 6-month-old infants. Infancy, 3(3), 395-402.

LeVine, R. A., Dixon, S., LeVine, S., Richman, A., Leiderman, P. H., Keefer, C. H., & Brazelton, T. B. (1994). Child care and culture: Lessons from Africa. New York: Cambridge University Press.

O'Connor, T. G., Marvin, R. S., Rotter, M., Olrich, J. T., Britner, P. A., & The English and Romanian Adoptees Study Team. (2003). Child-parent attachment following early institutional deprivation. Development and Psychopathology, 15, 19-38.

Sen, M. G., Yonas, A., & Knill, D. C. (2001). Development of infants' sensitivity to surface contour information for spatial layout. Perception, 30, 167-176.

Van Ijzendoorn, M. H., & Sagi, A. (n.d.). Cross-cultural patterns of attachment. In J. Cassidy & P. R. Shaver (Eds.), Handbook of attachment: Theory, research, and clinical applications (pp. 713-734). New York: Guilford.

Webb, S. J., Monk, C. S., & Nelson, C. A. (2001). Mechanisms of postnatal neurobiological development: Implications for human development. Developmental Neuropsychology, 19, 147-171.
CC licensed content, Shared previously

Physical Development

Overall Physical Growth

The average newborn in the United States weighs about 7.5 pounds and is about 20 inches in length. For the first few days of life, infants typically lose about 5 percent of their body weight as they eliminate waste and get used to feeding. This often goes unnoticed by most parents, but can be cause for concern for those who have a smaller infant. This weight loss is temporary, however, and is followed by a rapid period of growth. By the time an infant is 4 months old, it usually doubles in weight and by one year has tripled it birth weight. By age 2, the weight has quadrupled. The average length at one year is about 26-32 inches.

Body Proportions

Another dramatic physical change that takes place in the first several years of life is the change in body proportions. The head initially makes up about 50 percent of our entire length when we are developing in the womb. At birth, the head makes up about 25 percent of our length (think about how much of your length would be head if the proportions were still the same!). By age 25 it comprises about 20 percent our length. Imagine now how difficult it must be to raise one's head during the first year of life! And indeed, if you have ever seen a 2 to 4 month old infant lying on the stomach trying to raise the head, you know how much of a challenge this is.

The Brain in the First Two Years

Some of the most dramatic physical change that occurs during this period is in the brain. At birth, the brain is about 25 percent its adult weight and this is not true for any other part of the body. By age 2, it is at 75 percent its adult weight, at 95 percent by age 6 and at 100 percent by age 7 years.

While most of the brain's 100 to 200 billion neurons are present at birth, they are not fully mature and during the next several years dendrites or connections between neurons will undergo a period of transient exuberance or temporary dramatic growth. There is a proliferation of these dendrites during the first two years so that by age 2, a single neuron might have thousands of dendrites. After this dramatic increase, the neural pathways that are not used will be eliminated thereby making those that are used much stronger. This activity is occurring primarily in the cortex or the thin outer covering of the brain involved in voluntary activity and thinking. The prefrontal cortex that is located behind our forehead continues to grow and mature throughout childhood and experiences an addition growth spurt during adolescence. It is the last part of the brain to mature and will eventually comprise 85 percent of the brain's weight. Experience will shape which of these connections are maintained and which of these are lost. Ultimately, about 40 percent of these connections will be lost (Webb, Monk, and Nelson, 2001). As the prefrontal cortex matures, the child is increasingly able to regulate or control emotions, to plan activity, strategize, and have better judgment. Of course, this is not fully accomplished in infancy and toddlerhood, but continues throughout childhood and adolescence.

Another major change occurring in the central nervous system is the development of myelin, a coating of fatty tissues around the axon of the neuron. Myelin helps insulate the nerve cell and speed the rate of transmission of impulses from one cell to another. This enhances the building of neural pathways and improves coordination and control of movement and thought processes. The development of myelin continues into adolescence but is most dramatic during the first several years of life.

From Reflexes to Voluntary Movements

Infants are equipped with a number of reflexes which are involuntary movements in response to stimulation. These include the sucking reflex (infants suck on objects that touch their lips automatically), the rooting reflex, which involves turning toward any object that touches the cheek, the palmar grasp (the infant will tightly grasp any object placed in its palm), and the dancing reflex evidence when the infant is held in a standing position and moves its feet up and down alternately as if dancing. These movements occur automatically and are signals that the infant is functioning well neurologically. Within the first several weeks of life these reflexes are replaced with voluntary movements or motor skills.

Gross Motor Skills

These voluntary movements involve the use of large muscle groups and are typically large movements of the arms, legs, head, and torso. These skills begin to develop first. Examples include moving to bring the chin up when lying on the stomach, moving the chest up, rocking back and forth on hands and knees. But it also includes exploring an object with one's feet as many babies do as early as 8 weeks of age if seated in a carrier or other devise that frees the hips. This may be easier than reaching for an object with the hands, which requires much more practice (Berk, 2007). And sometimes an infant will try to move toward an object while crawling and surprisingly move backward because of the greater amount of strength in the arms than in the legs!

Fine Motor Skills

Fine motor skills are more exact movements of the hands and fingers and include the ability to reach and grasp an object. Newborns cannot grasp objects voluntarily but do wave their arms toward objects of interest. At about 4 months of age, the infant is able to reach for an object, first with both arms and within a few weeks, with only one arm. Grasping an object involves the use of the fingers and palm, but no thumbs. Stop reading for a moment and try to grasp an object using these fingers and the palm. How does that feel? How much control do you have over the object? If it is a pen or pencil, are you able to write with it? Can you draw a picture? The answer is probably not. Use of the thumb comes at about 9 months of age when the infant is able to grasp an object using the forefinger and thumb. This ability greatly enhances the ability to control and manipulate an object and infants take great delight in this newfound ability. They may spend hours picking up small objects from the floor and placing them in containers. By 9 months, an infant can also watch a moving object, reach for it as it approaches and grab it. This is quite a complicated set of actions if we remember how difficult this would have been just a few months earlier.

Sensory Development

Vision

The womb is a dark environment void of visual stimulation. Consequently, vision is the most poorly developed sense at birth. Newborns typically cannot see further than 8 to 16 inches away from their faces, have difficulty keeping a moving object within their gaze, and can detect contrast more than color differences. If you have ever seen a newborn struggle to see, you can appreciate the cognitive efforts being made to take in visual stimulation and build those neural pathways between the eye and the brain. When you glance at a person, where do you look? Chances are you look into their eyes. If so why? It is probably because there is more information there than in other parts of the face. Newborns do not scan objects this way; rather, they tend to look at the chin another less detailed part of the face. However, by 2 or 3 months, they will seek more detail when exploring an object visually and begin showing preferences for unusual images over familiar ones and for patterns over solids and faces over patterns and three-dimensional objects over flat images. Newborns have difficulty distinguishing between colors, but within a few months are able to discrimination between colors as well as do adults. Infants can also sense depth as binocular vision develops at about 2 months of age. By 6 months, the infant can perceive depth perception in pictures as well (Sen, Yonas, and Knill, 2001). Infants who have experience crawling and exploring will pay greater attention to visual cues of depth and modify their actions accordingly (Berk, 2007).

Hearing

The infant's sense of hearing is very keen at birth. If you remember, this ability to hear is evidenced as soon as the 5th month of prenatal development. In fact, an infant can distinguish between very similar sounds as early as one month after birth and can distinguish between a familiar and non-familiar voice even earlier. Some of this ability will be lost by 7 or 8 months as a child becomes familiar with the sounds of a particular language and less sensitive to sounds that are part of an unfamiliar language.

Other senses

Newborns can distinguish between sour, bitter, sweet, and salty flavors and show a preference for sweet flavors. They are sensitive to touch and can distinguish between their mother's scent and that of others.
CC licensed content, Shared previously

- Psyc 200 Lifespan Psychology. **Authored by**: Laura Overstreet. **Located at**: http://opencourselibrary.org/econ-201/. **License**: *CC BY: Attribution*

Nutrition

Breast milk is considered the ideal diet for newborns. It has the right amount of calories, fat, and protein to support overall physical and neurological development, it provides a source of iron more easily absorbed in the body than the iron found in dietary supplements, it provides a resistance against many diseases, it is more easily digested by infants than is formula, and it helps babies make a transition to solid foods more easily than if bottle fed. For all of these reasons, it is recommended that mothers breast feed their infants until at least 6 months of age and that breast milk be used in the diet throughout the first year (U.S. Department of Health and Human Services, 2004a in Berk, 2007).

However, most mothers who breastfeed in the United States stop breast feeding at about 6-8 weeks, often in order to return to work outside the home. Mothers can certainly continue to provide breast milk to their babies by expressing and freezing the milk to be bottle fed at a later time or by being available to their infants at feeding time, but some mothers find that after the initial encouragement they receive in the hospital to breast feed, the outside world is less supportive of such efforts. Some workplaces support breastfeeding mothers by providing flexible schedules and welcoming infants, but many do not. And the public support of breastfeeding is sometimes lacking. Women in Canada are more likely to breastfeed than are those in the United States and the Canadian health recommendation is for breastfeeding to continue until 2 years of age. Facilities in public places in Canada such as malls, ferries, and workplaces provide more support and comfort for the breastfeeding mother and child than found in the United States.

One early argument given to promote the practice of breastfeeding was that it promoted bonding and healthy emotional development for infants. However, this does not seem to be the case. Breastfed and bottle-fed infants adjust equally well emotionally (Ferguson and Woodward, 1999). This is good news for mothers who may be unable to breastfeed for a variety of reasons and for fathers who might feel left out as a result.

In addition to the nutritional benefits of breastfeeding, breast milk is free! Anyone who has priced formula recently can appreciate this added incentive to breastfeeding. Prices for a month's worth of formula can easily range from $130-200. Breastfeeding also stimulates contractions in the uterus to help it regain its normal size. And women who breastfeed are more likely to space their pregnancies further apart.

An historic look at breastfeeding

The use of wet nurses, or lactating women hired to nurse others' infants, during the middle ages eventually declined and mothers increasingly breastfed their own infants in the late 1800s. In the early part of the 20th century, breastfeeding began to go through another decline and by the 1950s, it was practiced less frequently by middle class, more affluent mothers as formula began to be viewed as superior to breast milk. In the late 1960s and 1970s, greater emphasis began to be placed on natural childbirth and breastfeeding and the benefits of breastfeeding were more widely publicized. Gradually rates of breastfeeding began to climb, particularly among middle-class educated mothers who received the strongest messages to breastfeed. Today, women receive consultation from lactation specialists before being discharged from the hospital to ensure that they are informed of the benefits of breastfeeding and given support and encouragement to get their infants to get used to taking the breast. This does not always happen immediately and first time mothers, especially, can become upset or discouraged. In this case, lactation specialists and nursing staff can encourage the mother to keep trying until baby and mother are comfortable with the feeding.

Global Considerations and Malnutrition

In the 1960s, formula companies led campaigns in developing countries to encourage mothers to feed their babies on infant formula. Many mothers felt that formula would be superior to breast milk and began using formula. The use of formula can certainly be healthy under conditions in which there is adequate, clean water with which to mix the formula and adequate means to sanitize bottles and nipples. However, in many of these countries such conditions were not available and babies often were given diluted, contaminated formula which made them become sick with diarrhea and become dehydrated. Rates of breast feeding declined in Peru from 90 percent to 10 percent in just 8 years time (Berger, 2001). These conditions continue today and now many hospitals prohibit the distribution of formula samples to new mothers in efforts to get them to rely on breast feeding. Many of these mothers do not understand the benefits of breast feeding and have to be encouraged and supported in order to promote this practice. Breast feeding could save the lives of millions of infants each year, according to the World Health Organization, yet fewer than 40 percent of infants are breastfed exclusively for the first 6 months of life. Find out more at the WHO's 10 facts on breastfeeding. Most women can breastfeed unless they are receiving chemotherapy or radiation therapy, have HIV, are dependent on illicit drugs, or have active, untreated tuberculosis.

Children in developing countries and countries experiencing the harsh conditions of war are at risk for two major types of malnutrition. Infantile marasmus refers to starvation due to a lack of calories and protein. Children who do not receive adequate nutrition lose fat and muscle until their bodies can no longer function. Babies who are breast fed are much less at risk of malnutrition than those who are bottle fed. After weaning, children who have diets deficient in protein may experience kwashiorkor or the "disease of the displaced child" often occurring after another child has been born and taken over breastfeeding. This results in a loss of appetite and swelling of the abdomen as the body begins to break down the vital organs as a source of protein.

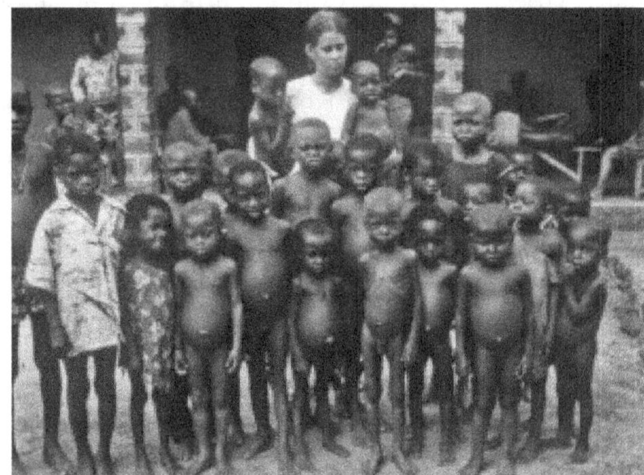

Kwashiorkor (Photo Courtesy Centers for Disease Control and Prevention)

The Breast Milk Industry

The benefits of breast milk are well-known and publicized. The collection and distribution of breast milk has become a million dollar industry supplying hospitals and others in need of the ideal diet. For more information, go to www.prolacta.com to see a current development in the story of breast milk.

Milk Anemia in the United States

About 9 million children in the United States are malnourished (Children's Welfare, 1998). More still suffer from milk anemia, a condition in which milk consumption leads to a lack of iron in the diet. This can be due to the practice of giving toddlers milk as a pacifier-when resting, when riding, when waking, and so on. Appetite declines somewhat during toddlerhood and a small amount of milk (especially with added chocolate syrup) can easily satisfy a child's appetite for many hours. The calcium in milk interferes with the absorption of iron in the diet as well. Many preschools and daycare centers give toddlers a drink after they have finished their meal in order to prevent spoiling their appetites.

CC licensed content, Shared previously

Cognitive Development

Piaget and Sensorimotor Intelligence

Remember our discussion of sensorimotor development during the first two years of life. Piaget describes intelligence in infancy as sensorimotor or based on direct, physical contact. Infants taste, feel, pound, push, hear, and move in order to experience the world. Let's explore the transition infants make from responding to the external world reflexively as newborns to solving problems using mental strategies as two year olds.

Stage One: Reflexive Action: (Birth through 1st month)

This active learning begins with automatic movements or reflexes. A ball comes into contact with an infant's cheek and is automatically sucked on and licked. But this is also what happens with a sour lemon, much to the infant's surprise!

Stage Two: First Adaptations to the Environment (1st through 4th month)

Fortunately, within a few days or weeks, the infant begins to discriminate between objects and adjust responses accordingly as reflexes are replaced with voluntary movements. An infant may accidentally engage in a behavior and find it interesting such as making a vocalization. This interest motivates trying to do it again and helps the infant learn a new behavior that originally occurred by chance. At first, most actions have to do with the body, but in months to come, will be directed more toward objects.

Stage Three: Repetition (4th through 8th months)

During the next few months, the infant becomes more and more actively engaged in the outside world and takes delight in being able to make things happen. Repeated motion brings particular interest as the infant is able to bang two lids together from the cupboard when seated on the kitchen floor.

Stage Four: New Adaptations and Goal-Directed Behavior (8th through 12th months)

Now the infant can engage in behaviors that others perform and anticipate upcoming events. Perhaps because of continued maturation of the prefrontal cortex, the infant become capable of having a thought and carrying out a planned, goal-directed activity such as seeking a toy that has rolled under the couch. The object continues to exist in the infant's mind even when out of sight and the infant now is capable of making attempts to retrieve it. Here is an example of a lack of object permanence.

Was Piaget correct? Infants seem to be able to recognize that objects have permanence at much younger ages (even as young as 3.5 months of age).

Dr. Rene Baillargeon explains in the following clip:

https://www.youtube.com/watch?v=hwgo2O5Vk_g

Stage Five: Active Experimentation of Little Scientists (12th through 18th months)

Infants from one year to 18 months of age more actively engage in experimentation to learn about the physical world. Gravity is learned by pouring water from a cup or pushing bowls from high chairs. The caregiver tries to help the child by picking it up again and placing it on the tray. And what happens? Another experiment! The child pushes it off the tray again causing it to fall and the caregiver to pick it up again! A closer examination of this stage causes us to really appreciate how much learning is going on at this time and how many things we come to take for granted must actually be learned. I remember handing my daughters (who are close in age) when they were both seated in the back seat of the car a small container of candy. They struggled to move the pieces up and out of the small box and became frustrated when their fingers would lose their grip on the treats before they made it up and out of the top of the boxes. They had not yet learned to simply use gravity and turn the box over in their hands! This is a wonderful and messy time of experimentation and most learning occurs by trial and error.

Stage Six: Mental Representations (18th month to 2 years of age)

The child is now able to solve problems using mental strategies, to remember something heard days before and repeat it, to engage in pretend play, and to find objects that have been moved even when out of sight. Take for instance, the child who is upstairs in a room with the door closed, supposedly taking a nap. The doorknob has a safety device on it that makes it impossible for the child to turn the knob. After trying several times in vain to push the door or turn the doorknob, the child carries out a mental strategy to get the door opened-he knocks on the door! Obviously, this is a technique learned from the past experience of hearing a knock on the door and observing someone opening the door. The child is now better equipped with mental strategies for problem-solving. This initial movement from the "hands-on" approach to knowing about the world to the more mental world of stage six marked the transition to preoperational intelligence that we will discuss in the next lesson. Part of this stage involves learning to use language.

CC licensed content, Shared previously

All rights reserved content

Language Development

Newborn Communication

Baby boy at 8 months.

Do newborns communicate? Certainly, they do. They do not, however, communicate with the use of language. Instead, they communicate their thoughts and needs with body posture (being relaxed or still), gestures, cries, and facial expressions. A person who spends adequate time with an infant can learn which cries indicate pain and which ones indicate hunger, discomfort, or frustration.

Intentional Vocalizations: Cooing and taking turns: Infants begin to vocalize and repeat vocalizations within the first couple of months of life. That gurgling, musical vocalization called cooing can serve as a source of entertainment to an infant who has been laid down for a nap or seated in a carrier on a car ride. Cooing serves as practice for vocalization as well as the infant hears the sound of his or her own voice and tries to repeat sounds that are entertaining. Infants also begin to learn the pace and pause of conversation as they alternate their vocalization with that of someone else and then take their turn again when the other person's vocalization has stopped. Cooing initially involves making vowel sounds like "oooo". Later, consonants are added to vocalizations such as "nananananana".

Babbling and gesturing: At about four to six months of age, infants begin making even more elaborate vocalizations that include the sounds required for any language. Guttural sounds, clicks, consonants, and vowel sounds stand ready to equip the child with the ability to repeat whatever sounds are characteristic of the language heard. Eventually, these sounds will no longer be used as the infant grow more accustomed to a particular language. Deaf babies also use gestures to communicate wants, reactions, and feelings. Because gesturing seems to be easier than vocalization for some toddlers, sign language is sometimes taught to enhance one's ability to communicate by making use of the ease of gesturing. The rhythm and pattern of language is used when deaf babies sign just as it is when hearing babies babble.

Understanding: At around ten months of age, the infant can understand more than he or she can say. You may have experienced this phenomenon as well if you have ever tried to learn a second language. You may have been able to follow a conversation more easily than to contribute to it.

Holophrasic speech: Children begin using their first words at about 12 or 13 months of age and may use partial words to convey thoughts at even younger ages. These one word expressions are referred to as holophrasic speech. For example, the child may say "ju" for the word "juice" and use this sound when referring to a bottle. The listener must interpret the meaning of the holophrase and when this is someone who has spent time with the child, interpretation is not too difficult. They know that "ju" means "juice" which means the baby wants some milk! But, someone who has not been around the child will have trouble knowing what is meant. Imagine the parent who to a friend exclaims, "Ezra's talking all the time now!" The friend hears only "ju da ga" which, the parent explains, means "I want some milk when I go with Daddy."

Underextension: A child who learns that a word stands for an object may initially think that the word can be used for only that particular object. Only the family's Irish Setter is a "doggie". This is referred to as underextension. More often, however, a child may think that a label applies to all objects that are similar to the original object. In overextension all animals become "doggies", for example.

First words and cultural influences: First words if the child is using English tend to be nouns. The child labels objects such as cup or ball. In a verb-friendly language such as Chinese, however, children may learn more verbs. This may also be due to the different emphasis given to objects based on culture. Chinese children may be taught to notice action and relationship between objects while children from the United States may be taught to name an object and its qualities (color, texture, size, etc.). These differences can be seen when comparing interpretations of art by older students from China and the United States.

Vocabulary growth spurt: One year olds typically have a vocabulary of about 50 words. But by the time they become toddlers, they have a vocabulary of about 200 words and begin putting those words together in telegraphic speech (I think of it now as 'text message' speech because texting is more common and is similar in that text messages typically only include the minimal amout of words to convey the message).

Two word sentences and telegraphic (text message?) speech: Words are soon combined and 18 month old toddlers can express themselves further by using expressions such as "baby bye-bye" or "doggie pretty". Words needed to convey messages are used, but the articles and other parts of speech necessary for grammatical correctness are not yet used. These expressions sound like a telegraph (or perhaps a better analogy today would be that they read like a text message) where unnecessary words are not used. "Give baby ball" is used rather than "Give the baby the ball." Or a text message of "Send money now!" rather than "Dear Mother. I really need some money to take care of my expenses" You get the idea.

Child-directed speech: Why is a horse a "horsie"? Have you ever wondered why adults tend to use "baby talk" or that sing-song type of intonation and exaggeration used when talking to children? This represents a universal tendency and is known as child-directed speech or motherese or parentese. It involves exaggerating the vowel and consonant sounds, using a high-pitched voice, and delivering the phrase with great facial expression. Why is this done? It may be in order to clearly articulate the sounds of a word so that the child can hear the sounds involved. Or it may be because when this type of speech is used, the infant pays more attention to the speaker and this sets up a pattern of interaction in which the speaker and listener are in tuned with one another. When I demonstrate this in class, the students certainly pay attention and look my way. Amazing! It also works in the college classroom!

Theories of Language Development

The first two theories of language development represent two extremes in the level of interaction required for language to occur (Berk, 2007).

Chomsky and the language acquisition device: The view known as nativism advocated by Noam Chomsky suggests that infants are equipped with a neurological construct referred to as the language acquisition device or LAD that makes infants ready for language. Language develops as long as the infant is exposed to it. No teaching, training, or reinforcement is required for language to develop.

Skinner and reinforcement: Learning theorist, B. F. Skinner, suggests that language develops through the use of reinforcement. Sounds, words, gestures and phrases are encouraged through by following the behavior with words of praise or treats or any thing that increases the likelihood that the behavior will be repeated.

Social pragmatics: Another view emphasizes the child's active engagement in learning language out of a need to communicate. The child seeks information, memorizes terms, imitates the speech heard from others and learns to conceptualize using words as language is acquired. Many would argue that all three of these dynamics foster the acquisition of language (Berger, 2004).
CC licensed content, Shared previously

Psychosocial Development and Attachment

Emotional Development

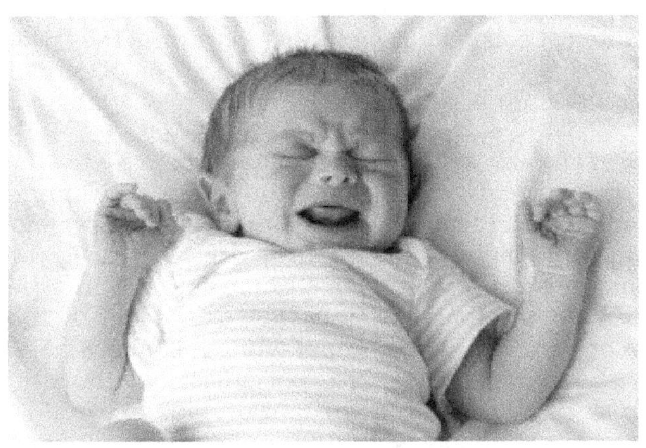

At birth, infants exhibit two emotional responses: attraction and withdrawal. They show attraction to pleasant situations that bring comfort, stimulation, and pleasure. And they withdraw from unpleasant stimulation such as bitter flavors or physical discomfort. At around two months, infants exhibit social engagement in the form of social smiling as they respond with smiles to those who engage their positive attention. Pleasure is expressed as laughter at 3 to 5 months of age, and displeasure becomes more specific fear, sadness, or anger between ages 6 and 8 months. This fear is often associated with the presence of strangers or the departure of significant others known respectively as stranger wariness and separation anxiety which appear sometime between 6 and 15 months. And there is some indication that infants may experience jealousy as young as 6 months of age (Hart & Carrington, 2002).

During the second year of life, children begin to recognize themselves as they gain a sense of self as object. This is illustrated in the 15 month old child's ability to recognize one's own reflection in a mirror. (The classic mirror test or rouge test involves showing a toddler a mirror after having secretly rubbed red coloring on the child's nose. Children who are younger than 15 months of age may try to wipe the color from the mirror. But a 15 month old child may wipe the color from his or her own nose.) Once a child has achieved self-awareness, the child is moving toward understanding social emotions such as guilt, shame or embarrassment as well as sympathy or empathy. These will require an understanding of the mental state of others that is acquired at around age 3 to 5 and will be explored in our next lesson (Berk, 2007).

Forming Attachments

The significance of early attachments: An attachment is desire for physical closeness with someone. The formation of attachments in infancy has been the subject of considerable research as attachments have been viewed as foundations for future relationships, as the basis for confidence and curiosity as toddlers, and as important influences on self-concept.

Measuring attachment styles: The classic model for studying styles of attachment involves having a caregiver and child come into a strange room filled with toys and observing the child's reactions. A securely attached child will play with the toys and bring one to the caregiver to show and describe from time to time. The child is content and secure as he or she explores the situation. An insecurely-resistant child will cling to the caregiver and refuse to go and play. An insecure-avoidant attachment style is indicated by a child who is neither curious nor clingy; rather the child sits and waits until time to go.

Attachment styles vary in the amount of security and closeness felt in the relationship and they can change with new experience. The type of attachment fostered in parenting styles varies by culture as well. For example, German parents value independence and Japanese mothers are typically by their children's sides. As a result, the rate of insecure-avoidant attachments is higher in Germany and insecure-resistant attachments are higher in Japan. These differences reflect cultural variation rather than true insecurity, however (van Ijzendoorn and Sagi, 1999). Keep in mind that methods for measuring attachment styles have been based on a model that reflects middle-class, U. S. values and interpretation. Newer methods for assessment attachment styles involve using a Q-sort technique in which a large number of behaviors are recorded on cards and the observer sorts the cards in a way that reflects the type of behavior that occurs within the situation.

As we explore styles of attachment below, consider how these are evidenced also in adult relationships.

Types of Attachments

Secure: A secure attachment is one in which the child feels confident that needs will be met in a timely and consistent way. In North America, this interaction may include emotional connection in addition to adequate care. However, even in cultures where mothers do not talk, cuddle, and play with their infants, secure attachments can develop (LeVine et. al., 1994). Secure attachments can form provided the child has consistent contact and care from one or more caregivers. Consistency of contacts may be jeopardized if the infant is cared for in a day care with a high turn-over of caregivers or if institutionalized and given little more than basic physical care. And while infants who, perhaps because of being in orphanages with inadequate care, have not had the opportunity to attach in infancy can form initial secure attachments several years later, they may have more emotional problems of depression, anger, or be overly friendly as they make adjustments (O'Connor et. als., 2003).

Insecure Resistant: This attachment style is marked by insecurity and a resistance to engaging in activities or play away from the caregiver. It is as if the child fears that the caregiver will abandon them and clings accordingly. (Keep in mind that clingy behavior can also just be part of a child natural disposition or temperament and does not necessarily reflect some kind of parental neglect.) The child may cry if separated from the caregiver and also cry upon their return. They seek constant reassurance that never seems to satisfy their doubt. This type of insecure attachment might be a result of not having needs met in a consistent or timely way. Consequently the infant is never sure that the world is a trustworthy place or that he or she can rely on others without some anxiety. A caregiver who is unavailable, perhaps because of marital tension, substance abuse, or preoccupation with work, may send a message to the infant he or she cannot rely on having needs met. A caregiver that attends to a child's frustration can help teach them to be calm and to relax. But an infant who receives only sporadic attention when experiencing discomfort may not learn how to calm down.

Insecure-Avoidant: This too is an attachment style marked by insecurity. But this style is also characterized by a tendency to avoid contact with the caregiver and with others. This child may have learned that needs typically go unmet and learns that the caregiver does not provide care and cannot be relied upon for comfort, even sporadically. An insecure-avoidant child learns to be more independent and disengaged. Such a child might sit passively in a room filled with toys until it is time to go.

Disorganized: This represents the most insecure style of attachment and occurs when the child is given mixed, confused, and inappropriate responses from the caregiver. For example, a mother who suffers from schizophrenia may laugh when a child is hurting or cry when a child exhibits joy. The child does not learn how to interpret emotions or to connect with the unpredictable caregiver.

How common are the attachment styles among children in the United States? It is estimated that about 65 percent of children in the United States are securely attached. Twenty percent exhibit avoidant styles and 10 to 15 percent are resistant. Another 5 to 10 percent may be characterized as disorganized. How would this compare with adults in the United States? (We will look at this in our lesson on early adulthood.)
CC licensed content, Shared previously

- Psyc 200 Lifespan Psychology. **Authored by**: Laura Overstreet. **Located at**: http://opencourselibrary.org/econ-201/. **License**: *CC BY: Attribution*

Public domain content

- crying baby. **Authored by**: Evan-Amos. **Located at**: https://en.wikipedia.org/wiki/Infant#/media/File:Human-Male-White-Newborn-Baby-Crying.jpg. **License**: *Public Domain: No Known Copyright*

Temperament

Perhaps you have spent time with a number of infants. How were they alike? How did they differ? Or compare yourself with your siblings or other children you have known well. You may have noticed that some seemed to be in a better mood than others and that some were more sensitive to noise or more easily distracted than others. These differences may be attributed to temperment. Temperament is an inborn quality noticeable soon after birth. According to Chess and Thomas (1996), children vary on 9 dimensions of temperament. These include activity level, regularity (or predictability), sensitivity thresholds, mood, persistence or distractibility, among others. The New York Longitudinal Study was a long term study of infants on these dimensions which began in the 1950s. Most children do not have their temperament clinically measured, but categories of temperament have been developed and are seen as useful in understanding and working with children. These categories include easy or flexible, slow to warm up or cautious, difficult or feisty, and undifferentiated (or those who can't easily be categorized).

Think about how you might approach each type of child in order to improve your interactions with them. An easy or flexible child will not need much extra attention unless you want to find out whether they are having difficulties that have gone unmentioned. A slow to warm up child may need to be given advance warning if new people or situations are going to be introduced. A difficult or feisty child may need to be given extra time to burn off their energy. A caregiver's ability to work well and accurately read the child will enjoy a goodness of fit meaning their styles match and communication and interaction can flow. Rather than believing that discipline alone will bring about improvements in children's behavior, our knowledge of temperament may help a parent, teacher or other gain insight to work more effectively with a child.

Temperament doesn't change dramatically as we grow up, but we may learn how to work around and manage our temperamental qualities. Temperament may be one of the things about us that stays the same throughout development.

CC licensed content, Shared previously

- Psyc 200 Lifespan Psychology. **Authored by**: Laura Overstreet. **Located at**: http://opencourselibrary.org/econ-201/. **License**: *CC BY: Attribution*

Public domain content

- smiling baby. **Authored by**: PublicDomainPictures. **Located at**: https://pixabay.com/en/baby-boy-child-face-happy-joy-84708/. **License**: *Public Domain: No Known Copyright*

Psychosocial Development

Erikson's Stages for Infants and Toddlers

Trust vs. mistrust: Erikson maintained that the first year to year and a half of life involves the establishment of a sense of trust. Infants are dependent and must rely on others to meet their basic physical needs as well as their needs for stimulation and comfort. A caregiver who consistently meets these needs instills a sense of trust or the belief that the world is a trustworthy place. The caregiver should not worry about overly indulging a child's need for comfort, contact or stimulation. This view is in sharp contrast with the Freudian view that a parent who overly indulges the infant by allowing them to suck too long or be picked up too frequently will be spoiled or become fixated at the oral stage of development.

Problems establishing trust: Consider the implications for establishing trust if a caregiver is unavailable or is upset and ill-prepared to care for a child. Or if a child is born prematurely, is unwanted, or has physical problems that make him or her less desirable to a parent. Unwanted pregnancies can be experienced by busy, upper-middle class professional couples as well as young, unmarried mothers, or couples in the midst of relational strains. Under these circumstances, we cannot assume that the parent is going to provide the child with a feeling of trust. However, keep in mind that children can also exhibit strong resiliency to harsh circumstances. Resiliency can be attributed to certain personality factors, such as an easy-going temperament and receiving support from others. So a positive and strong support group can help a parent and child build a strong foundation by offering assistance and positive attitudes toward the newborn and parent.

Autonomy vs. shame and doubt: As the child begins to walk and talk, an interest in independence or autonomy replaces a concern for trust. The toddler tests the limits of what can be touched, said, and explored. Erikson believed that toddlers should be allowed to explore their environment as freely as safety allows and in so doing will develop a sense of independence that will later grow to self-esteem, initiative, and overall confidence. If a caregiver is overly anxious about the toddler's actions for fear that the child will get hurt or violate other's expectation, the caregiver can give the child the message that he or she should be ashamed of their behavior and instill a sense of doubt in their own abilities. Parenting advice based on these ideas would be to keep your toddler safe, but let him or her learn by doing. A sense of pride seems to rely on doing rather than being told how capable one is as well (Berger, 2005).

Conclusion

We have explored the dramatic story of the first two years of life. Rapid physical growth, neurological development, language acquisition, the movement from hands on to mental learning, an expanding emotional repertoire, and the initial conceptions of self and others make this period of life very exciting. These abilities are shaped into more sophisticated mental processes, self-concepts, and social relationships during the years of early childhood.

CC licensed content, Shared previously

Module 5: Early Childhood

Introduction to Early Childhood

Learning Objectives

Objectives: At the end of this lesson, you will be able to

Summarize overall physical growth during early childhood.
Describe growth of structures in the brain during early childhood.
Identify examples of gross and fine motor skill development in early childhood.
Identify nutritional concerns for children in early childhood.
Examine nutritional content in popular foods consumed by children in early childhood.
Describe sexual development in early childhood.
Define preoperational intelligence.
Illustrate animism, egocentrism, and centration using children's games or media.
Describe language development in early childhood.
Illustrate scaffolding.
Explain private speech.
Explain theory of mind.
Explain Erikson's stages of psychosocial development for toddlers and children in early childhood.
Contrast models of parenting styles.
Examine concerns about child care.
Explain theories of self from Cooley and Mead.
Summarize theories of gender role development.
Examine concerns about childhood stress and development.

REFERENCES

Ariès, P. (1962). Centuries of childhood; a social history of family life. New York: Knopf.

Baumrind, D. (1971). Current patterns of parental authority. Developmental Psychology Monograph, 4(1), part 2.

Berk, L. E. (2007). Development through the life span (4th ed.). Boston: Allyn and Bacon.

Carroll, J. L. (2007). Sexuality now: Embracing diversity (2nd ed.). Belmont, CA: Thomson.

Cohen, P. N., & Bianchi, S. M. (1999). Marriage, children, and women's employment: What do we know? Monthly Labor Review, 22-31.

Cooley, C. H. (1964). Human nature and the social order. New York: Schocken Books.

Employment Characteristics of Families Summary. (2010). U.S. Bureau of Labor Statistics. Retrieved May 05, 2011, from http://www.bls.gov/news.release/famee.nr0.htm

Gecas, V., & Self, M. (1991). Families and adolescents. In A. Booth (Ed.), Contemporary families: Looking forward, looking back (National Council on Family Relations). Minneapolis.

Imai, M., Li, L., Haryu, E., Hirsh-Pasek, K., Golinkoff, R. M., & Shigematsu, J. (2008). Novel noun and verb learning in Chinese, English, and Japanese children: Universality and language-specificity in novel noun and verb learning. Child Development, 79, 979-1000.

Kimmel, M. S. (2008). The gendered society (3rd ed.). Oxford: Oxford University Press.

Kohn, M. L. (1977). Class and conformity. (2nd ed.). Chicago: University of Chicago Press.

LeMasters, E. E., & DeFrain, J. D. (1989). Parents in contemporary America: a sympathetic view. Belmont, CA: Wadsworth.

Maccoby, E., & Jacklin, C. (1987). Gender segregation in childhood. Advances in Child Development and Behavior, 20, 239-287.

Martinson, F. M. (1981). Eroticism in infancy and childhood. In L. L. Constantine & F. M. Martinson (Eds.), Children and sex: New findings, new perspectives. (pp. 23-35). Boston: Little, Brown.

Mead, G. H., & Morris, C. W. (1967). Mind, self, and society; from the standpoint of a social behaviorist. Chicago, IL: University of Chicago Press.

Middlebrooks, J. S., & Audage, N. C. (2008). The effects of childhood stress on health across the lifespan. (United States, Center for Disease Control, National Center for Injury Prevention and Control). Atlanta, GA.

Nance-Nash, S. (2009, March 5). President's Fund Repays Liberia's Market Women | Womens eNews. Women's ENews. Retrieved May 05, 2011, from http://womensenews.org/story/business/090305/presidents-fund-repays-liberias-market-women

Okami, P., Olmstead, R., & Abramson, P. R. (1997). Sexual experiences in early childhood: 18-year longitudinal data from UCLA Family Lifestyles Project. Journal of Sex Research, 34(4), 339-347.

Rice, F. P. (1997). Human development: A life-span approach. Upper Saddle River, NJ: Prentice Hall.

Sadker, M., & Sadker, D. M. (1994). Failing at fairness: How America's schools cheat girls. New York: C. Scribner's Sons.

Sandberg, J. F., & Hofferth, S. L. (2001). Changes in children's time with parents: United States, 1981-1997. Demography, 38, 423-436.

Schwartz, I. M. (1999). Sexual activity prior to coitus initiation: A comparison between males and females. Archives of Sexual Behavior, 28(1), 63-69.

Vygotskiĭ, L. S. (1962). Thought and language. Cambridge: M.I.T. Press, Massachusetts Institute of Technology.

WHO | Gender and genetics: Sex selection and the law. (2010). Retrieved May 05, 2011, from http://www.who.int/genomics/gender/en/index4.html
CC licensed content, Shared previously

- Psyc 200 Lifespan Psychology. **Authored by**: Laura Overstreet. **Located at**: http://opencourselibrary.org/econ-201/. **License**: CC BY: Attribution

Physical Development

Growth in early childhood

Children between the ages of 2 and 6 years tend to grow about 3 inches in height each year and gain about 4 to 5 pounds in weight each year. The average 6 year old weighs about 46 pounds and is about 46 inches in height. The 3 year old is very similar to a toddler with a large head, large stomach, short arms and legs. But by the time the child reaches age 6, the torso has lengthened and body proportions have become more like those of adults.

This growth rate is slower than that of infancy and is accompanied by a reduced appetite between the ages of 2 and 6. This change can sometimes be surprising to parents and lead to the development of poor eating habits.

Nutritional concerns

Caregivers who have established a feeding routine with their child can find this reduction in appetite a bit frustrating and become concerned that the child is going to starve. However, by providing adequate, sound nutrition, and limiting sugary snacks and drinks, the caregiver can be assured that 1) the child will not starve; and 2) the child will receive adequate nutrition. Preschoolers can experience iron deficiencies if not given well-balanced nutrition and if given too much milk. Calcium interferes with the absorption of iron in the diet as well.

Caregivers need to keep in mind that they are setting up taste preferences at this age. Young children who grow accustomed to high fat, very sweet and salty flavors may have trouble eating foods that have more subtle flavors such as fruits and vegetables. Consider the following advice about establishing eating patterns for years to come (Rice, F.P., 1997). Notice that keeping mealtime pleasant, providing sound nutrition and not engaging in power struggles over food are the main goals:

Tips for Establishing Healthy Eating Patterns

1. Don't try to force your child to eat or fight over food. Of course, it is impossible to force someone to eat. But the real advice here is to avoid turning food into some kind of ammunition during a fight. Do not teach your child to eat to or refuse to eat in order to gain favor or express anger toward someone else.
2. Recognize that appetite varies. Children may eat well at one meal and have no appetite at another. Rather than seeing this as a problem, it may help to realize that appetites do vary. Continue to provide good nutrition, but do not worry excessively if the child does not eat.
3. Keep it pleasant. This tip is designed to help caregivers create a positive atmosphere during mealtime. Mealtimes should not be the time for arguments or expressing tensions. You do not want the child to

have painful memories of mealtimes together or have nervous stomachs and problems eating and digesting food due to stress.

4. No short order chefs. While it is fine to prepare foods that children enjoy, preparing a different meal for each child or family member sets up an unrealistic expectation from others. Children probably do best when they are hungry and a meal is ready. Limiting snacks rather than allowing children to "graze" continuously can help create an appetite for whatever is being served.

5. Limit choices. If you give your preschool aged child choices, make sure that you give them one or two specific choices rather than asking "What would you like for lunch?" If given an open choice, children may change their minds or choose whatever their sibling does not choose!

6. Serve balanced meals. This tip encourages caregivers to serve balanced meals. A box of macaroni and cheese is not a balanced meal. Meals prepared at home tend to have better nutritional value than fast food or frozen dinners. Prepared foods tend to be higher in fat and sugar content as these ingredients enhance taste and profit margin because fresh food is often more costly and less profitable. However, preparing fresh food at home is not costly. It does, however, require more activity. Preparing meals and including the children in kitchen chores can provide a fun and memorable experience.

7. Don't bribe. Bribing a child to eat vegetable by promising desert is not a good idea. For one reason, the child will likely find a way to get the desert without eating the vegetables (by whining or fidgeting, perhaps, until the caregiver gives in), and for another reason, because it teaches the child that some foods are better than others. Children tend to naturally enjoy a variety of foods until they are taught that some are considered less desirable than others. A child, for example, may learn the broccoli they have enjoyed is seen as yucky by others unless it's smothered in cheese sauce!

To what extent do these tips address cultural practices? How might these tips vary by culture?

Brain Maturation

Brain weight: If you recall, the brain is about 75 percent its adult weight by two years of age. By age 6, it is at 95 percent its adult weight. Myelination and the development of dendrites continues to occur in the cortex and as it does, we see a corresponding change in what the child is capable of doing. Greater development in the prefrontal cortex, the area of the brain behind the forehead that helps us to think, strategizes, and controls emotion, makes it increasingly possible to control emotional outbursts and to understand how to play games. Consider 4 or 5 year old children and how they might approach a game of soccer. Chances are every move would be a response to the commands of a coach standing nearby calling out, "Run this way! Now, stop. Look at the ball. Kick the ball!" And when the child is not being told what to do, he or she is likely to be looking at the clover on the ground or a dog on the other side of the fence! Understanding the game, thinking ahead, and coordinating movement improve with practice and myelination. Not being too upset over a loss, hopefully, does as well.

Visual Pathways

Have you ever examined the drawings of young children? If you look closely, you can almost see the development of visual pathways reflected in the way these images change as pathways become more mature. Early scribbles and dots illustrate the use of simple motor skills. No real connection is made between an image being visualized and what is created on paper.

At age 3, the child begins to draw wispy creatures with heads and not much other detail. Gradually pictures begin to have more detail and incorporate more parts of the body. Arm buds become arms and faces take on noses, lips and eventually eyelashes. Look for drawings that you or your child has created to see this fascinating trend. Here are some examples of pictures drawn by my daughters from ages 2 to 7 years.

Growth in the hemispheres and corpus callosum: Between ages 3 and 6, the left hemisphere of the brain grows dramatically. This side of the brain or hemisphere is typically involved in language skills. The right hemisphere continues to grow throughout early childhood and is involved in tasks that require spatial skills such as recognizing shapes and patterns. The corpus callosum which connects the two hemispheres of the brain undergoes a growth spurt between ages 3 and 6 as well and results in improved coordination between right and left hemisphere tasks. (I once saw a 5 year old hopping on one foot, rubbing his stomach and patting his head all at the same time. I asked him what he was doing and he replied, "My teacher said this would help my corpus callosum!" Apparently, his kindergarten teacher had explained the process!)

Motor Skill Development

Early childhood is a time when children are especially attracted to motion and song. Days are filled with moving, jumping, running, swinging and clapping and every place becomes a playground. Even the booth at a restaurant affords the opportunity to slide around in the seat or disappear underneath and imagine being a sea creature in a cave! Of course, this can be frustrating to a caregiver, but it's the business of early childhood. Children continue to improve their gross motor skills as they run and jump. And frequently ask their caregivers to "look at me" while they hop or roll down a hill. Children's songs are often accompanied by arm and leg movements or cues to turn around or move from left to right. Fine motor skills are also being refined in activities such as pouring water into a container, drawing, coloring, and using scissors. Some children's songs promote fine motor skills as well (have you ever heard of the song "itsy, bitsy, spider"?). Mastering the fine art of cutting one's own fingernails or tying shoes will take a lot of practice and maturation. Motor skills continue to develop in middle childhood-but for preschoolers, play that deliberately involves these skills is emphasized.

Go ahead. Sing along and practice your fine motor skills.

Sexual Development in Early Childhood

Historically, children have been thought of as innocent or incapable of sexual arousal (Aries, 1962). Yet, the physical dimension of sexual arousal is present from birth. But to associate the elements of seduction, power, love, or lust that is part of the adult meanings of sexuality would be inappropriate. Sexuality begins in childhood as a response to physical states and sensation and cannot be interpreted as similar to that of adults in any way (Carroll, 2007).

Infancy: Boys and girls are capable of erections and vaginal lubrication even before birth (Martinson, 1981). Arousal can signal overall physical contentment and stimulation that accompanies feeding or warmth. And infants begin to explore their bodies and touch their genitals as soon as they have the sufficient motor skills. This stimulation is for comfort or to relieve tension rather than to reach orgasm (Carroll, 2007).

Early Childhood: Self-stimulation is common in early childhood for both boys and girls. Curiosity about the body and about others' bodies is a natural part of early childhood as well. Consider this example. A mother is asked by her young daughter: "So it's okay to see a boy's privates as long as it's the boy's mother or a doctor?" The mother hesitates a bit and then responds, "Yes. I think that's alright." "Hmmm," the girl begins, "When I grow up, I want to be a doctor!" Hopefully, this subject is approached in a way that teaches children to be safe and know what is appropriate without frightening them or causing shame.

As children grow, they are more likely to show their genitals to siblings or peers, and to take off their clothes and touch each other (Okami et al., 1997). Masturbation is common for both boys and girls. Boys are often shown by other boys how to masturbate. But girls tend to find out accidentally. And boys masturbate more often and touch themselves more openly than do girls (Schwartz, 1999).

Hopefully, parents respond to this without undue alarm and without making the child feel guilty about their bodies. Instead, messages about what is going on and the appropriate time and place for such activities help the child learn what is appropriate.

CC licensed content, Shared previously

- Psyc 200 Lifespan Psychology. **Authored by**: Laura Overstreet. **Located at**: http://opencourselibrary.org/econ-201/. **License**: *CC BY: Attribution*
- picky eater image. **Authored by**: David Goehring. **Located at**: https://www.flickr.com/photos/carbonnyc/6144729060. **License**: *CC BY: Attribution*

Cognitive Development

Early childhood is a time of pretending, blending fact and fiction, and learning to think of the world using language. As young children move away from needing to touch, feel, and hear about the world toward learning some basic principles about how the world works, they hold some pretty interesting initial ideas. For example, how many of you are afraid that you are going to go down the bathtub drain? Hopefully, none of you do! But a child of three might really worry about this as they sit at the front of the bathtub. A child might protest if told that something will happen "tomorrow" but be willing to accept an explanation that an event will occur "today after we sleep." Or the young child may ask, "How long are we staying? From here to here?" while pointing to two points on a table. Concepts such as tomorrow, time, size and distance are not easy to grasp at this young age. Understanding size, time, distance, fact and fiction are all tasks that are part of cognitive development in the preschool years.

Preoperational Intelligence

Piaget's stage that coincides with early childhood is the **preoperational stage.** The word operational means logical, so these children were thought to be illogical. However, they were learning to use language or to think of the world symbolically. Let's examine some Piaget's assertions about children's cognitive abilities at this age.

Pretend Play: Pretending is a favorite activity at this time. A toy has qualities beyond the way it was designed to function and can now be used to stand for a character or object unlike anything originally intended. A teddy bear, for example, can be a baby or the queen of a faraway land!

Piaget believed that children's pretend play helped children solidify new schemes they were developing cognitively. This play, then, reflected changes in their conceptions or thoughts. However, children also learn as they pretend and experiment. Their play does not simply represent what they have learned (Berk, 2007).

Egocentrism: Egocentrism in early childhood refers to the tendency of young children to think that everyone sees things in the same way as the child. Piaget's classic experiment on egocentrism involved showing children a 3 dimensional model of a mountain and asking them to describe what a doll that is looking at the mountain from a different angle might see. Children tend to choose a picture that represents their own, rather than the doll's view. However, when children are speaking to others, they tend to use different sentence structures and vocabulary when addressing a younger child or an older adult. This indicates some awareness of the views of others.

Syncretism: Syncretism refers to a tendency to think that if two events occur simultaneously, one caused the other. I remember my daughter asking that if she put on her bathing suit whether it would turn to summer!

Animism: Animism refers to attributing life-like qualities to objects. The cup is alive, the chair that falls down and hits the child's ankle is mean, and the toys need to stay home because they are tired. Watch this segment in which the actor Robin Williams sings a song to teach children the difference between what is alive and what is not alive. (Interesting, the puppets in the background sing and dance the phrase "it's not alive". This might be a bit confusing to the viewers!). Cartoons frequently show objects that appear alive and take on lifelike qualities. Young children do seem to think that objects that move may be alive but after age 3, they seldom refer to objects as being alive (Berk, 2007).

https://www.youtube.com/watch?v=3p47bGlZuDA&feature=youtu.be

Classification Errors: Preoperational children have difficulty understanding that an object can be classified in more than one way. For example, if shown three white buttons and four black buttons and asked whether there are more black buttons or buttons, the child is likely to respond that there are more black buttons. As the child's vocabulary improves and more schemes are developed, the ability to classify objects improves.

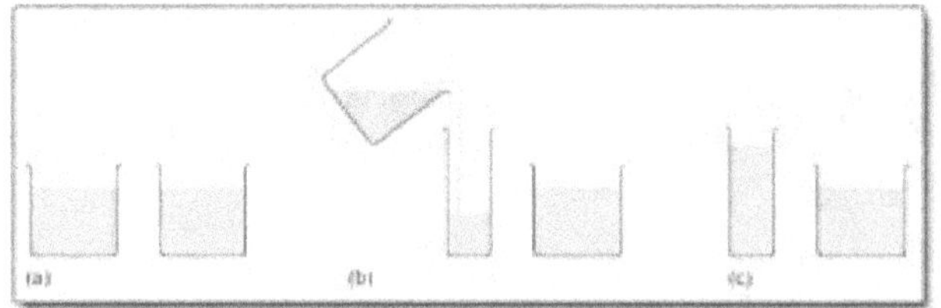

Conservation of Liquid. Does pouring liquid in a tall, narrow container make it have more?

Conservation Errors: Conservation refers to the ability to recognize that moving or rearranging matter does not change the quantity. Imagine a 2 year old and a 4 year old eating lunch. The 4 year old has a whole peanut butter and jelly sandwich. He notices, however, that his younger sister's sandwich is cut in half and protests, "She has more!" Watch the following examples of conversation errors of quantity and volume:

https://www.youtube.com/watch?v=GLj0IZFLKvg&feature=youtu.be

Theory of Mind

Imagine showing a child of three a bandaid box and asking the child what is in the box. Chances are, the child will reply, "bandaids." Now imagine that you open the box and pour out crayons. If you ask the child what they thought was in the box before it was opened, they may respond, "crayons". If you ask what a friend would have thought was in the box, the response would still be "crayons". Why? Before about 4 years of age, a child does not recognize that the mind can hold ideas that are not accurate. So this 3 year old changes his or her response once shown that the box contains crayons. The theory of mind is the understanding that the mind can be tricked or that the mind is not always accurate. At around age 4, the child would reply, "Crayons" and understand that thoughts and realities do not always match.

This awareness of the existence of mind is part of social intelligence or the ability to recognize that others can think differently about situations. It helps us to be self-conscious or aware that others can think of us in different ways and it helps us to be able to be understanding or empathic toward others. This mind reading ability helps us to anticipate and predict the actions of others (even though these predictions are sometimes inaccurate).

The awareness of the mental states of others is important for communication and social skills. A child who demonstrates this skill is able to anticipate the needs of others. This video describes a research in which theory of mind is linked to popularity.

Language Development

Vocabulary growth: A child's vocabulary expands between the ages of 2 to 6 from about 200 words to over 10,000 words through a process called fast-mapping. Words are easily learned by making connections between new words and concepts already known. The parts of speech that are learned depend on the language and what is emphasized. Children speaking verb-friendly languages such as Chinese and Japanese as well as those speaking English tend to learn nouns more readily. But those learning less verb-friendly languages such as English seem to need assistance in grammar to master the use of verbs (Imai, et als, 2008). Children are also very creative in creating their own words to use as labels such as a "take-care-of" when referring to John, the character on the cartoon, Garfield, who takes care of the cat.

Literal meanings: Children can repeat words and phrases after having heard them only once or twice. But they do not always understand the meaning of the words or phrases. This is especially true of expressions or figures of speech which are taken literally. For example, two preschool aged girls began to laugh loudly while listening to a tape-recording of Disney's "Sleeping Beauty" when the narrator reports, "Prince Phillip lost his head!" They image his head popping off and rolling down the hill as he runs and searches for it. Or a classroom full of preschoolers hears the teacher say, "Wow! That was a piece of cake!" The children began asking "Cake? Where is my cake? I want cake!"

Overregularization: Children learn rules of grammar as they learn language but may apply these rules inappropriately at first. For instance, a child learns to ad "ed" to the end of a word to indicate past tense. Then form a sentence such as "I goed there. I doed that." This is typical at ages 2 and 3. They will soon learn new words such as went and did to be used in those situations.

The Impact of Training: Remember Vygotsky and the Zone of Proximal Development? Children can be assisted in learning language by others who listen attentively, model more accurate pronunciations and encourage elaboration. The child exclaims, "I'm goed there!" and the adult responds, "You went there? Say, 'I went there.' Where did you go?" Children may be ripe for language as Chomsky suggests, but active participation in helping them learn is important for language development as well. The process of scaffolding is one in which the guide provides needed assistance to the child as a new skill is learned.

Private Speech: Do you ever talk to yourself? Why? Chances are, this occurs when you are struggling with a problem, trying to remember something, or feel very emotional about a situation. Children talk to themselves too. Piaget interpreted this as egocentric speech or a practice engaged in because of a child's inability to seeing things from others points of views. Vygotsky, however, believed that children talk to themselves in order to solve problems or clarify thoughts. As children learn to think in words, they do so aloud before eventually closing their lips and engaging in private speech or inner speech. Thinking out loud eventually becomes thought accompanied by internal speech and talking to oneself becomes a practice only engaged in when we are trying to learn something or remember something, etc. This inner speech is not as elaborate as the speech we use when communicating with others (Vygotsky, 1962).

CC licensed content, Shared previously

- Psyc 200 Lifespan Psychology. **Authored by**: Laura Overstreet. **Located at**: http://opencourselibrary.org/econ-201/. **License**: *CC BY: Attribution*

All rights reserved content

- Piaget - Stage 2 - Preoperational - Lack of Conservation. **Provided by**: Fi3021's channel. **Located at**: https://www.youtube.com/watch?v=GLj0IZFLKvg&feature=youtu.be. **License**: *Other*. **License Terms**: Standard YouTube License
- Classic Sesame Street - Robin Williams on what is alive. **Provided by**: sawing14s. **Located at**: https://www.youtube.com/watch?v=3p47bGlZuDA&feature=youtu.be. **License**: *Other*. **License Terms**: Standard YouTube License

Psychosocial Development

A Look at Self-Concept, Gender Identity, and Family Life

Self-Concept

Early childhood is a time of forming an initial sense of self. A self-concept or idea of who we are, what we are capable of doing, and how we think and feel is a social process that involves taking into consideration how others view us. It might be said, then, that in order to develop a sense of self, you must have interaction with others. Interactionist theorists, Cooley and Mead offer two interesting explanations of how a sense of self develops.

Interactionism and Views of Self

Cooley: Charles Horton Cooley (1964) suggests that our self concept comes from looking at how others respond to us. This process, known as the looking-glass self involves looking at how others seem to view us and interpreting this as we make judgments about whether we are good or bad, strong or weak, beautiful or ugly, and so on. Of course, we do not always interpret their responses accurately so our self-concept is not simply a mirror reflection of the views of others. After forming an initial self-concept, we may use it as a mental filter screening out those responses that do not seem to fit our ideas of who we are. So compliments may be negated, for example. Think of times in your life when you feel self-conscious. The process of the looking-glass self is pronounced when we are preschoolers, or perhaps when we are in a new school or job or are taking on a new role in our personal lives and are trying to gauge our own performances. When we feel more sure of who we are we focus less on how we appear to others.

Mead: Herbert Mead (1967) offers an explanation of how we develop a social sense of self by being able to see ourselves through the eyes of others. There are two parts of the self: the "I" which is the part of the self that is spontaneous, creative, innate, and is not concerned with how others view us and the "me" or the social definition of who we are.

When we are born, we are all "I" and act without concern about how others view us. But the socialized self begins when we are able to consider how one important person views us. This initial stage is called "taking the role of the significant other". For example, a child may pull a cat's tail and be told by his mother, "No! Don't do that, that's bad" while receiving a slight slap on the hand. Later, the child may mimic the same behavior toward the self and say aloud, "No, that's bad" while patting his own hand. What has happened? The child is able to see himself through the eyes of the mother. As the child grows and is exposed to many situations and rules of culture, he begins to view the self in the eyes of many others through these cultural norms or rules. This is referred to as "taking the role of the generalized other" and results in a sense of self with many dimensions. The child comes to have a sense of self as student, as friend, as son, and so on.

Exaggerated Sense of Self

One of the ways to gain a clearer sense of self is to exaggerate those qualities that are to be incorporated into the self. Preschoolers often like to exaggerate their own qualities or to seek validation as the biggest or smartest or child who can jump the highest. I wonder if messages given in children's books or television shows that everyone is special are really meaningful to children who want to separate themselves from others on such qualities. This exaggeration tends to be replaced by a more realistic sense of self in middle childhood.

Erikson: Initiative vs. Guilt

The trust and autonomy of previous stages develop into a desire to take initiative or to think of ideas and initiative action. Children may want to build a fort with the cushions from the living room couch or open a lemonade stand in the driveway or make a zoo with their stuffed animals and issue tickets to those who want to come. Or they may just want to get themselves ready for bed without any assistance. To reinforce taking initiative, caregivers should offer praise for the child's efforts and avoid being critical of messes or mistakes. Soggy washrags and toothpaste left in the sink pales in comparison to the smiling face of a five year old that emerges from the bathroom with clean teeth and pajamas!

Gender Identity, Gender Constancy and Gender Roles

Another important dimension of the self is the sense of self as male or female. Preschool aged children become increasingly interested in finding out the differences between boys and girls both physically and in terms of what activities are acceptable for each. While 2 year olds can identify some differences and learn whether they are boys or girls, preschoolers become more interested in what it means to be male or female. This self-identification or gender identity is followed sometime later with gender constancy or the knowledge that gender does not change. Gender roles or the rights and expectations that are associated with being male or female are learned throughout childhood and into adulthood.

Freud and the phallic stage: Freud believed that masculinity and femininity were learned during the phallic stage or psychosexual development. During the phallic stage, the child develops an attraction to the opposite sexed parent but after recognizing that that parent is unavailable, learns to model their own behavior after the same sexed parent. The child develops his or her own sense of masculinity or femininity from this resolution. And, according to Freud, a person who does not exhibit gender appropriate behavior, such as a woman who competes with men for jobs or a man who lacks self-assurance and dominance, has not successfully completed this stage of development. Consequently, such a person continues to struggle with his or her own gender identity.

Chodorow and mothering: Chodorow, a neoFreudian, believed that mothering promotes gender stereotypic behavior. Mothers push their sons away too soon and direct their attention toward problem-solving and independence. As a result, sons grow up confident in their own abilities but uncomfortable with intimacy. Girls are kept dependent too long and are given unnecessary and even unwelcome assistance from their mothers. Girls learn to underestimate their abilities and lack assertiveness, but feel comfortable with intimacy.

Both of these models assume that early childhood experiences result in lifelong gender self-concepts. However, gender socialization is a process that continues throughout life. Children, teens, and adults refine and can modify their sense of self based on gender.

Learning through reinforcement and modeling: Learning theorists suggest that gender role socialization is a result of the ways in which parents, teachers, friends, schools, religious institutions, media and others send messages about what is acceptable or desirable behavior as males or females. This socialization begins early-in fact, it may even begin the moment a parent learns that a child is on the way. Knowing the sex of the child can conjure up images of the child's behavior, appearance, and potential on the part of a parent. And this stereotyping continues to guide perception through life. Consider parents of newborns, shown a 7 pound, 20 inch baby, wrapped in blue (a color designating males) describe the child as tough, strong, and angry when crying. Shown the same infant in pink (a color used in the United States for baby girls), these parents are likely to describe the baby as pretty, delicate, and frustrated when crying. (Maccoby & Jacklin, 1987). Female infants are held more, talked to more frequently and given direct eye contact, while male infants play is often mediated through a toy or activity.

Sons are given tasks that take them outside the house and that have to be performed only on occasion while girls are more likely to be given chores inside the home such as cleaning or cooking that is performed daily. Sons are encouraged to think for themselves when they encounter problems and daughters are more likely to be given assistance even when they are working on an answer. This impatience is reflected in teachers waiting less time when asking a female student for an answer than when asking for a reply from a male student (Sadker and Sadker, 1994). Girls are given the message from teachers that they must try harder and endure in order to succeed while boys successes are attributed to their intelligence. Of course, the stereotypes of advisors can also influence which kinds of courses or vocational choices girls and boys are encouraged to make.

Friends discuss what is acceptable for boys and girls and popularity may be based on modeling what is considered ideal behavior or looks for the sexes. Girls tend to tell one another secrets to validate others as best friends while boys compete for position by emphasizing their knowledge, strength or accomplishments. This focus on accomplishments can even give rise to exaggerating accomplishments in boys, but girls are discouraged from showing off and may learn to minimize their accomplishments as a result.

Gender messages abound in our environment. But does this mean that each of us receives and interprets these messages in the same way? Probably not. In addition to being recipients of these cultural expectations, we are individuals who also modify these roles (Kimmel, 2008).

How much does gender matter? In the United States, gender differences are found in school experiences (even into college and professional school, girls are less vocal in the classrooms and much more at risk for sexual harassment from teachers, coaches, classmates, and professors), in social interactions and in media messages. The stereotypes that boys should be strong, forceful, active, dominant, and rational and that girls should be pretty, subordinate, unintelligent, emotional, and gabby are portrayed in children's toys, books, commercials, video games, movies, television shows and music. In adulthood, these differences are reflected in income gaps between men and women where women working full-time earn about 74 percent the income of men, in higher rates of women suffering rape and domestic violence, higher rates of eating disorders for females, and in higher rates of violent death for men in young adulthood. Each of these differences will be explored further in subsequent chapters.

The impact in India: Gender differences in India can be a matter of life and death as preferences for male children have been strong historically and are still held, especially in rural areas. (WHO, 2010). Male children are given preference for receiving food, breast milk, medical care and other resources. It is no longer legal to give parents information on the sex of their developing child for fear that they will abort a female fetus. Clearly, gender socialization and discrimination still impact development in a variety of ways across the globe.
CC licensed content, Shared previously

- Psyc 200 Lifespan Psychology. **Authored by**: Laura Overstreet. **Located at**: http://opencourselibrary.org/econ-201/. **License**: *CC BY: Attribution*
- Baby reflection in mirror. **Provided by**: Wikipedia. **Located at**: https://en.wikipedia.org/wiki/Mirror_test#/media/File:Mirror_baby.jpg. **License**: *CC BY: Attribution*

Family Life

Parenting Styles

Relationships between parents and children continue to play a significant role in children's development during early childhood. We will explore two models of parenting styles. Keep in mind that these most parents do not follow any model completely. Real people tend to fall somewhere in between these styles. And sometimes parenting styles change from one child to the next or in times when the parent has more or less time and energy for parenting. Parenting styles can also be affected by concerns the parent has in other areas of his or her life. For example, parenting styles tend to become more authoritarian when parents are tired and perhaps more authoritative when they are more energetic. Sometimes parents seem to change their parenting approach when others are around, maybe because they become more self-conscious as parents or are concerned with giving others the impression that they are a "tough" parent or an "easy-going" parent. And of course, parenting styles may reflect the type of parenting someone saw modeled while growing up.

Baumrind (1971) offers a model of parenting that includes three styles. The first, **authoritarian**, is the traditional model of parenting in which parents make the rules and children are expected to be obedient. Baumrind suggests that authoritarian parents tend to place maturity demands on their children that are unreasonably high and tend to be aloof and distant. Consequently, children reared in this way may fear rather than respect their parents and, because their parents do not allow discussion, may take out their frustrations on safer targets-perhaps as bullies toward peers.

Permissive parenting involves holding expectations of children that are below what could be reasonably expected from them. Children are allowed to make their own rules and determine their own activities. Parents are warm and communicative, but provide little structure for their children. Children fail to learn self-discipline and may feel somewhat insecure because they do not know the limits.

Authoritative parenting involves being appropriately strict, reasonable, and affectionate. Parents allow negotiation where appropriate and discipline matches the severity of the offense. A popular parenting program that is offered in many school districts is called "Love and Logic" and reflects the authoritative or democratic style of parenting just described. Uninvolved parents are disengaged from their children. They do not make demands on their children and are non-responsive. These children can suffer in school and in their relationships with their peers (Gecas & Self, 1991).

Lemasters and Defrain (1989) offer another model of parenting. This model is interesting because it looks more closely at the motivations of the parent and suggests that parenting styles are often designed to meet the psychological needs of the parent rather than the developmental needs of the child. The **martyr** is a parent who will do anything for the child; even tasks that the child should do for himself or herself. All of the good deeds performed for the child, in the name of being a "good parent", may be used later should the parent want to gain compliance from the child. If a child goes against the parent's wishes, the parent can remind the child of all of the times the parent helped the child and evoke a feeling of guilt so that the child will do what the parent wants. The child learns to be dependent and manipulative as a result. (Beware! A parent busy whipping up cookies may really be thinking "control"!)

The **pal** is like the permissive parent described in Baumrind's model above. The pal wants to be the child's friend. Perhaps the parent is lonely or perhaps the parent is trying to win a popularity contest against an ex-spouse. Pals let children do what they want and focus most on being entertaining and fun and set few limitations. Consequently, the child may have little self-discipline and may try to test limits with others.

The **police officer/drill sergeant** style of parenting is similar to the authoritarian parent described above. The parent focuses primarily making sure that the child is obedient and that the parent has full control of the child. Sometimes this can be taken to extreme by giving the child tasks that are really designed to check on their level of obedience. For example, the parent may require that the child fold the clothes and place items back in the drawer in a particular way. If not, the child might be scolded or punished for not doing things "right". This type of parent has a very difficult time allowing the child to grow and learn to make decisions independently. And the child may have a lot of resentment toward the parent that is displaced on others.

The **teacher-counselor** parent is one who pays a lot of attention to expert advice on parenting and who believes that as long as all of the steps are followed, the parent can rear a perfect child. "What's wrong with that?" you might ask. There are two major problems with this approach. First, the parent is taking all of the responsibility for the child's behavior-at least indirectly. If the child has difficulty, the parent feels responsible and thinks that the solution lies in reading more advice and trying more diligently to follow that advice. Parents can certainly influence children, but thinking that the parent is fully responsible for the child's outcome if faulty. A parent can only do so much and can never have full control over the child. Another problem with this approach is that the child may get an unrealistic sense of the world and what can be expected from others. For example, if a teacher-counselor parent decides to help the child build self-esteem and has read that telling the child how special he or she is or how important it is to compliment the child on a job well done, the parent may convey the message that everything the child does is exceptional or extraordinary. A child may come to expect that all of his efforts warrant praise and in the real world, this is not something one can expect. Perhaps children get more of a sense of pride from assessing their own performance than from having others praise their efforts.

So what is left? Lemasters and Defrain (1989) suggest that the **athletic coach style of parenting** is best. Before you draw conclusions here, set aside any negative experiences you may have had with coaches in the past. The principles of coaching are what are important to Lemasters and Defrain. A coach helps players form strategies, supports their efforts, gives feedback on what went right and what went wrong, and stands at the sideline while the players perform. Coaches and referees make sure that the rules of the game are followed and that all players adhere to those rules. Similarly, the athletic coach as parent helps the child understand what needs to happen in certain situations whether in friendships, school, or home life, and encourages and advises the child about how to manage these situations. The parent does not intervene or do things for the child. Rather, the parent's role is to provide guidance while the child learns first hand how to handle these situations. And the rules for behavior are consistent and objective and presented in that way. So, a child who is late for dinner might hear the parent respond in this way, "Dinner was at six o'clock." Rather than, "You know good and well that we always eat at six. If you expect me to get up and make something for you now, you have got another thing coming! Just who do you think you are showing up late and looking for food? You're grounded until further notice!"

The most important thing to remember about parenting is that you can be a better, more objective parent when you are directing your actions toward the child's needs and while considering what they can reasonably be expected to do at their stage of development. Parenting is more difficult when you are tired and have psychological needs that interfere with the relationship. Some of the best advice for parents is to try not to take the child's actions personally and be as objective as possible.

The impact of class and culture cannot be ignored when examining parenting styles. The two models of parenting described above assume that authoritative and athletic coaching styles are best because they are designed to help the parent raise a child who is independent, self-reliant and responsible. These are qualities favored in "individualistic" cultures such as the United States, particularly by the middle class. African-American, Hispanic and Asian parents tend to be more authoritarian than non-Hispanic whites. However, in "collectivistic" cultures such as China or Korea, being obedient and compliant are favored behaviors. Authoritarian parenting has been used historically and reflects cultural need for children to do as they are told. In societies where family members' cooperation is necessary for survival, as in the case of raising crops, rearing children who are independent and who strive to be on their own makes no sense. But in an economy based on being mobile in order to find jobs and where one's earnings are based on education, raising a child to be independent is very important.

Working class parents are more likely than middle class parents to focus on obedience and honesty when raising their children. In a classic study on social class and parenting styles called Class and Conformity, Kohn (1977) explains that parents tend to emphasize qualities that are needed for their own survival when parenting their children. Working class parents are rewarded for being obedient, reliable, and honest in their jobs. They are not paid to be independent or to question the management; rather, they move up and are considered good employees if they show up on time, do their work as they are told, and can be counted on by their employers. Consequently, these parents reward honesty and obedience in their children. Middle class parents who work as professionals are rewarded for taking initiative, being self-directed, and assertive in their jobs. They are required to get the job done without being told exactly what to do. They are asked to be innovative and to work independently. These parents encourage their children to have those qualities as well by rewarding independence and self-reliance. Parenting styles can reflect many elements of culture.

Child Care Concerns

About 77.3 percent of mothers of school-aged and 64.2 percent of mothers of preschool aged children in the United States work outside the home (Cohen and Bianchi, 1999; Bureau of Labor Statistics, 2010). Since more women have been entering the workplace, there has been a concern that families do not spend as much time with their children. This, however, is not true. Between 1981 and 1997, the amount of time that parents spent with children has increased overall (Sandberg and Hofferth, 2001).

Seventy-five percent of children under age 5 are in scheduled child care programs. Others are cared for by family members, friends, or are in Head Start Programs. Older children are often in after school programs, before school programs, or stay at home alone after school once they are older. Quality childcare programs can enhance a child's social skills and can provide rich learning experiences. But long hours in poor quality care can have negative consequences for young children in particular. What determines the quality of child care? One consideration is the **teacher/child ratio**. States specify the maximum number of children that can be supervised by one teacher. In general, the younger the children, the more teachers required for a given number of children. The higher the teacher to child ratio, the more time the teacher has for involvement with the children and the less stressed the teacher may be so that the interactions can be more relaxed, stimulating and positive. The more children there are in a program, the less desirable the program as well. This is because the center may be more rigid in rules and structure to accommodate the large number of children in the facility.

The **physical environment** should be colorful, stimulating, clean, and safe. The **philosophy** of the organization and the **curriculum** available should be child-centered, positive, and stimulating. Providers should be trained in early childhood education as well. A majority of states do not require training for their child care providers. And while formal education is not required for a person to provide a warm, loving relationship to a child, knowledge of a child's development is useful for addressing their social, emotional, and cognitive needs in an effective way. By working toward improving the quality of childcare and increasing family-friendly workplace policies such as more flexible scheduling and perhaps childcare facilities at places of employment, we can accommodate families with smaller children and relieve parents of the stress sometimes associated with managing work and family life.

Global Concerns: The Market Women of Liberia

Work and mothering go hand in hand in many parts of the world. Consider the market women of Liberia. These are women who work as street vendors and are primary providers for their families. They come together in marketplaces along with their children to sell their goods while keeping a watchful eye on their children. Recently, they have been supported by President Sirleaf whose grandmother was a market woman. President Sirleaf has worked to raise funds to improve the marketplaces and conditions for mothers and children. The hope has been to make these marketplaces more safe, to provide childcare, and social services to improve the lives of mothers and children (Nance-Nash, 2009).

https://www.youtube.com/watch?v=heYBJd2uvZo&feature=youtu.be

Childhood Stress and Development

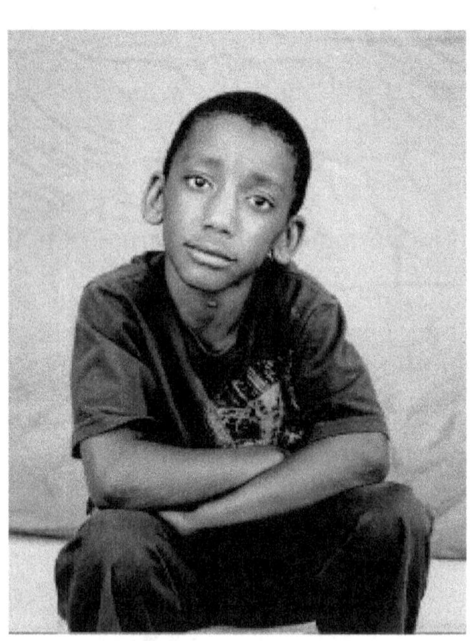

What is the impact of stress on child development? Children experience different types of stressors. Normal, everyday stress can provide an opportunity for young children to build coping skills and poses little risk to development. Even more long-lasting stressful events such as changing schools or losing a loved one can be managed fairly well. But children who experience toxic stress or who live in extremely stressful situations of abuse over long periods of time can suffer long-lasting effects. The structures in the midbrain or limbic system such as the hippocampus and amygdala can be vulnerable to prolonged stress during early childhood (Middlebrooks and Audage, 2008). High levels of the stress hormone cortisol can reduce the size of the hippocampus and effect the child's memory abilities. Stress hormones can also reduce immunity to disease. The brain exposed to long periods of severe stress can develop a low threshold making the child hypersensitive to stress in the future. However, the effects of stress can be minimized if the child has the support of caring adults.

In the next lesson, we continue to look at childhood as we examine the period between starting school and entering adolescence known as middle childhood.

CC licensed content, Shared previously

Assignment 2

Read this article: Domestic Violence, Children and Toxic Stress

(You may be asked to enter your *My*FM username and password to access article)
Write a 2 page double spaced paper answering the following questions:

a) What is the impact of trauma/toxic stress on human development across the lifespan?

b) What is ACE's and why are they important as we study human development?

c) What did you learn by reading this article?

d) What questions (at least 3) remain for you related to this topic?

All rights reserved content

Module 6: Middle Childhood

Introduction to Middle Childhood

Learning Objectives

Objectives: At the end of this lesson, you will be able to

Describe physical growth during middle childhood.
Prepare recommendations to avoid health risks in school-aged children.
Describe recognized examples of concrete operational intelligence.
Define conservation, reversibility, and identity in concrete operational intelligence.
Explain information processing theory of memory.
Characterize language development in middle childhood.
Compare preconventional, conventional, and postconventional moral development.
Define learning disability and describe dyslexia and attention deficit hyperactivity disorder.
Evaluate the impact of labeling on children's self-concept and social relationships.
Explain the rationale for identifying childhood conditions as spectrum disorders.
Explain the controversy over the use of standardized testing in schools.
Compare Gardner's theory of multiple intelligences and Sternberg's triarchic theory of intelligence.
Compare aptitude and achievement tests.
Apply the ecological systems model to explore children's experiences in schools.
Examine social relationships in middle childhood.
Characterized the incidence and impact of sexual abuse in middle childhood.
Analyze the impact of family structure on children's development.
Describe the developmental stages of stepfamilies.

Introduction

Middle childhood is the period of life that begins when children enter school and lasts until they reach adolescence. Think for a moment about children this age that you may know. What are their lives like? What kinds of concerns do they express and with what kinds of activities are their days filled? If it were possible, would you want to return to this period of life? Why or why not? Early childhood and adolescence seem to get much more attention than middle childhood. Perhaps this is because growth patterns slow at this time, the id becomes hidden during the latent stage, according to Freud, and children spend much more time in schools, with friends, and in structured activities. It may be easy for parents to lose track of their children's development unless they stay directly involved in these worlds. I think it is important to stop and give full attention to middle childhood to stay in touch with these children and to take notice of the varied influences on their lives in a larger world.

REFERENCES:

Arditti, J. A. (1999). Rethinking relationships between divorced mothers and their children: Capitalizing on family strengths. Family Relations, 48, 109-119.

Asperger syndrome: MedlinePlus Medical Encyclopedia. (2006). National Library of Medicine – National Institutes of Health. Retrieved May 05, 2011, from http://www.nlm.nih.gov/medlineplus/ency/article/001549.htm

Berk, L. (2007). Development through the life span (4th ed.). Boston: Allyn and Bacon.

Boulton, M. J. (1999). Concurrent and longitudinal relations between children's playground behavior and social preference, victimization, and bullying. Child Development, 70, 944-954.

Chao, R. (2001). Extending research on the consequences of parenting styles for Chinese Americans and European Americans. Child Development, 72, 1832-1843.

Cillesen, A. H., & Mayeaux, L. (2004). From censure to reinforcement: Developmental changes in the association between aggression and social status.. Child Development, 75, 147-163.

Considered, A. T. (n.d.). Youth Soccer Coaches Encouraged to Ease Regimen : NPR. NPR : National Public Radio : News & Analysis, World, US, Music & Arts : NPR. Retrieved May 05, 2011, from http://www.npr.org/templates/story/story.php?storyId=5428473

Davis, N. J. (1999). Youth crisis: Growing up in the high-risk society. Westport, CT: Praeger.

Drexler, P. (2005). Raising boys without men. Emmaus, PA: Rodale.

Finkelhor, D. (1984). Child sexual abuse: New theory and research. New York: Free Press.

Finkelhor, D., Hotaling, G., Lewis, I. A., & Smith, C. (1990). Sexual abuse in a national survey of adult men and women: Prevalence, characteristics, and risk factors. Child Abuse and Neglect, 14, 19-28.

Furstenberg, F. F., & Cherlin, A. J. (1991). Divided families: What happens to children when parents part. Cambridge, MA: Harvard University Press.

Gardner, H. (1983). Frames of mind: The theory of multiple intelligences. New York: Basic Books.

Gardner, H. (1998). Are there additional intelligences? The case for naturalist, spiritual, and existentialist intelligences. In J. Kane (Ed.), Education, information, and transformation: Essays on learning and thinking. Englewood Cliffs, NJ: Prentice-Hall.

Gardner, H. (1999). Intelligence reframed: Multiple intelligences for the 21st century. New York, NY: Basic Books.

Guttmann, J. (1993). Divorce in psychosocial perspective: Theory and research. Hillsdale, NJ: L. Erlbaum Associates.

Harmanci, R. (2006, December 17). Sex inuendo: Under the tree over the punch bowl. Cultural shift: Little girls, sexy dolls-toy industry markets to 'Kids growing older younger. Retrieved January 3, 2007, from http://www.sfgate.com/cgi-bin/article.cgi?file=/c/a/2006/12/17/MNGoMN18MP1.DTL

Hetherington, E. M., & Kelly, J. (2002). For better or for worse: Divorce reconsidered. New York: W.W. Norton.

Horvat, E. M. (2004). Moments of social inclusion and exclusion: Race, class, and cultural capital in family-school relationships. In A. Lareau (Author) & J. H. Ballantine & J. Z. Spade (Eds.), Schools and society: A sociological approach to education (2nd ed., pp. 276-286). Belmont, CA: Wadsworth.

Irvine, M. (2006). 10 is the new 15 as kids grow up faster. Retrieved January 3, 2007, from http://ww.foxnews.com/wires/2006Nov26/0.4670.TeenTweens.00.html

Kohlberg, L. (1963). The development of children's oreintations toward a moral order: Sequence in the development of moral thought. Vita Humana, 16, 11-36.

McLanahan, S., & Sandefur, G. D. (1994). Growing up with a single parent: What hurts, what helps. Cambridge, MA: Harvard University Press.

McLaren, P. (1999). Schooling as a ritual performance: Toward a political economy of educational symbols and gestures (3rd ed.). Lanham, MD: Rowman & Littlefield.

Papernow, P. L. (1993). Becoming a stepfamily: Patterns of development in remarried families. San Francisco:

Jossey-Bass.

Pervasive Developmental Disorders Information Page. (n.d.). National Institute of Neurological Disorders and Stroke (NINDS). Retrieved May 05, 2011, from http://www.ninds.nih.gov/disorders/pdd/pdd.htm

Seccombe, K., & Warner, R. L. (2004). Marriages and families: Relationships in social context. Belmont, CA: Wadsworth/Thomson Learning.

Spade, J. Z. (2004). Learning the student role: Kindergarten as Academic Boot Camp. In H. Gracey (Author) & J. H. Ballantine (Ed.), Schools and society: A sociological approach to education (2nd ed., pp. 144-148). Belmont, CA: Wadsworth.

Special issues for tweens and teens. (n.d.). Retrieved December 23, 2006, from http://www.media-awareness.ca/english/parents/marketing/issues_teens_marketing.cfm?RenderForPrint=1

Squires, R. (2006, November 3). Marketers hijack sexuality: Expert decries young girls' loss of childhood. Winnipeg Sun. Retrieved January 3, 2007, from http://www.jeankilbourne.com/news.htm.

Sternberg, R. J. (1997). Successful intelligence: How practical and creative intelligence determine success in life. New York: Plume.

Sternberg, R. J. (1999). A triarchic approach to understanding and assessment of intelligence in multicultural populations. Journal of School Psychology, 37, 145-159.

Stewart, A. J., Copeland, Chester, Malley, & Barenbaum. (1997). Separating together: How divorce transforms families. New York: Guilford Press.

Turnbull, J. K. (1985). To dream the impossible dream: An agenda for discussion with stepparents. In S. K. Turnbull (Author) & L. Cargen (Ed.), Marriage and family: Coping with change. Belmont, CA: Wadsworth.

Tyre, P. (2006, September 11). The new first grade: Too much too soon? Newsweek, 34-44.

United States, Center for Disease Control, Department of Health and Human Services. (2006, April 5). Autism. Retrieved from http://www.cdc.gov/ncbddd/autism/index.htm

United States, Center for Disease Control, Metropolitan Atlanta Developmental Disabilities Surveillance Program. (2005, January 21). Retrieved December 30, 2006, from http://www.cdc.gov/ncbddd/autism/ask_common.htm

United States, U. S. Department of Health and Human Services, U. S. Government Printing Office. (2005). Health United States (2005g). Washington, D. C.

Valentine, S. M. (2005). Sexual abuse of boys. Journal of Child and Adolescent Psychiatric Nursing, 18(1), 10-16.

Visher, E. B., & Visher, J. S. (1985). Stepfamilies are different. Journal of Family Therapy, 7(1), 9-18.

Woitalla, M. (2006, January 30). Remember, it's playtime. Retrieved December 23, 2006, from http://www.socceramerica.com/article.asp?Art_ID=562136883
CC licensed content, Shared previously

Physical Development

Growth Rates and Motor Skills

Rates of growth generally slow during Middle Childhood. Typically, a child will gain about 5-7 pounds a year and grow about 2 inches per year. They also tend to slim down and gain muscle strength and lung capacity making it possible to engage in strenuous physical activity for long periods of time. The brain reaches its adult size at about age 7. The school-aged child can is better able to plan, coordinate activity using both left and right hemispheres of the brain, and to control emotional outbursts. Paying attention is also improved as the prefrontal cortex matures. And as the myelin continues to develop, the child's reaction time also improves as well. One result of the slower rate of growth is an improvement in motor skills. Children of this age tend to sharpen their abilities to perform both gross motor skills such as riding a bike and fine motor skills such as cutting their fingernails.

Organized Sports: Pros and Cons

Middle childhood seems to be a great time to introduce children to organized sports. And in fact, many parents do. Nearly 3 million children play soccer in the United States (listen to NPR's "Youth Soccer Coaches Encouraged to Ease Regimen" story from 5/24/06). This activity promises to help children build social skills, improve athletically and learn a sense of competition. It has been suggested, however, that the emphasis on competition and athletic skill can be counterproductive and lead children to grow tired of the game and want to quit. In many respects, it appears that children's activities are no longer children's activities once adults become involved and approach the games as adults rather than children. The U. S. Soccer Federation recently advised coaches to reduce the amount of drilling engaged in during practice and to allow children to play more freely and to choose their own positions. The hope is that this will build on their love of the game and foster their natural talents.

New Concerns

Childhood Obesity

Rates: About 16 to 33 percent of American children are obese (U. S. Department of Health and Human Services, 2005). This is defined as being at least 20 percent over their ideal weight. The percentage of obesity in school aged children has increased substantially since the 1960s and has in fact doubled since the 1980s.

Reasons: This is true in part because of the introduction of a steady diet of television and other sedentary activities. In addition, we have come to emphasize high fat, fast foods as a culture. Pizza, hamburgers, chicken nuggets and "lunchables" with soda have replaced more nutritious foods as staples.

Consequences: Children who are overweight tend to be ridiculed and teased by others. This can certainly be damaging to their self-image and popularity. In addition, obese children run the risk of suffering orthopedic problems such as knee injuries, and an increase risk of heart disease and stroke in adulthood. It's hard for a child who is obese to become a non-obese adult. In addition, the number of cases of pediatric diabetes has risen dramatically in recent years.

Recommendations: Dieting is not really the answer. If you diet, your basal metabolic rate tends to decrease thereby making the body burn even fewer calories in order to maintain the weight. Increased activity is much more effective in lowering the weight and improving the child's health and psychological well-being. Exercise reduces stress and being an overweight child, subjected to the ridicule of others can certainly be stressful. Parents should take caution against emphasizing diet alone to avoid the development of any obsession about dieting that can lead to eating disorders as teens. Again, increasing a child's activity level is most helpful.

A Look at School Lunches: Many children in the United States buy their lunches in the school cafeteria, so it might be worthwhile to look at the nutritional content of school lunches. You can obtain this information through your local school district's website. An example of a school menu and nutritional analysis from a school district in north central Texas is a meal consisting of pasta alfredo, bread stick, peach cup, tomato soup, and a brownie, and 2% milk and is in compliance with Federal Nutritional Guidelines of 108% calories, 24 % protein, 55 % carbohydrates, 27% fat, and 8% saturated fats, according to the website. Students may also purchase chips, cookies, or ice cream along with their meals. Many school districts rely on the sale of desert and other items in the lunchrooms to make additional revenues. Many children purchase these additional items and so our look at their nutritional intake should also take this into consideration.

Consider another menu from an elementary school in the state of Washington. This sample meal consists of chicken burger, tater tots, fruit and veggies and 1% or nonfat milk. This meal is also in compliance with Federal Nutrition Guidelines but has about 300 fewer calories. And, children are not allowed to purchase additional deserts such as cookies or ice cream.

Of course, children eat away from school as well. Listen to NPR's Kids Have Easy Access to Junk Food to hear a story about how advertising and fast food restaurant locations may influence children's diets.
CC licensed content, Shared previously

Cognitive Development

Recall from our last lesson on early childhood are in the **preoperational** stage, according to Piaget, and during this stage children are learning to think symbolically about the world.

Concrete Operational Thought

From ages 7 to 11, the school-aged child is in what Piaget referred to as the concrete operational stage of cognitive development. This involves mastering the use of logic in concrete ways. The child can use logic to solve problems tied to their own direct experience but has trouble solving hypothetical problems or considering more abstract problems. The child uses inductive reasoning which means thinking that the world reflects one's own personal experience. For example, a child has one friend who is rude, another friend who is also rude, and the same is true for a third friend. The child may conclude that friends are rude. (We will see that this way of thinking tends to change during adolescence being replaced with deductive reasoning.)

The word concrete refers to that which is tangible; that which can be seen or touched or experienced directly. The concrete operational child is able to make use of logical principles in solving problems involving the physical world. For example, the child can understand principles of cause and effect, size, and distance.

Classification: As children's experiences and vocabularies grow, they build schema and are able to classify objects in many different ways. Look at the word below and write a list of the ways in which it could be classified:

BALL

(Compare your list with the one at the end of the lesson.)

Identity: One feature of concrete operational thought is the understanding that objects have an identity or qualities that do not change even if the object is altered in some way. For instance, mass of an object does not change by rearranging it. A piece of chalk is still chalk even when the piece is broken in two.

Reversibility: The child learns that some things that have been changed can be returned to their original state. Water can be frozen and then thawed to become liquid again. But eggs cannot be unscrambled. Arithmetic operations are reversible as well: $2 + 3 = 5$ and $5 - 3 = 2$. Many of these cognitive skills are incorporated into the school's curriculum through mathematical problems and in worksheets about which situations are reversible or irreversible. (If you have access to children's school papers, look for examples of these.)

Reciprocity: Remember the example in our last lesson of children thinking that a tall beaker filled with 8 ounces of water was "more" than a short, wide bowl filled with 8 ounces of water? Concrete operational children can understand the concept of reciprocity which means that changing one quality (in this example, height or water level) can be compensated for by changes in another quality (width). So there is the same amount of water in each container although one is taller and narrower and the other is shorter and wider.

These new cognitive skills increase the child's understanding of the physical world. Operational or logical thought about the abstract world comes later.

Information Processing Theory

Information processing theory is a classic theory of memory that compares the way in which the mind works to computer storing, processing and retrieving information.

There are three levels of memory:

1) **Sensory register:** Information first enters our sensory register. Stop reading and look around the room very quickly. (Yes, really. Do it!) Okay. What do you remember? Chances are, not much. Everything you saw and heard entered into your sensory register. And although you might have heard yourself sigh, caught a glimpse of your dog walking across the room, and smelled the soup on the stove, you did not register those sensations. Sensations are continuously coming into our brains, and yet most of these sensations are never really perceived or stored in our minds. They are lost after a few seconds because they were immediately filtered out as irrelevant. If the information is not perceived or stored, it is discarded quickly.

2) **Working memory** (short-term memory): If information is meaningful (either because it reminds us of something else or because we must remember it for something like a history test we will be taking in 5 minutes), it makes its way into our working memory. This consists of information of which we are immediately aware. All of the things on your mind at this moment are part of your working memory. There is a limited amount of information that can be kept in the working memory at any given time. So, if you are given too much information at a time, you may lose some of it. (Have you ever been writing down notes in a class and the instructor speaks too quickly for you to get it all in your notes? You are trying to get it down and out of your working memory to make room for new information and if you cannot "dump" that information onto your paper and out of your mind quickly enough, you lose what has been said.)

Information in our working memory must be stored in an effective way in order to be accessible to us for later use. It is stored in our long-term memory or knowledge base.

3) **Knowledge base** (long-term memory): This level of memory has an unlimited capacity and stores information for days, months or years. It consists of things that we know of or can remember if asked. This is where you want information to ultimately be stored. The important thing to remember about storage is that it must be done in a meaningful or effective way. In other words, if you simply try to repeat something several times in order to remember it, you may only be able to remember the sound of the word rather than the meaning of the concept. So if you are asked to explain the meaning of the word or to apply a concept in some way, you will be lost. Studying involves organizing information in a meaningful way for later retrieval. Passively reading a text is usually inadequate and should be thought of as the first step in learning material. Writing key words, thinking of examples to illustrate their meaning, and considering ways that concepts are related are all techniques helpful for organizing information for effective storage and later retrieval.

During middle childhood, children are able to learn and remember due to an improvement in the ways they attend to and store information. As children enter school and learn more about the world, they develop more categories for concepts and learn more efficient strategies for storing and retrieving information. One significant reason is that they continue to have more experiences on which to tie new information. New experiences are similar to old ones or remind the child of something else about which they know. This helps them file away new experiences more easily.

They also have a better understanding of how well they are performing on a task and the level of difficulty of a task. As they become more realistic about their abilities, they can adapt studying strategies to meet those needs. While preschoolers may spend as much time on an unimportant aspect of a problem as they do on the main point, school aged children start to learn to prioritize and gage what is significant and what is not. They develop metacognition or the ability to understand the best way to figure out a problem. They gain more tools and strategies (such as "i before e except after c" so they know that "receive" is correct but "recieve" is not.)

Vocabulary

One of the reasons that children can classify objects in so many ways is that they have acquired a vocabulary to do so. By 5th grade, a child's vocabulary has grown to 40,000 words. It grows at the rate of 20 words per day, a rate that exceeds that of preschoolers. This language explosion, however, differs from that of preschoolers because it is facilitated by being able to association new words with those already known and because it is accompanied by a more sophisticated understanding of the meanings of a word.

New Understanding

The child is also able to think of objects in less literal ways. For example, of asked for the first word that comes to mind when one hears the word "pizza", the preschooler is likely to say "eat" or some word that describes what is done with a pizza. However, the school-aged child is more likely to place pizza in the appropriate category and say "food" or "carbohydrate".

This sophistication of vocabulary is also evidenced in the fact that school-aged children are able to tell jokes and delight in doing do. They may use jokes that involve plays on words such as "knock-knock" jokes or jokes with punch lines. Preschoolers do not understand plays on words and rely on telling "jokes" that are literal or slapstick such as "A man fell down in the mud! Isn't that funny?"

Grammar and Flexibility

School-aged children are also able to learn new rules of grammar with more flexibility. While preschoolers are likely to be reluctant to give up saying "I goed there", school-aged children will learn this rather quickly along with other rules of grammar.

While the preschool years might be a good time to learn a second language (being able to understand and speak the language), the school years may be the best time to be taught a second language (the rules of grammar).

How many ways can you classify "ball"? It's a word, a round object, a toy, a shape, a rolling object, a piece of playground equipment, another word for "fun", etc.

Kohlberg's Stages of Moral Development

Lawrence Kohlberg (1963) built on the work of Piaget and was interested in finding out how our moral reasoning changes as we get older. He wanted to find out how people decide what is right and what is wrong. In order to explore this area, he read a story containing a moral dilemma to boys of different age groups. In the story, a man is trying to obtain an expensive drug that his wife needs in order to treat her cancer. The man has no money and no one will loan him the money he requires. He begs the pharmacist to reduce the price, but the pharmacist refuses. So, the man decides to break into the pharmacy to steal the drug. Then Kohlberg asked the children to decide whether the man was right or wrong in his choice. Kohlberg was not interested in whether they said the man was right or wrong, he was interested in finding out how they arrived at such a decision. He wanted to know what they thought made something right or wrong.

Pre-conventional Moral Development

The youngest subjects seemed to answer based on what would happen to the man as a result of the act. For example, they might say the man should not break into the pharmacy because the pharmacist might find him and beat him. Or they might say that the man should break in and steal the drug and his wife will give him a big kiss. Right or wrong, both decisions were based on what would physically happen to the man as a result of the act. This is a self-centered approach to moral decision-making. He called this most superficial understanding of right and wrong pre-conventional moral development.

Conventional Moral Development

Middle childhood boys seemed to base their answers on what other people would think of the man as a result of his act. For instance, they might say he should break into the store, and then everyone would think he was a good husband. Or, he shouldn't because it is against the law. In either case, right and wrong is determined by what other people think. A good decision is one that gains the approval of others or one that complies with the law. This he called conventional moral development.

Post-conventional Moral Development

Older children were the only ones to appreciate the fact that this story has different levels of right and wrong. Right and wrong are based on social contracts established for the good of everyone or on universal principles of right and wrong that transcend the self and social convention. For example, the man should break into the store because, even if it is against the law, the wife needs the drug and her life is more important than the consequences the man might face for breaking the law. Or, the man should not violate the principle of the right of property because this rule is essential for social order. In either case, the person's judgment goes beyond what happens to the self. It is based on a concern for others; for society as a whole or for an ethical standard rather than a legal standard. This level is called post-conventional moral development because it goes beyond convention or what other people think to a higher, universal ethical principle of conduct that may or may not be reflected in the law. Notice that such thinking (the kind supreme justices do all day in deliberating whether a law is moral or ethical, etc.) requires being able to think abstractly. Often this is not accomplished until a person reaches adolescence or adulthood.

Developmental Problems

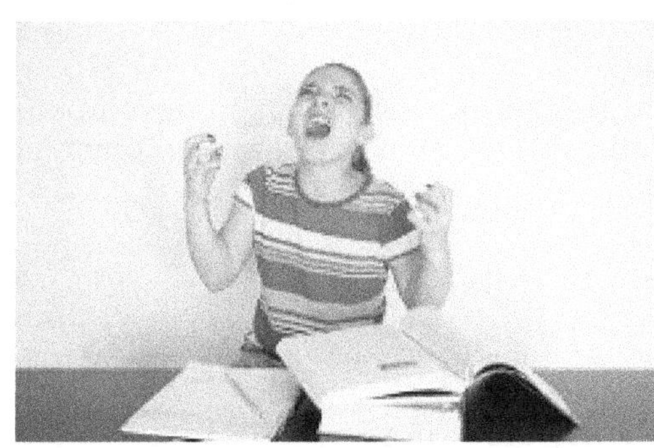

Children's cognitive and social skills are evaluated as they enter and progress through school. Sometimes this evaluation indicates that a child needs special assistance with language or in learning how to interact with others. Evaluation and diagnosis of a child can be the first step in helping to provide that child with the type of instruction and resources needed. But diagnosis and labeling also have social implications. It is important to consider that children can be misdiagnosed and that once a child has received a diagnostic label, the child, teachers, and family members may tend to interpret actions of the child through that label. The label can also influence the child's self-concept. Consider, for example, a child who is misdiagnosed as learning disabled. That child may expect to have difficulties in school, lack confidence, and out of these expectations, have trouble indeed. This self-fulfilling prophecy or tendency to act in such a way as to make what you predict will happen comes true, calls our attention to the power that labels can have whether or not they are accurately applied. It is also important to consider that children's difficulties can change over time; a child who has problems in school, may improve later or may live under circumstances as an adult where the problem (such as a delay in math skills or reading skills) is no longer relevant. That person, however, will still have a label as learning disabled. It should be recognized that the distinction between abnormal and normal behavior is not always clear; some abnormal behavior in children is fairly common. Misdiagnosis may be more of a concern when evaluating learning difficulties than in cases of autism spectrum disorder where unusual behaviors are clear and consistent.

Keeping these cautionary considerations in mind, let's turn our attention to some developmental and learning difficulties.

Autism Spectrum Disorders

The estimate published by the Center for Disease Control (2006) is that about 1 out of every 166 children in the United States has an autism spectrum disorder. Autism spectrum disorders include autism, Asperger's disorder and pervasive developmental disabilities. Many of these children are not identified until they reach school age. In 2003, about 141,000 children received special education through the public schools (Center for Disease Control, 2006). These disorders are found in all racial and ethnic groups and are more common in boys than in girls. All of these disorders are marked by difficulty in social interactions, problems in various areas of communication, and in difficulty with altering patterns or daily routines. There is no single cause of ASDs and the causes of these disorders are to a large extent, unknown. In cases involving identical twins, if one twin has autism, the other is also autistic about 75 percent of the time. Rubella, fragile X syndrome and PKU that has been untreated are some of the medical conditions associated with risks of autism.

None of these disorders is curable. Some individuals benefit from medications that alleviate some of the symptoms of ASDs. But the most effective treatments involve behavioral intervention and teaching techniques used to promote the development of language and social skills, and to structure learning environments that accommodate the needs of these children.

Autism is a developmental disorder more commonly known than Asperger's or Pervasive Developmental disorders. A person with autism has difficulty with and a lack of interest in learning language. An autistic child may respond to a question by repeating the question or might rarely speak. Sometimes autistic children learn more difficult words before simple words or complicated tasks before easier ones. The person has difficulty reading social cues such as the meanings of non-verbal gestures such as a wave of the hand or the emotion associated with a frown. Intense sensitivity to touch or visual stimulation may also be experienced. Autistic children have poor social skills and are unable to communicate with others or empathize with others emotionally. An autistic views the world differently and learns differently than others. Autistic children tend to prefer routines and patterns and become upset when routines are altered. For example, moving the furniture or changing the daily schedule can be very upsetting.

Asperger's syndrome is considered by some to be the same as high functioning autism. Others suggest that Asperger's disorder is different from autism in that language development is generally not delayed (Medline Plus, 2006). A person with Asperger's syndrome does not experience cognitive developmental delays, but has difficulty in social interactions. This person may be identified as strange by others, may have difficulty reading or identifying with other people's emotions, and may prefer routine and become upset if routines are disrupted. Many people with Asperger's syndrome may have above average intelligence and may have an intense focus of interests in a particular field. For example, a person may be extremely interested in and knowledgeable about cars. Another might be very interested in the smell of people's shoes.

Pervasive developmental disorder is a term used to refer to difficulties in socialization and delays in developing communicative skills. This is usually recognized before 3 years of age. A child with PDD may interact in unusual ways with toys, people, or situations, and may engage in repetitive movement.

Learning Disabilities

What is a learning disability? The spectrum disorders just described impact many areas of the child's life. And if a child is mentally retarded, that child is typically slow in all areas of learning. However, a child with a learning disability has problems in a specific area or with a specific task or type of activity related to education. A learning difficulty refers to a deficit in a child's ability to perform an expected academic skill (Berger, 2005). These difficulties are identified in school because this is when children's academic abilities are being tested, compared, and measured. Consequently, once academic testing is no longer essential in that person's life (as when they are working rather than going to school) these disabilities may no longer be noticed or relevant, depending on the person's job and the extent of the disability.

Dyslexia is one of the most commonly diagnosed disabilities and involves having difficulty in the area of reading. This diagnosis is used for a number of reading difficulties. For example, the child may reverse letters or have difficulty reading from left to right or may have problems associating letters with sounds. It appears to be rooted in some neurological problems involving the parts of the brain active in recognizing letters, verbally responding, or being able to manipulate sounds (National Institute of Neurological Disorders and Stroke, 2006). Treatment typically involves altering teaching methods to accommodate the person's particular problematic area.

Attention Deficit Hyperactivity Disorder is considered a neurological and behavioral disorder in which a person has difficulty staying on task, screening out distractions, and inhibiting behavioral outbursts. The most commonly recommended treatment involves the use of medication, structuring the classroom environment to keep distractions at a minimum, tutoring, and teaching parents how to set limits and encourage age-appropriate behavior (NINDS, 2006).

Learning and Intelligence

Schools and Testing

Children's academic performance is often measured with the use of standardized tests. **Achievement tests** are used to measure what a child has already learned. Achievement tests are often used as measures of teaching effectiveness within a school setting and as a method to make schools that receive tax dollars (such as public schools, charter schools, and private schools that receive vouchers) accountable to the government for their performance. In 2001, President George W. Bush signed into effect the No Child Left Behind Act mandating that schools administer achievement tests to students and publish those results so that parents have an idea of their children's performance and the government has information on the gaps in educational achievement between children from various social class, racial, and ethnic groups. Schools that show significant gaps in these levels of performance are to work toward narrowing these gaps. Educators have criticized the policy for focusing too much on testing as the only indication of performance levels.

Aptitude tests are designed to measure a student's ability to learn or to determine if a person has potential in a particular program. These are often used at the beginning of a course of study or as part of college entrance requirements. The Scholastic Aptitude Test (SAT) and Preliminary Scholastic Aptitude Test (PSAT) are perhaps the most familiar aptitude tests to students in grades 6 and above. Learning test taking skills and preparing for SATs has become part of the training that some students in these grades receive as part of their pre-college preparation. Other aptitude tests include the MCAT (Medical College Admission Test), the LSAT (Law School Admission Test), and the GRE (Graduate Record Examination). Intelligence tests are also a form of aptitude test which designed to measure a person's ability to learn.

Theories of Intelligence

Intelligence tests and psychological definitions of intelligence have been heavily criticized since the 1970s for being biased in favor of Anglo-American, middle-class respondents and for being inadequate tools for measuring non-academic types of intelligence or talent. Intelligence changes with experience and intelligence quotients or scores do not reflect that ability to change. What is considered smart varies culturally as well and most intelligence tests do not take this variation into account. For example, in the west, being smart is associated with being quick. A person who answers a question the fastest is seen as the smartest. But in some cultures, being smart is associated with considering an idea thoroughly before giving an answer. A well-thought out, contemplative answer is the best answer.

Multiple Intelligences

Gardner (1983, 1998, 1999) suggests that there are not one, but nine domains of intelligence. The first three are skills that are measured by IQ tests:

- **Logical-mathematical:** the ability to solve mathematical problems; problems of logic, numerical patterns
- **Linguistic**: vocabulary, reading comprehension, function of language
- **Spatial**: visual accuracy, ability to read maps, understand space and distance

The next six represent skills that are not measured in standard IQ tests but are talents or abilities that can also be important for success in a variety of fields: These are:

- **Musical**: ability to understand patterns in music, hear pitches, recognize rhythms and melodies
- **Bodily-kinesthetic**: motor coordination, grace of movement, agility, strength
- **Naturalistic**: knowledge of plants, animals, minerals, climate, weather
- **Interpersonal**: understand the emotion, mood, motivation of others; able to communicate effectively
- **Intrapersonal**: understanding of the self, mood, motivation, temperament, realistic knowledge of strengths, weaknesses
- **Existential**: concern about and understanding of life's larger questions, meaning of life, or spiritual matters

Gardner contends that these are also forms of intelligence. A high IQ does not always ensure success in life or necessarily indicate that a person has common sense, good interpersonal skills or other abilities important for success.

Triarchic Theory of Intelligence

Another alternative view of intelligence is presented by Sternberg (1997; 1999). Sternberg offers three types of intelligences. Sternberg provided background information about his view of intelligence in a conference I attended several years ago. He described his frustration as a committee member charged with selecting graduate students for a program in psychology. He was concerned that there was too much emphasis placed on aptitude test scores and believed that there were other, less easily measured, qualities necessary for success in a graduate program and in the world of work. Aptitude test scores indicate the first type of intelligence-academic.

- **Academic** (componential): includes the ability to solve problems of logic, verbal comprehension, vocabulary, and spatial abilities.

Sternberg noted that students who have high academic abilities may still not have what is required to be a successful graduate student or a competent professional. To do well as a graduate student, he noted, the person needs to be creative. The second type of intelligence emphasizes this quality.

- **Creative** (experiential): the ability to apply newly found skills to novel situations.

A potential graduate student might be strong academically and have creative ideas, but still be lacking in the social skills required to work effectively with others or to practice good judgment in a variety of situations. This common sense is the third type of intelligence.

- **Practical** (contextual): the ability to use common sense and to know what is called for in a situation.

This type of intelligence helps a person know when problems need to be solved. Practical intelligence can help a person know how to act and what to wear for job interviews, when to get out of problematic relationships, how to get along with others at work, and when to make changes to reduce stress.

Let's apply these theories of intelligence to the world of children. To what extent are these types of intelligences cultivated at home and in the schools?

The World of School

Remember the ecological systems model that we explored in Lesson 2? This model helps us understand an individual by examining the contexts in which the person lives and the direct and indirect influences on that person's life. School becomes a very important component of children's lives during middle childhood and one way to understand children is to look at the world of school. We have discussed educational policies that impact the curriculum in schools above. Now let's focus on the school experience from the standpoint of the student, the teacher and parent relationship, and the cultural messages or hidden curriculum taught in school in the United States.

Parental Involvement in School: Parents vary in their level of involvement with their children's schools. Teachers often complain that they have difficulty getting parents to participate in their child's education and devise a variety of techniques to keep parents in touch with daily and overall progress. For example, parents may be required to sign a behavior chart each evening to be returned to school or may be given information about the school's events through websites and newsletters. There are other factors that need to be considered when looking at parental involvement. To explore these, first ask yourself if all parents who enter the school with concerns about their child be received in the same way? If not, what would make a teacher or principal more likely to consider the parent's concerns? What would make this less likely?

Lareau and Horvat (2004) found that teachers seek a particular type of involvement from particular types of parents. While teachers thought they were open and neutral in their responses to parental involvement, in reality teachers were most receptive to support, praise and agreement coming from parents who were most similar in race and social class with the teachers. Parents who criticized the school or its policies were less likely to be given voice. Parents who have higher levels of income, occupational status, and other qualities favored in society have family capital. This is a form of power that can be used to improve a child's education. Parents who do not have these qualities may find it more difficult to be effectively involved. Lareau and Horvat (2004) offer three cases of African-American parents who were each concerned about discrimination in the schools. Despite evidence that such discrimination existed, their children's white, middle-class teachers were reluctant to address the situation directly. Note the variation in approaches and outcomes for these three families:

The Masons: This working class, African-American couple, a minister and a beautician, voiced direct complaints about discrimination in the schools. Their claims were thought to undermine the authority of the school and as a result, their daughter was kept in a lower reading class. However, her grade was boosted to "avoid a scene" and the parents were not told of this grade change.

The Irvings: This middle class, African-American couple was concerned that the school was discriminating against black students. They fought against it without using direct confrontation by staying actively involved in their daughter's schooling and making frequent visits to the school so make sure that discrimination could not occur. They also talked with other African-American teachers and parents about their concerns.

Ms. Caldron: This poor, single-parent was concerned about discrimination in the school. She was a recovering drug addict receiving welfare. She did not discuss her concerns with other parents because she did not know the other parents and did not monitor her child's progress or get involved with the school. She felt that her concerns would not receive attention. She requested spelling lists from the teacher on several occasions but did not receive them. The teacher complained that Ms. Caldron did not sign forms that were sent home for her signature.

Working within the system without direct confrontation seemed to yield better results for the Irvings, although the issue of discrimination in the school was not completely addressed. Ms. Caldron was the least involved and felt powerless in the school setting. Her lack of family capital and lack of knowledge and confidence keep her from addressing her concerns with the teachers. What do you think would happen if she directly addressed the teachers and complained about discrimination? Chances are, she would be dismissed as undermining the authority of the school, just as the Masons, and might be thought to lack credibility because of her poverty and drug addiction. The authors of this study suggest that teachers closely examine their biases against parents. Schools may also need to examine their ability to dialogue with parents about school policies in more open ways. What happens when parents have concerns over school policy or view student problems as arising from flaws in the educational system? How are parents who are critical of the school treated? And are their children treated fairly even when the school is being criticized? Certainly, any efforts to improve effective parental involvement should address these concerns.

Student Perspectives

Imagine being a 3rd-grader for one day in public school. What would the daily routine involve? To what extent would the institution dictate the activities of the day and how much of the day would you spend on those activities? Would always be 'on task'? What would you say if someone asked you how your day went? Or "What happened in school today?" Chances are, you would be more inclined to talk about whom you sat at lunch with or who brought a puppy to class than to describe how fractions are added.

Ethnographer and Professor of Education Peter McLaren (1999) describes the student's typical day as filled with constrictive and unnecessary ritual that has a damaging effect on the desire to learn. Students move between various states as they negotiate the demands of the school system and their own personal interests. The majority of the day (298 minutes) takes place in the **student state**. This state is one in which the student focuses on a task or tries to stay focused on a task, is passive, compliant, and often frustrated. Long pauses before getting out the next book or finding materials sometimes indicate that frustration. The **street corner state** is one in which the child is playful, energetic, excited, and expresses personal opinions, feelings, and beliefs. About 66 minutes a day take place in this state. Children try to maximize this by going slowly to assemblies or when getting a hall pass- always eager to say 'hello' to a friend or to wave if one of their classmates is in another room. This is the state in which friends talk and play. In fact, teachers sometimes reward students with opportunities to move freely or to talk or to be themselves. But when students initiate the street corner state on their own, they risk losing recess time, getting extra homework, or being ridiculed in front of their peers. The **home state** occurs when parents or siblings visit the school. Children in this state may enjoy special privileges such as going home early or being exempt from certain school rules in the mother's presence. Or it can be difficult if the parent is there to discuss trouble at school with a staff member. The sanctity state is a time in which the child is contemplative, quiet, or prayerful and is a very brief part of the day.

Since students seem to have so much enthusiasm and energy in street corner states, what would happen if the student and street corner states could be combined? Would it be possible? Many educators feel concern about the level of stress children experience in school. Some stress can be attributed to problems in friendship. And some can be a result of the emphasis on testing and grades, as reflected in a Newsweek article entitled "The New First Grade: Are Kids Getting Pushed Too Fast Too Soon?" (Tyre, 2006). This article reports concerns of a principal who worries that students begin to burn out as early as 3rd grade. In the book, The Homework Myth: Why Our Kids Get Too Much of a Bad Thing, Kohn (2006) argues that neither research nor experience support claims that homework reinforces learning and builds responsibility. Why do schools assign homework so frequently? A look at cultural influences on education my provide some answers.

Cultural Influences

Another way to examine the world of school is to look at the cultural values, concepts, behaviors and roles that are part of the school experience but are not part of the formal curriculum. These are part of the **hidden curriculum** but are nevertheless very powerful messages. The hidden curriculum includes ideas of patriotism, gender roles, the ranking of occupations and classes, competition, and other values. Teachers, counselors, and other students specify and make known what is considered appropriate for girls and boys. The gender curriculum continues into high school, college, and professional school. Students learn a ranking system of occupations and social classes as well. Students in gifted programs or those moving toward college preparation classes may be viewed as superior to those who are receiving tutoring.

Gracy (2004) suggests that cultural training occurs early. Kindergarten is an "academic boot camp" in which students are prepared for their future student role-that of complying with an adult imposed structure and routine designed to produce docile, obedient, children who do not question meaningless tasks that will become so much of their future lives as students. A typical day is filled with structure, ritual, and routine that allows for little creativity or direct, hands-on contact. "Kindergarten, therefore, can be seen as preparing children not only for participation in the bureaucratic organization of large modern school systems, but also for the large-scale occupational bureaucracies of modern society." (Gracy, 2004, p. 148)

What do you think? Let's examine a kindergarten class schedule taken from a website found by going to Google and typing in "kindergarten schedule". You can find more of these on your own. Most look similar to this one:

7:55 to 8:20 Math tubs (manipulatives) and small group math lessons

8:20 to 8:35 Class meeting/restroom and drinks
8:35 to 8:55 Math board/calendar
8:55 to 9:10 Whole class math lesson
9:10 to 9:20 Daily news chart
9:20 to 9:50 Shared reading (big books/poem and song charts)
9:50 to 10:15 Language Arts Centers
10:15 to 10:30 Morning recess
10:30 to 10:50 Alphabet/phonics lesson and paper
10:50 to 11:10 Reading Workshop (more centers)
11:10 to 11:20 Picture and word chart
11:20 to 11:40 Writing workshop (journals)
11:40 to 12:20 Lunch and recess
12:20 to 12:50 Rainbow Reading Lab (sequenced file folder activities) or computer lab or internet computers. Children are divided into two groups and do one of these activities each day, title 1 teacher is in my room at this time.
12:50 to 1:20 Theme related activity or art class one day per week
1:20 to 1:35 Afternoon recess (or still in art one day per week)
1:35 to 2:10 Nap/rest time
2:10 to 2:50 Special classes (music, counseling, pe, or library)
2:50 to 3:05 Show and Tell and get ready to go home

(Source: Classroom_Schedules).

To what extent do you think that students are being prepared for their future student role? What are the pros and cons of such preparation? Look at the curriculum for kindergarten and the first few grades in your own school district. Emphasizing math and reading in preschool and kindergarten classes is becoming more common in some school districts. It is not without controversy, however. Some suggest that emphasis is warranted in order to help students learn math and reading skills that will be needed throughout school and in the world of work. This will also help school districts improve their accountability through test performance. Others argue that learning is becoming too structured to be enjoyable or effective and that students are being taught only to focus on performance and test taking. Students learn student incivility or lack of sincere concern for politeness and consideration of others is taught in kindergarten through 12th grades through the "what is on the test" mentality modeled by teachers. Students are taught to accept routinized, meaningless information in order to perform well on tests. And they are experiencing the stress felt by teachers and school districts focused on test scores and taught that their worth comes from their test scores. Genuine interest, an appreciation of the process of learning, and valuing others are important components of success in the workplace that are not part of the hidden curriculum in today's schools.
CC licensed content, Shared previously

Public domain content

Psychosocial Development

Now let's turn our attention to concerns related to self-concept, the world of friendships, and family life.

Self-Concept

Children in middle childhood have a more realistic sense of self than do those in early childhood. That exaggerated sense of self as "biggest" or "smartest" or "tallest" gives way to an understanding of one's strengths and weaknesses. This can be attributed to greater experience in comparing one's own performance with that of others and to greater cognitive flexibility. A child's self-concept can be influenced by peers and family and the messages they send about a child's worth. Contemporary children also receive messages from the media about how they should look and act. Movies, music videos, the internet, and advertisers can all create cultural images of what is desirable or undesirable and this too can influence a child's self-concept.

The Tweens

Advertisers have created a new consumer group known as the "tweens". This group spends an estimated $51 billion dollars annually and has another $170 billion a year spent on them (Irvine, 2006). Tweens range in age from 8 to 12 years and are characterized as sophisticated, early-maturing teenagers concerned primarily with their appearance, weight, and sexuality ("The 'Tween Market'" Media Awareness Network, 2007). Tweens are primarily targeted as consumers of media, clothing, and products that make them look "cool" and feel independent. For example, attitude t-shirts have been very popular among female tweens for the past several years and the slogans on these shirts reflect what might be considered "cool". Here are a few found in a national retail clothing store that focuses on fashion for tweens.

- Your boyfriend gave me this shirt.
- I live to shop
- It's all about me
- You wish

In general, toys are not marketed to this age group as they once were. However, some toys designed to appeal to slightly younger children tend to sexualize children (Harmanci, 2006). For an example of such sexy children's dolls, go to www.bratz.com. Jean Kilbourne, a noted expert on the impact of advertising on self-image, responds to the promotion of such products as examples of how "marketers are hijacking our children's sexuality" at the expense of childhood (Squire, 2006).

Sexual Abuse in Middle Childhood

Being sexually abused as a child can have a powerful impact on self-concept. Childhood sexual abuse is defined as any sexual contact between a child and an adult or a much older child. Incest refers to sexual contact between a child and family members. In each of these cases, the child is exploited by an older person without regard for the child's developmental immaturity and inability to understand the sexual behavior (Steele, 1986). The concept of **false self-training** (Davis, 1999) refers to holding a child to adult standards while denying the child's developmental needs. Sexual abuse is just one example of false self-training. Children are held to adult standards of desirableness and sexuality while their level of cognitive, psychological, and emotional immaturity is ignored. Consider how confusing it might be for a 9 year old girl who has physically matured early to be thought of as a potential sex partner. Her cognitive, psychological, and emotional state do not equip her to make decisions about sexuality or, perhaps, to know that she can say no to sexual advances. She may feel like a 9 year old in all ways and be embarrassed and ashamed of her physical development. Girls who mature early have problems with low self-esteem because of the failure of others (family members, teachers, ministers, peers, advertisers, and others) to recognize and respect their developmental needs. Overall, youth are more likely to be victimized because they do not have control over their contact with offenders (parents, babysitters, etc.) and have no means of escape (Finkelhor and Dzuiba-Leatherman, in Davis, 1999).

Researchers estimate that 1 out of 4 girls and one out of 10 boys has been sexually abused (Valente, 2005). The median age for sexual abuse is 8 or 9 years for both boys and girls (Finkelhor et. al. 1990). Most boys and girls are sexually abused by a male. Although rates of sexual abuse are higher for girls than for boys, boys may be less likely to report abuse because of the cultural expectation that boys should be able to take care of themselves and because of the stigma attached to homosexual encounters (Finkelhor et. al. 1990). Girls are more likely to be abused by family member and boys by strangers. Sexual abuse can create feelings of self-blame, betrayal, and feelings of shame and guilt (Valente, 2005). Sexual abuse is particularly damaging when the perpetrator is someone the child trusts and may lead to depression, anxiety, problems with intimacy, and suicide (Valente, 2005). The topic of the sexualization of girls in media and society was of chief concern by the American Psychological Association in 2007 and their findings and recommendations to reduce this problem can be accessed here.

Industry vs. Inferiority

According to Erikson, children in middle childhood are very busy or industrious. They are constantly doing, planning, playing, getting together with friends, achieving. This is a very active time and a time when they are gaining a sense of how they measure up when compared with friends. Erikson believed that if these industrious children can be successful in their endeavors, they will get a sense of confidence for future challenges. If not, a sense of inferiority can be particularly haunting during middle childhood.

The Society of Children

Friendships take on new importance as judges of one's worth, competence, and attractiveness. Friendships provide the opportunity for learning social skills such as how to communicate with others and how to negotiate differences. Children get ideas from one another about how to perform certain tasks, how to gain popularity, what to wear, say, and listen to, and how to act. This society of children marks a transition from a life focused on the family to a life concerned with peers. Peers play a key role in a child's self-esteem at this age as any parent who has tried to console a rejected child will tell you. No matter how complimentary and encouraging the parent may be, being rejected by friends can only be remedied by renewed acceptance.

Peer Relationships: Most children want to be liked and accepted by their friends. Some popular children are nice and have good social skills. These popular-prosocial children tend to do well in school and are cooperative and friendly. Popular-antisocial children may gain popularity by acting tough or spreading rumors about others (Cillessen & Mayeux, 2004). Rejected children are sometimes excluded because they are shy and withdrawn. The withdrawn-rejected children are easy targets for bullies because they are unlikely to retaliate when belittled (Boulton, 1999). Other rejected children are ostracized because they are aggressive, loud, and confrontational. The aggressive-rejected children may be acting out of a feeling of insecurity. Unfortunately, their fear of rejection only leads to behavior that brings further rejection from other children. Children who are not accepted are more likely to experience conflict, lack confidence, and have trouble adjusting.

Family Life

During middle childhood, children spend less time with parents and more time with peers. And parents may have to modify their approach to parenting to accommodate the child's growing independence. Using reason and engaging in joint decision-making whenever possible may be the most effective approach (Berk, 2007). However, Asian-American, African-American, and Mexican-American parents are more likely than European-Americans to use an authoritarian style of parenting. This authoritarian style of parenting that using strict discipline and focuses on obedience is also tempered with acceptance and warmth on the part of the parents. And children raised in this manner tend to be confident, successful and happy (Chao, 2001; Stewart and Bond, 2002).

Family Tasks

One of the ways to assess the quality of family life is to consider the tasks of families.

Berger (2005) lists five family functions:

> Providing food, clothing and shelter
> Encouraging Learning
> Developing self-esteem
> Nurturing friendships with peers
> Providing harmony and stability

Notice that in addition to providing food, shelter, and clothing, families are responsible for helping the child learn, relate to others, and have a confident sense of self. The family provides a harmonious and stable environment for living. A good home environment is one in which the child's physical, cognitive, emotional, and social needs are adequately met. Sometimes families emphasize physical needs, but ignore cognitive or emotional needs. Other times, families pay close attention to physical needs and academic requirements, but may fail to nurture the child's friendships with peers or guide the child toward developing healthy relationships. Parents might want to consider how it feels to live in the household. Is it stressful and conflict-ridden? Is it a place where family members enjoy being?

Family Change

Divorce: A lot of attention has been given to the impact of divorce on the life of children. The assumption has been that divorce has a strong, negative impact on the child and that single-parent families are deficient in some way. However, 75-80 percent of children and adults who experience divorce suffer no long term effects (Hetherington & Kelly, 2002). Children of divorce and children who have not experienced divorce are more similar than different (Hetherington & Kelly, 2002).

Mintz (2004) suggests that the alarmist view of divorce was due in part to the newness of divorce when rates in the United States began to climb in the late 1970s. Adults reacting to the change grew up in the 1950s when rates were low. As divorce has become more common and there is less stigma associated with divorce, this view has changed somewhat. Social scientists have operated from the divorce as deficit model emphasizing the problems of being from a "broken home" (Seccombe &Warner, 2004). But more recently, a more objective view of divorce, repartnering, and remarriage indicates that divorce, remarriage and life in stepfamilies can have a variety of effects. The exaggeration of the negative consequences of divorce has left the majority of those who do well hidden and subjected them to unnecessary stigma and social disapproval (Hetherington & Kelly, 2002).

The tasks of families listed above are functions that can be fulfilled in a variety of family types-not just intact, two-parent households. Harmony and stability can be achieved in many family forms and when it is disrupted, either through divorce, or efforts to blend families, or any other circumstances, the child suffers (Hetherington & Kelly, 2002).

Factors Affecting the Impact of Divorce

As you look at the consequences (both pro and con) of divorce and remarriage on children, keep these family functions in mind. Some negative consequences are a result of financial hardship rather than divorce per se (Drexler, 2005). Some positive consequences reflect improvements in meeting these functions. For instance, we have learned that a positive self-esteem comes in part from a belief in the self and one's abilities rather than merely being complimented by others. In single-parent homes, children may be given more opportunity to discover their own abilities and gain independence that fosters self-esteem. If divorce leads to fighting between the parents and the child is included in these arguments, the self-esteem may suffer.

The impact of divorce on children depends on a number of factors. The degree of conflict prior to the divorce plays a role. If the divorce means a reduction in tensions, the child may feel relief. If the parents have kept their conflicts hidden, the announcement of a divorce can come as a shock and be met with enormous resentment. Another factor that has an great impact on the child concerns financial hardships they may suffer, especially if financial support is inadequate. Another difficult situation for children of divorce is the position they are put into if the parents continue to argue and fight-especially if they bring the children into those arguments.

Short-term consequences: In roughly the first year following divorce, children may exhibit some of these short-term effects:

1. **Grief over losses suffered**. The child will grieve the loss of the parent they no longer see as frequently. The child may also grieve about other family members that are no longer available. Grief sometimes comes in the form of sadness, but it can also be experienced as anger or withdrawal. Preschool-aged boys may act out aggressively while the same aged girls may become more quiet and withdrawn. Older children may feel depressed.

2. **Reduced Standard of Living**. Very often, divorce means a change in the amount of money coming into the household. Children experience in new constraints on spending or entertainment. School-aged children, especially, may notice that they can no longer have toys, clothing or other items to which they've grown accustomed. Or it may mean that there is less eating out or being able to afford satellite television, and so on. The custodial parent may experience stress at not being able to rely on child support payments or having the same level of income as before. This can affect decisions regarding healthcare, vacations, rents, mortgages and other expenditures. And the stress can result in less happiness and relaxation in the home. The parent who has to take on more work may also be less available to the children.

3. **Adjusting to Transitions**. Children may also have to adjust to other changes accompanying a divorce. The divorce might mean moving to a new home and changing schools or friends. It might mean leaving a neighborhood that has meant a lot to them as well.

Long-Term consequences: Here are some effects are found after the first year.

1. **Economic/Occupational Status**. One of the most commonly cited long-term effects of divorce is that children of divorce may have lower levels of education or occupational status. This may be a consequence of lower income and resources for funding education rather than to divorce per se. In those households where economic hardship does not occur, there may be no impact on economic status (Drexler, 2005).

2. **Improved Relationships with the Custodial Parent** (usually the mother): In the United States and Canada, children reside with the mother in 88 percent of single-parent households (Berk, 2007). Children from single-parent families talk to their mothers more often than children of two-parent families (McLanahan and Sandefur, 1994). Most children of divorce lead happy, well-adjusted lives and develop stronger, positive relationships with their custodial parent (Seccombe and Warner, 2004). In a study of college-age respondents, Arditti (1999) found that increasing closeness and a movement toward more democratic parenting styles was experienced. Others have also found that relationships between mothers and children become closer and stronger (Guttman, 1993) and suggest that greater equality and less rigid parenting is beneficial after divorce (Steward, Copeland, Chester, Malley, and Barenbaum, 1997).

3. **Greater emotional independence in sons**. Drexler (2005) notes that sons who are raised by mothers only develop an emotional sensitivity to others that is beneficial in relationships.

4. **Feeling more anxious in their own love relationships.** Children of divorce may feel more anxious about their own relationships as adults. This may reflect a fear of divorce if things go wrong, or it may be a result of setting higher expectations for their own relationships.

5. **Adjustment of the custodial parent**. Furstenberg and Cherlin (1991) believe that the primary factor influencing the way that children adjust to divorce is the way the custodial parent adjusts to the divorce. If that parent is adjusting well, the children will benefit. This may explain a good deal of the variation we find in children of divorce. Adults going though divorce should consider good self-care as beneficial to the children-not as self-indulgent.

Here are some tips for taking care of the self during divorce:

> Take care of your own mental health. Don't be a martyr. Do what is necessary to heal.
> Allow children to grieve and express their feelings without becoming defensive. Give the child the freedom to express feelings and be supportive and neutral as they voice their emotions over the loss.
> Try to have an amicable relationship with the ex-spouse and keep the children's best interests in mind.
> Do not put-down or badmouth the ex-spouse. This puts the child in a very uncomfortable position. You don't have to hide the truth from them either, but they will uncover the truth on their own. Be neutral. Children want to love their parents, regardless of the circumstances.
> Focus on establishing a comfortable, consistent healthy environment for the children as they adjust.

Repartnering

Repartnering refers to forming new, intimate relationships after divorce. This includes dating, cohabitation and remarriage.

Parental considerations about dating: Dating as a single parent can pose certain challenges. Time and money are considerations. A single mother may not have time for dating and may not have the money needed for child-care while she is out. Children can also resent a parent taking time away to date. Parents may struggle with whether or not to introduce a date to the children or to demonstrate affection in front of the children. When a dating relationship becomes serious, a boyfriend or girlfriend might expect the parent to prove their concern for them above the children. This puts a parent in a very uncomfortable situation. Sometimes, this vying for attention does not occur until the couple begins to consider sharing a long-term relationship.

Parental considerations about cohabitation: Having time, money and resources to date can be difficult. And having privacy for a dating relationship can also be problematic. Divorced parents may cohabit as a result. Cohabitation involves living together in a sexually intimate relationship without being married. This can be difficult for children to adjust to because cohabiting relationships in the United States tend to be short-lived. About 50 percent last less than 2 years (Brown, 2000). The child who starts a relationship with the parent's live-in partner may have to sever this relationship later. And even in long-term cohabiting relationships, once it's over, continued contact with the child is rare.

Is remarriage more difficult than divorce? The remarriage of a parent may be a more difficult adjustment for a child than the divorce of a parent (Seccombe & Warner, 2004). Parents and children typically have different ideas of how the stepparent should act. Parents and stepparents are more likely to see the stepparent's role as that of parent. A more democratic style of parenting may become more authoritarian after a parent remarries. And biological parents are more likely to continue to be involved with their children jointly when neither parent has remarried. They are least likely to jointly be involved if the father has remarried and the mother has not.

Characteristics of Stepfamilies

About 60 percent of divorced parents remarry within a few years (Berk, 2007). Largely due to high rates of divorce and remarriage, we have seen the number of stepfamilies in America grow considerably in the last 20 years although rates of remarriage are declining (Seccombe & Warner, 2004). Stepfamilies are not new. In the 1700-1800s there were many stepfamilies, but they were created because someone died and remarried. Most stepfamilies today are a result of divorce and remarriage. And such origins lead to new considerations. Stepfamilies are different from intact families and more complex in a number of ways that can pose unique challenges to those who seek to form successful stepfamily relationships (Visher & Visher, 1985). Stepfamilies are also known as blended families and stepchildren as "bonus children" by social scientists interested in emphasizing the positive qualities of these families.

Stepfamilies have a biological parent outside the stepfamily and a same sex adult in the family as natural parent. This can lead to animosity on part of a rejecting child. This can also lead to confusion on part of stepparent as to what their role is within the family.

Child may be a part of two households, each with different rules.

Members may not be as sure that others care and may require more demonstrations of affection for reassurance. For example, stepparents expect more gratitude and acknowledgment from the stepchild than they would with a biological child. Stepchildren experience more uncertainty/insecurity in their relationship with the parent and fear the parents will see them as sources of tension. And stepparents may feel guilty for a lack of feelings they may initially have toward their partner's children. Children who are required to respond to the parent's new mate as though they were the child's "real" parent often react with hostility, rebellion, or withdrawal. Especially if there has not been time for the relationship to develop.

Stepfamilies are born of loss. Members may have lost a home, a neighborhood, family members or at least their dream of how they thought life would be. These losses must be acknowledged and mourned.

Remarriage quickly after a divorce makes expressing grief more difficult. Family members are looking for signs that all is well at the same time that members are experiencing grief over losses.

Stepfamilies are structurally more complex. There are lost of triangles and lots of ways to divide and conquer the new couple.

Sexual attractions are more common in stepfamilies. Members have not grown up together and sexual attractions need to be understood, and controlled. Also a new couple may need to tone down sexual displays when around the children (can bring on jealousy, etc.) until there is greater acceptance of the new partner.

Sociologist Andrew Cherlin suggests that one reason people remarry is because divorce is so socially awkward. There are no clear guidelines for family/friends, how to treat divorcees, etc. As a result, people remarry to avoid this "displacement." The problem is that remarriage is similarly ill-defined. This is reflected in the lack of language to support the institution of remarriage. What does one call their stepparent? Who is included when thinking of "the family"? For couples with joint custody, where is "home"? And there are few guidelines about how ex-spouses and new spouses or other kin should interact. This is especially an issue when children are involved

In light of this incompleteness, here are some tips for those in stepfamilies. Most of these tips are focused on the stepparent. These come from an article entitled "The Ten Commandments of Step parenting" by Turnbull and Turnbull.

Provide neutral territory. If there is a way to do so, relocate the new family in a new, more neutral home. Houses have histories and there are many memories attached to family homes. This territoriality can cause resentments.

Don't try to fit a preconceived role. Stepparents need to realize that they cannot just walk into a situation and expect to fill a role. They need to stay in tuned with what works in this new family rather than being dogmatic about their new role.

Set limits and enforce them. Don't allow children to take advantage of the parent's guilt or adjustment by trying to gain special privileges as a result of the change. Limits provide security, especially if they are reasonable limits.

Allow an outlet for feelings by the children for their natural parent. This tip is for the natural parent. Avoid the temptation to "encourage" the child to go against your ex-spouse. Instead, remain neutral when comments are made.

Expect ambivalence, not instant love. Stepparents need to realize that their acceptance has to be earned, and sometimes it is long in coming. The relationship has to be given time to grow. Trust has to be established. One day they may be loved, the next, hated. Adjustment takes time.

Developmental Stages of Step-famililes

Stepfamilies go through periods of adjustments and developmental stages that take about 7 years for completion (Papernow, 1993). The early stages of stepfamily adjustment include periods of fantasy in which members may hope for immediate acceptance. This is followed by the immersion stage in which children have to adjust to their parent's date being transformed into a new stepfather or stepmother. This acceptance can be accompanied by a sense of betrayal toward the natural parent on the part of the children. The awareness stage involves members beginning to become aware of how they feel in the family and taking steps to map our their territory. Children may begin to feel as if they've been set aside for other family members and the couple may begin to focus their attention toward one another. Biological parents may feel resentful.

The middle stages include mobilization, in which family members begin to recognize their differences. Stepparents may be less interested in pleasing family members and more interested in taking a stand and being respected as family members. Children may start to voice their frustrations at being pulled in different directions by biological and stepparents. The next step is that of taking action. Now step-couples and stepparents begin to reorganize the family based on more realistic expectations and understandings of how members feel.

The later stages include contact between stepfamily members that is more intimate and genuine. A clearer role for the stepparent emerges. Finally, the stepfamily seems to have more security and stability than ever before.

Conclusions

Middle childhood is a complex period of the life span. New understandings and social situations bring variety to children's lives as they form new strategies for the world ahead. We next turn our attention to adolescents.
CC licensed content, Shared previously

- Psyc 200 Lifespan Psychology. **Authored by**: Laura Overstreet. **Located at**: http://opencourselibrary.org/econ-201/. **License**: *CC BY: Attribution*

Public domain content

- mirror. **Authored by**: ClkrFreeVectorImages. **Located at**: https://pixabay.com/en/frame-mirror-picture-baroque-empty-308791/. **License**: *CC0: No Rights Reserved*

Module 7: Adolescence

Introduction to Adolescense

Adolescence is a period that begins with puberty and ends with the transition to adulthood (approximately ages 10–20). Physical changes associated with puberty are triggered by hormones. Cognitive changes include improvements in complex and abstract thought, as well as development that happens at different rates in distinct parts of the brain and increases adolescents' propensity for risky behavior because increases in sensation-seeking and reward motivation precede increases in cognitive control. Adolescents' relationships with parents go through a period of redefinition in which adolescents become more autonomous, and aspects of parenting, such as distal monitoring and psychological control, become more salient. Peer relationships are important sources of support and companionship during adolescence yet can also promote problem behaviors. Same-sex peer groups evolve into mixed-sex peer groups, and adolescents' romantic relationships tend to emerge from these groups. Identity formation occurs as adolescents explore and commit to different roles and ideological positions. Nationality, gender, ethnicity, socioeconomic status, religious background, sexual orientation, and genetic factors shape how adolescents behave and how others respond to them, and are sources of diversity in adolescence.

Adolescence Defined

Adolescence is a developmental stage that has been defined as starting with puberty and ending with the transition to adulthood (approximately ages 10–20). Adolescence has evolved historically, with evidence indicating that this stage is lengthening as individuals start puberty earlier and transition to adulthood later than in the past. Puberty today begins, on average, at age 10–11 years for girls and 11–12 years for boys. This average age of onset has decreased gradually over time since the 19th century by 3–4 months per decade, which has been attributed to a range of factors including better nutrition, obesity, increased father absence, and other environmental factors (Steinberg, 2013[1]). Completion of formal education, financial independence from parents, marriage, and parenthood have all been markers of the end of adolescence and beginning of adulthood, and all of these transitions happen, on average, later now than in the past. In fact, the prolonging of adolescence has prompted the introduction of a new developmental period called *emerging adulthood* that captures these developmental changes out of adolescence and into adulthood, occurring from approximately ages 18 to 29 (Arnett, 2000[2]).

Adolescence is often characterized as a period of transformation, primarily, in terms of physical, cognitive, and social-relational change. [Image: Lorenia]

Steinberg, L. (2013). Adolescence (10th ed.). New York, NY: McGraw-Hill.
Arnett, J. J. (2000). Emerging adulthood: A theory of development from the late teens through the twenties. American Psychologist, 55, 469–480.

Physical Development

Adolescence begins with puberty. While the sequence of physical changes in puberty is predictable, the onset and pace of puberty vary widely. Several physical changes occur during puberty, such as adrenarche and gonadarche, the maturing of the adrenal glands and sex glands, respectively. Also during this time, primary and secondary sexual characteristics develop and mature. Primary sexual characteristics are organs specifically needed for reproduction, like the uterus and ovaries in females and testes in males. Secondary sexual characteristics are physical signs of sexual maturation that do not directly involve sex organs, such as development of breasts and hips in girls, and development of facial hair and a deepened voice in boys. Girls experience menarche, the beginning of menstrual periods, usually around 12–13 years old, and boys experience spermarche, the first ejaculation, around 13–14 years old.

During puberty, both sexes experience a rapid increase in height (i.e., growth spurt). For girls this begins between 8 and 13 years old, with adult height reached between 10 and 16 years old. Boys begin their growth spurt slightly later, usually between 10 and 16 years old, and reach their adult height between 13 and 17 years old. Both nature (i.e., genes) and nurture (e.g., nutrition, medications, and medical conditions) can influence height.

Because rates of physical development vary so widely among teenagers, puberty can be a source of pride or embarrassment. Early maturing boys tend to be stronger, taller, and more athletic than their later maturing peers. They are usually more popular, confident, and independent, but they are also at a greater risk for substance abuse and early sexual activity (Flannery, Rowe, & Gulley, 1993; Kaltiala-Heino, Rimpela, Rissanen, & Rantanen, 2001). Early maturing girls may be teased or overtly admired, which can cause them to feel self-conscious about their developing bodies. These girls are at a higher risk for depression, substance abuse, and eating disorders (Ge, Conger, & Elder, 2001; Graber, Lewinsohn, Seeley, & Brooks-Gunn, 1997; Striegel-Moore & Cachelin, 1999). Late blooming boys and girls (i.e., they develop more slowly than their peers) may feel self-conscious about their lack of physical development. Negative feelings are particularly a problem for late maturing boys, who are at a higher risk for depression and conflict with parents (Graber et al., 1997) and more likely to be bullied (Pollack & Shuster, 2000).

The adolescent brain also remains under development. Up until puberty, brain cells continue to bloom in the frontal region. Adolescents engage in increased risk-taking behaviors and emotional outbursts possibly because the frontal lobes of their brains are still developing. Recall that this area is responsible for judgment, impulse control, and planning, and it is still maturing into early adulthood (Casey, Tottenham, Liston, & Durston, 2005).

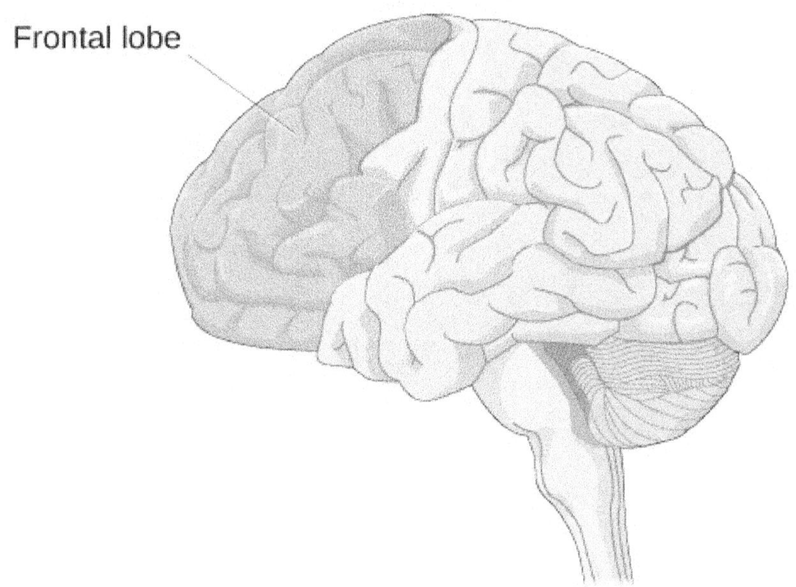

Example

According to neuroscientist Jay Giedd in the Frontline video "Inside the Teenage Brain" (2013), "It's sort of unfair to expect [teens] to have adult levels of organizational skills or decision-making before their brains are finished being built." Watch this segment on "The Wiring of the Adolescent Brain" to find out more about the developing brain during adolescence.

CC licensed content, Shared previously

- Stages of Development. **Provided by**: OpenStax College. **Located at**: http://cnx.org/contents/4abf04bf-93a0-45c3-9cbc-2cefd46e68cc@4.100:1/Psychology. **License**: *CC BY: Attribution*. **License Terms**: Download for free at http://cnx.org/content/col11629/latest/.

Cognitive Development

More complex thinking abilities emerge during adolescence. Some researchers suggest this is due to increases in processing speed and efficiency rather than as the result of an increase in mental capacity—in other words, due to improvements in existing skills rather than development of new ones (Bjorkland, 1987; Case, 1985). During adolescence, teenagers move beyond concrete thinking and become capable of abstract thought. Recall that Piaget refers to this stage as formal operational thought. Teen thinking is also characterized by the ability to consider multiple points of view, imagine hypothetical situations, debate ideas and opinions (e.g., politics, religion, and justice), and form new ideas. In addition, it's not uncommon for adolescents to question authority or challenge established societal norms.

Early in adolescence, changes in the brain's dopaminergic system contribute to increases in adolescents' sensation-seeking and reward motivation. Later in adolescence, the brain's cognitive control centers in the prefrontal cortex develop, increasing adolescents' self-regulation and future orientation. The difference in timing of the development of these different regions of the brain contributes to more risk taking during middle adolescence because adolescents are motivated to seek thrills that sometimes come from risky behavior, such as reckless driving, smoking, or drinking, and have not yet developed the cognitive control to resist impulses or focus

equally on the potential risks (Steinberg, 2008[1]). One of the world's leading experts on adolescent development, Laurence Steinberg, likens this to engaging a powerful engine before the braking system is in place. The result is that adolescents are more prone to risky behaviors than are children or adults.

Cognitive empathy, also known as theory-of-mind (which we discussed earlier with regard to egocentrism), relates to the ability to take the perspective of others and feel concern for others (Shamay-Tsoory, Tomer, & Aharon-Peretz, 2005). Cognitive empathy begins to increase in adolescence and is an important component of social problem solving and conflict avoidance. According to one longitudinal study, levels of cognitive empathy begin rising in girls around 13 years old, and around 15 years old in boys (Van der Graaff et al., 2013). Teens who reported having supportive fathers with whom they could discuss their worries were found to be better able to take the perspective of others (Miklikowska, Duriez, & Soenens, 2011).

Teenage thinking is characterized by the ability to reason logically and solve hypothetical problems such as how to design, plan, and build a structure. (credit: U.S. Army RDECOM)

Steinberg, L. (2013). Adolescence (10th ed.). New York, NY: McGraw-Hill.

- Second paragraph on cognitive development. **Authored by**: Jennifer Lansford. **Provided by**: Duke University. **Located at**: http://nobaproject.com/modules/adolescent-development?r=LDE2MjU3. **Project**: The Noba Project. **License**: *CC BY-NC-SA: Attribution-NonCommercial-ShareAlike*
- Stages of Development. **Authored by**: OpenStax College. **Located at**: http://cnx.org/contents/4abf04bf-93a0-45c3-9cbc-2cefd46e68cc@4.100:1/Psychology. **License**: *CC BY: Attribution*. **License Terms**: Download for free at http://cnx.org/content/col11629/latest/.

Social Development

Psychosocial Development

Adolescents continue to refine their sense of self as they relate to others. Erikson referred to the task of the adolescent as one of identity versus role confusion. Thus, in Erikson's view, an adolescent's main questions are "Who am I?" and "Who do I want to be?" Some adolescents adopt the values and roles that their parents expect for them. Other teens develop identities that are in opposition to their parents but align with a peer group. This is common as peer relationships become a central focus in adolescents' lives.

As adolescents work to form their identities, they pull away from their parents, and the peer group becomes very important (Shanahan, McHale, Osgood, & Crouter, 2007). Despite spending less time with their parents, most teens report positive feelings toward them (Moore, Guzman, Hair, Lippman, & Garrett, 2004). Warm and healthy parent-child relationships have been associated with positive child outcomes, such as better grades and fewer school behavior problems, in the United States as well as in other countries (Hair et al., 2005).

It appears that most teens don't experience adolescent storm and stress to the degree once famously suggested by G. Stanley Hall, a pioneer in the study of adolescent development. Only small numbers of teens have major conflicts with their parents (Steinberg & Morris, 2001), and most disagreements are minor. For example, in a study of over 1,800 parents of adolescents from various cultural and ethnic groups, Barber (1994) found that conflicts occurred over day-to-day issues such as homework, money, curfews, clothing, chores, and friends. These types of arguments tend to decrease as teens develop (Galambos & Almeida, 1992).

Social Changes

Parents. Although peers take on greater importance during adolescence, family relationships remain important too. One of the key changes during adolescence involves a renegotiation of parent–child relationships. As adolescents strive for more independence and autonomy during this time, different aspects of parenting become more salient. For example, parents' distal supervision and monitoring become more important as adolescents spend more time away from parents and in the presence of peers. Parental monitoring encompasses a wide range of behaviors such as parents' attempts to set rules and know their adolescents' friends, activities, and whereabouts, in addition to adolescents' willingness to disclose information to their parents (Stattin & Kerr, 2000[1]). *Psychological control*, which involves manipulation and intrusion into adolescents' emotional and cognitive world through invalidating adolescents' feelings and pressuring them to think in particular ways (Barber, 1996[2]), is another aspect of parenting that becomes more salient during adolescence and is related to more problematic adolescent adjustment.

Peers

As children become adolescents, they usually begin spending more time with their peers and less time with their families, and these peer interactions are increasingly unsupervised by adults. Children's notions of friendship often focus on shared activities, whereas adolescents' notions of friendship increasingly focus on intimate exchanges of thoughts and feelings. During adolescence, peer groups evolve from primarily single-sex to mixed-sex. Adolescents within a peer group tend to be similar to one another in behavior and attitudes, which has been explained as being a function of *homophily* (adolescents who are similar to one another choose to spend time together in a "birds of a feather flock together" way) and influence (adolescents who spend time together shape each other's behavior and attitudes). One of the most widely studied aspects of adolescent peer influence is known as *deviant peer contagion* (Dishion & Tipsord, 2011[3]), which is the process by which peers reinforce problem behavior by laughing or showing other signs of approval that then increase the likelihood of future problem behavior.

Peers can serve both positive and negative functions during adolescence. Negative peer pressure can lead adolescents to make riskier decisions or engage in more problematic behavior than they would alone or in the presence of their family. For example, adolescents are much more likely to drink alcohol, use drugs, and commit crimes when they are with their friends than when they are alone or with their family. However, peers also serve as an important source of social support and companionship during adolescence, and adolescents with positive peer relationships are happier and better adjusted than those who are socially isolated or have conflictual peer relationships.

Crowds refer to different collections of people, like the "theater kids" or the "environmentalists." In a way, they are kind of like clothing brands that label the people associated with that crowd. [Image: Garry Knight]

Crowds are an emerging level of peer relationships in adolescence. In contrast to friendships (which are reciprocal dyadic relationships) and cliques (which refer to groups of individuals who interact frequently), crowds are characterized more by shared reputations or images than actual interactions (Brown & Larson, 2009[4]). These crowds reflect different prototypic identities (such as jocks or brains) and are often linked with adolescents' social status and peers' perceptions of their values or behaviors.

Romantic relationships

Adolescence is the developmental period during which romantic relationships typically first emerge. Initially, same-sex peer groups that were common during childhood expand into mixed-sex peer groups that are more characteristic of adolescence. Romantic relationships often form in the context of these mixed-sex peer groups (Connolly, Furman, & Konarski, 2000[5]). Although romantic relationships during adolescence are often short-lived rather than long-term committed partnerships, their importance should not be minimized. Adolescents spend a great deal of time focused on romantic relationships, and their positive and negative emotions are more tied to romantic relationships (or lack thereof) than to friendships, family relationships, or school (Furman & Shaffer, 2003[6]). Romantic relationships contribute to adolescents' identity formation, changes in family and peer relationships, and adolescents' emotional and behavioral adjustment.

Furthermore, romantic relationships are centrally connected to adolescents' emerging sexuality. Parents, policymakers, and researchers have devoted a great deal of attention to adolescents' sexuality, in large part because of concerns related to sexual intercourse, contraception, and preventing teen pregnancies. However, sexuality involves more than this narrow focus. For example, adolescence is often when individuals who are lesbian, gay, bisexual, or transgender come to perceive themselves as such (Russell, Clarke, & Clary, 2009[7]). Thus, romantic relationships are a domain in which adolescents experiment with new behaviors and identities.

Identity formation

Theories of adolescent development often focus on identity formation as a central issue. For example, in Erikson's (1968[8]) classic theory of developmental stages, identity formation was highlighted as the primary indicator of successful development during adolescence (in contrast to role confusion, which would be an indicator of not successfully meeting the task of adolescence). Marcia (1966[9]) described identify formation during adolescence as involving both decision points and commitments with respect to ideologies (e.g., religion, politics) and occupations. He described four identity statuses: foreclosure, identity diffusion, moratorium, and identity achievement. *Foreclosure* occurs when an individual commits to an identity without exploring options. *Identity diffusion* occurs when adolescents neither explore nor commit to any identities. *Moratorium* is a state in which adolescents are actively exploring options but have not yet made commitments. *Identity achievement* occurs when individuals have explored different options and then made identity commitments. Building on this work, other researchers have investigated more specific aspects of identity. For example, Phinney (1989[10]) proposed a model of ethnic identity development that included stages of unexplored ethnic identity, ethnic identity search, and achieved ethnic identity.

Aggression and antisocial behavior

Early, antisocial behavior leads to befriending others who also engage in antisocial behavior, which only perpetuates the downward cycle of aggression and wrongful acts. [Image: Philippe Put]

Several major theories of the development of antisocial behavior treat adolescence as an important period.

Patterson's (1982[11]) early versus late starter model of the development of aggressive and antisocial behavior distinguishes youths whose antisocial behavior begins during childhood (early starters) versus adolescence (late starters). According to the theory, early starters are at greater risk for long-term antisocial behavior that extends into adulthood than are late starters. Late starters who become antisocial during adolescence are theorized to experience poor parental monitoring and supervision, aspects of parenting that become more salient during adolescence. Poor monitoring and lack of supervision contribute to increasing involvement with deviant peers, which in turn promotes adolescents' own antisocial behavior. Late starters desist from antisocial behavior when changes in the environment make other options more appealing. Similarly, Moffitt's (1993[12]) life-course persistent versus adolescent-limited model distinguishes between antisocial behavior that begins in childhood versus adolescence. Moffitt regards adolescent-limited antisocial behavior as resulting from a "maturity gap" between adolescents' dependence on and control by adults and their desire to demonstrate their freedom from adult constraint. However, as they continue to develop, and legitimate adult roles and privileges become available to them, there are fewer incentives to engage in antisocial behavior, leading to desistance in these antisocial behaviors.

Anxiety and depression

Developmental models of anxiety and depression also treat adolescence as an important period, especially in terms of the emergence of gender differences in prevalence rates that persist through adulthood (Rudolph, 2009[13]). Starting in early adolescence, compared with males, females have rates of anxiety that are about twice as high and rates of depression that are 1.5 to 3 times as high (American Psychiatric Association, 2013[14]). Although the rates vary across specific anxiety and depression diagnoses, rates for some disorders are markedly higher in adolescence than in childhood or adulthood. For example, prevalence rates for specific phobias are about 5% in children and 3%–5% in adults but 16% in adolescents. Anxiety and depression are particularly concerning because suicide is one of the leading causes of death during adolescence. Developmental models focus on interpersonal contexts in both childhood and adolescence that foster depression and anxiety (e.g., Rudolph, 2009[15]). Family adversity, such as abuse and parental psychopathology, during childhood sets the stage for social and behavioral problems during adolescence. Adolescents with such problems generate stress in their relationships (e.g., by resolving conflict poorly and excessively seeking reassurance) and select into more maladaptive social contexts (e.g., "misery loves company" scenarios in which depressed youths select other depressed youths as friends and then frequently co-ruminate as they discuss their problems, exacerbating negative affect and stress). These processes are intensified for girls compared with boys because girls have more relationship-oriented goals related to intimacy and social approval, leaving them more vulnerable to disruption in these relationships. Anxiety and depression then exacerbate problems in social relationships, which in turn contribute to the stability of anxiety and depression over time.

Academic achievement

Adolescents spend more waking time in school than in any other context (Eccles & Roeser, 2011[16]). Academic achievement during adolescence is predicted by interpersonal (e.g., parental engagement in adolescents' education), intrapersonal (e.g., intrinsic motivation), and institutional (e.g., school quality) factors. Academic achievement is important in its own right as a marker of positive adjustment during adolescence but also because academic achievement sets the stage for future educational and occupational opportunities. The most serious consequence of school failure, particularly dropping out of school, is the high risk of unemployment or underemployment in adulthood that follows. High achievement can set the stage for college or future vocational training and opportunities.

Diversity

Adolescent development does not necessarily follow the same pathway for all individuals. Certain features of adolescence, particularly with respect to biological changes associated with puberty and cognitive changes associated with brain development, are relatively universal. But other features of adolescence depend largely on circumstances that are more environmentally variable. For example, adolescents growing up in one country might have different opportunities for risk taking than adolescents in a different country, and supports and sanctions for different behaviors in adolescence depend on laws and values that might be specific to where adolescents live. Likewise, different cultural norms regarding family and peer relationships shape adolescents' experiences in these domains. For example, in some countries, adolescents' parents are expected to retain control over major decisions, whereas in other countries, adolescents are expected to begin sharing in or taking control of decision making.

Even within the same country, adolescents' gender, ethnicity, immigrant status, religion, sexual orientation, socioeconomic status, and personality can shape both how adolescents behave and how others respond to them, creating diverse developmental contexts for different adolescents. For example, early puberty (that occurs before most other peers have experienced puberty) appears to be associated with worse outcomes for girls than boys, likely in part because girls who enter puberty early tend to associate with older boys, which in turn is associated with early sexual behavior and substance use. For adolescents who are ethnic or sexual minorities, discrimination sometimes presents a set of challenges that nonminorities do not face.

Finally, genetic variations contribute an additional source of diversity in adolescence. Current approaches emphasize gene X environment interactions, which often follow a *differential susceptibility* model (Belsky & Pluess, 2009[17]). That is, particular genetic variations are considered riskier than others, but genetic variations also can make adolescents more or less susceptible to environmental factors. For example, the association between the CHRM2genotype and adolescent externalizing behavior (aggression and delinquency)has been found in adolescents whose parents are low in monitoring behaviors (Dick et al., 2011[18]). Thus, it is important to bear in mind that individual differences play an important role in adolescent development.

Conclusions

Adolescent development is characterized by biological, cognitive, and social changes. Social changes are particularly notable as adolescents become more autonomous from their parents, spend more time with peers, and begin exploring romantic relationships and sexuality. Adjustment during adolescence is reflected in identity formation, which often involves a period of exploration followed by commitments to particular identities. Adolescence is characterized by risky behavior, which is made more likely by changes in the brain in which reward-processing centers develop more rapidly than cognitive control systems, making adolescents more sensitive to rewards than to possible negative consequences. Despite these generalizations, factors such as country of residence, gender, ethnicity, and sexual orientation shape development in ways that lead to diversity of experiences across adolescence.

Outside Resources

Podcasts: Society for Research on Adolescence website with links to podcasts on a variety of topics related to adolescent development
http://www.s-r-a.org/sra-news/podcasts
Study: Add Health website on one of the biggest longitudinal studies of adolescence to date
http://www.cpc.unc.edu/projects/addhealth
Video: A selection of TED talks on adolescent brain development
http://tinyurl.com/lku4a3k
Web: UNICEF website on adolescents around the world
http://www.unicef.org/adolescence/index.html

Stattin, H., & Kerr, M. (2000). Parental monitoring: A reinterpretation. Child Development, 71, 1072-1085.

Barber, B. K. (1996). Parental psychological control: Revisiting a neglected construct. Child Development, 67, 3296-3319.

Dishion, T. J., & Tipsord, J. M. (2011). Peer contagion in child and adolescent social and emotional development. Annual Review of Psychology, 62, 189-214.

Brown, B. B., & Larson, J. (2009). Peer relationships in adolescence. In R. M. Lerner & L. Steinberg (Eds.), Handbook of adolescent psychology (pp. 74-103). New York, NY: Wiley.

Connolly, J., Furman, W., & Konarski, R. (2000). The role of peers in the emergence of heterosexual romantic relationships in adolescence. Child Development, 71, 1395-1408.

Furman, W., & Shaffer, L. (2003). The role of romantic relationships in adolescent development. In P. Florsheim (Ed.), Adolescent romantic relations and sexual behavior: Theory, research, and practical implications (pp. 3-22). Mahwah, NJ: Erlbaum.

Russell, S. T., Clarke, T. J., & Clary, J. (2009). Are teens "post-gay"? Contemporary adolescents' sexual identity labels. Journal of Youth and Adolescence, 38, 884-890.

Erikson, E. H. (1968). Identity, youth, and crisis. New York, NY: Norton.

Marcia, J. E. (1966). Development and validation of ego identity status. Journal of Personality and Social Psychology, 3, 551–558.

Phinney, J. (1989). Stages of ethnic identity in minority group adolescents. Journal of Early Adolescence, 9, 34–49.

Patterson, G. R. (1982). Coercive family process. Eugene, OR: Castalia Press.

Moffitt, T. E. (1993). Adolescence-limited and life course persistent antisocial behavior: Developmental taxonomy. Psychological Review, 100, 674–701.

Rudolph, K. D. (2009). The interpersonal context of adolescent depression. In S. Nolen-Hoeksema & L. M. Hilt (Eds.), Handbook of depression in adolescents (pp. 377–418). New York, NY: Taylor and Francis.

American Psychiatric Association. (2013). Diagnostic and statistical manual of mental disorders (5th ed.). Arlington, VA: American Psychiatric Publishing.

Rudolph, K. D. (2009). The interpersonal context of adolescent depression. In S. Nolen-Hoeksema & L. M. Hilt (Eds.), Handbook of depression in adolescents (pp. 377–418). New York, NY: Taylor and Francis.

Eccles, J. S., & Roeser, R. W. (2011). Schools as developmental contexts during adolescence. Journal of Research on Adolescence, 21, 225–241.

Belsky, J., & Pluess, M. (2009). Beyond diathesis-stress: Differential susceptibility to environmental influences. Psychological Bulletin, 135, 885–908.

Dick, D. M., Meyers, J. L., Latendresse, S. J., Creemers, H. E., Lansford, J. E., … Huizink, A. C. (2011). CHRM2, parental monitoring, and adolescent externalizing behavior: Evidence for gene-environment interaction. Psychological Science, 22, 481–489.

Assignment 3

Write a 2 page double spaced paper reflecting on your own adolescence.

Use the concepts discussed in Module 7 to relate to your experience.

Provide examples of times when you think your experience was different from those of our peers.

How do those differences show something unique about you?

Module 8: Early Adulthood

Introduction to Early Adulthood

Learning Objectives

Objectives: At the end of this lesson, you will be able to

Discuss the developmental tasks of early adulthood.
Describe physical development in early adulthood.
Explain how early adulthood is a healthy, yet risky time of life.
Summarize Levinson's theory of adult transitions.
Distinguish between formal and postformal thought.
Explain dialectical thought.
Describe Erikson's stage of intimacy vs. isolation.
Question Erikson's assertion about the focus on intimacy in early adulthood.
Identify trends in mate selection, age at first marriage, and cohabitation in the United States.
Discuss fertility issues in early adulthood.
Explain social exchange theory of mate selection.
Define the principle of least interest.
Apply Sternberg's theory of love to specific examples of relationships.
Apply Lee's love styles to specific examples of relationships.
Compare frames of relationships.
Explain the wheel theory of love.
Explain the process of disaffection.
Describe some current concerns in education in today's colleges.

Developmental Tasks of Early Adulthood

Early adulthood can be a very busy time of life. Havighurst (1972) describes some of the developmental tasks of young adults. These include:

- Achieving autonomy: trying to establish oneself as an independent person with a life of one's own
- Establishing identity: more firmly establishing likes, dislikes, preferences, and philosophies
- Developing emotional stability: becoming more stable emotionally which is considered a sign of maturing
- Establishing a career: deciding on and pursuing a career or at least an initial career direction and pursuing an education
- Finding intimacy: forming first close, long-term relationships
- Becoming part of a group or community: young adults may, for the first time, become involved with various groups in the community. They may begin voting or volunteering to be part of civic organizations (scouts, church groups, etc.). This is especially true for those who participate in organizations as parents.
- Establishing a residence and learning how to manage a household: learning how to budget and keep a home maintained.
- Becoming a parent and rearing children: learning how to manage a household with children. Making marital adjustments and learning to parent.

Photo Courtesy of Joshua Gray

REFERENCES

American Society of Reproductive Medicine (1996-2011): quick facs about infertility. (n.d.). American Society for Reproductive Medicine: News and Publications. Retrieved May 07, 2011, from http://www.reproductivefacts.org

Basseches, M. (1984). Dialectical thinking and adult development. Norwood, NJ: Ablex Pub.

Benokraitis, N. V. (2005). Marriages and families: Changes, choices, and constraints (5th ed.). Upper Saddle River, NJ: Pearson.

Berger, K. S. (n.d.). The developing person through the life span (6th ed.). New York: Worth.

Bianchi, S., & Casper, L. (2000). American families. (Dec. ed., Vol. 55) (United States, Population Reference Bureau). Washington, DC: Population Bulletin.

Bok, D. (2005, December 18). Are colleges failing? – The Boston Globe. Boston.com – Boston, MA News, Breaking News, Sports, Video. Retrieved May 07, 2011, from http://www.boston.com/news/education/higher/articles/2005/12/18/are_colleges_failing?

Bok, D. C. (2006). Our underachieving colleges: A candid look at how much students learn and why they should be learning more. Princeton, NJ: Princeton University Press.

Brooks, J. M. (1997). Beyond teaching and learning paradigms: Trekking into the Virtual University. Teaching Sociology, 27, 1-14.

Carroll, J. L. (2007). Sexuality now: Embracing diversity (2nd ed.). Belmont, CA: Thomson Learning.

Casper, L. M., & Bianchi, S. M. (2002). Continuity and change in the American family. Thousand Oaks, CA: Sage.

Collins, L. (1999). Emotional adultery: Cybersex anc commitment. Social Theory and Practice, 25(2), 243-270.

Davidson, J. K. (1991). Marriage and family. Dubuque, IA: William C. Brown.

Frieden, T. (2011, January 14). Morbidity and Mortality Weekly Report for the Centers for Disease Control (United States, Center for Disease Control). Retrieved February 12, 2011, from http://www.cdc.gov/mmwr/preview/mmwrhtml/su6001a1.htm?s_su6001a1_w

Gwinnell, E. (1998). Online seductions: Falling in love with strangers on the Internet. New York: Johnson Publishing.

Havighurst, R. J. (1972). Developmental tasks and education, (3rd ed.). New York: D. McKay.

Heron, M. P., & Smith, B. L. (2007). Products – Health E Stats – Homepage. Centers for Disease Control and Prevention. Retrieved May 07, 2011, from http://www.cdc.gov/nchs/products/pubs/pubd/hestats/leadingdeath03/leadingdeath03.htm

HRC | Marriage & relationship recognition. (n.d.). HRC | Human Rights Campaign | Home. Retrieved May 07, 2011, from http://www.hrc.org/issues/marriage.asp

Kerckhoff, A., & Davis, K. (1962). Value consensus and need complementarity in mate selection. American Sociological Review, 27(June), 295-303.

Lee, J. A. (1973). The colors of love: An exploration of the ways of loving. Don Mills, Ont.: New Press.

Of, T. (2006, September 21). Families and living arrangements, formerly households and families. Census Bureau Home Page. Retrieved May 07, 2011, from http://www.census.gov/population/www/socdemo/hh-fam.html

Reiss, I. (1960). Toward a sociology of the heterosexual love relationship. Marriage and Family Living, 22(May), 139-145.

Ridley, C. A., Peterman, D. J., & Avery, A. W. (1978). Cohabitation: Does it make for a better marriage? The Family Coordinator, April, 126-136.

Seccombe, K., & Warner, R. L. (2004). Marriages and families: Relationships in social context. Belmont, CA: Wadsworth/Thomson Learning.

Sternberg, R. (1988). A triangular theory of love. New York: Basic.

Tannen, D. (1990). You just don't understand: Women and men in conversation. New York: Morrow.

United States, U. S. Department of Education. (2006). A test of leadership: Charting the future of U. S. higher education. Washington, D. C.

Volko, N. D. (2004, September 19). Exploring the Whys of Adolescent Drug Use. (United States, National Institute on Drug Abuse). Retrieved January 23, 2007, from http://www.drugabuse.gov/NIDA_notes/NNvol19N3/DirRepVol19N3.html

Physical Development

The Physiological Peak: People in their twenties and thirties are considered young adults. If you are in your early twenties, good news-you are probably at the peak of your physiological development. Your reproductive system, motor ability, strength, and lung capacity are operating at their best. Now here is the bad news. These systems will now start a slow, gradual decline so that by the time you reach your mid to late 30s, you will begin to notice signs of aging. This includes a decline in your immune system, your response time, and in your ability to recover quickly from physical exertion. For example, you may have noticed that it takes you quite some time to stop panting after running to class or taking the stairs. But, here is more good news. Getting out of shape is not an inevitable part of aging; it is probably due to the fact that you have become less physically active and have experienced greater stress. How is that good news, you ask? It's good news because it means that there are thing you can do to combat many of these changes. So keep in mind, as we continue to discuss the life span that many of the changes we associate with aging can be turned around if we adopt healthier lifestyles.

A Healthy, but Risky Time: Doctor's visits are less frequent in early adulthood than for those in midlife and late adulthood and are necessitated primarily by injury and pregnancy (Berger, 2005). However, among the top five causes of death in young adulthood are non-intentional injury (including motor vehicle accidents), homicide, and suicide (Heron, M. P. & B. L. Smith, 2007). Cancer and heart disease complete the list. Rates of violent death (homicide, suicide, and accidents) are highest among young adult males, and vary among by race and ethnicity. Rates of violent death are higher in the United States than in Canada, Mexico, Japan, and other selected countries. Males are 3 times more likely to die in auto accidents than are females (Frieden, 2011).

Substance Abuse: Rates of violent death are influenced by substance abuse which peaks during early adulthood. Illicit drug use peaks between the ages of 19 and 22 and then begins to decline (Berk, 2007). And twenty-five percent of those who smoke cigarettes, a third of those who smoke marijuana, and 70 percent of those who abuse cocaine began using after age 17 (Volkow, 2004). Some young adults use as a way of coping with stressors from family, personal relationships, or concerns over being on one's own. Others use because they have friends who use and in the early 20s, there is still a good deal of pressure to conform. Half of all alcohol consumed in the United States is in the form of binge drinking (Frieden, 2011).

Drugs impair judgment, reduce inhibitions, and alter mood, all of which can lead to dangerous behavior. Reckless driving, violent altercations, and forced sexual encounters are some examples. Binge drinking on college campuses has received considerable media and public attention. The role alcohol plays in predicting acquaintance rape on college campuses is of particular concern. In the majority of cases of rape, the victim knows the rapist. Being intoxicated increases a female's risk of being the victim of date or acquaintance rape (Fisher et als. in Carroll, 2007). And, she is more likely to blame herself and to be blamed by others if she was intoxicated when raped. Males increase their risk of being accused of rape if they are drunk when an incidence occurred (Carroll, 2007).

Drug and alcohol use increase the risk of sexually transmitted infections because people are more likely to engage in risky sexual behavior when under the influence. This includes having sex with someone who has had multiple partners, having anal sex without the use of a condom, having multiple partners, or having sex with someone whose history is unknown. And, as we previously discussed in our lesson on Beginnings, drugs and alcohol ingested during pregnancy have a teratogenic effect.

Sexual Responsiveness and Reproduction in Early Adulthood

Sexual Responsiveness: Men and women tend to reach their peak of sexual responsiveness at different ages. For men, sexual responsiveness tends to peak in the late teens and early twenties. Sexual arousal can easily occur in response to physical stimulation or fantasizing. Sexual responsiveness begins a slow decline in the late twenties and into the thirties although a man may continue to be sexually active. Through time, a man may require more intense stimulation in order to become aroused. Women often find that they become more sexually responsive throughout their 20s and 30s and may peak in the late 30s or early 40s. This is likely due to greater self-confidence and reduced inhibitions about sexuality.

Reproduction: For many couples, early adulthood is the time for having children. However, delaying childbearing until the late 20s or early 30s has become more common in the United States.

Couples delay childbearing for a number of reasons. Women are more likely to attend college and begin careers before starting families. And both men and women are delaying marriage until they are in their late 20s and early 30s.

Infertility: Infertility affects about 6.1 million women or 10 percent of the reproductive age population (American Society of Reproductive Medicine [ASRM], 2000-2007). Male factors create infertility in about a third of the cases. For men, the most common cause is a lack of sperm production or low sperm production. Female factors cause infertility in another third of cases. For women, one of the most common causes of infertility is the failure to ovulate. Another cause of infertility is pelvic inflammatory disease, an infection of the female genital tract (Carroll, 2007). Pelvic inflammatory disease is experienced by 1 out of 7 women in the United States and leads to infertility about 20 percent of the time. One of the major causes of pelvic inflammatory disease is Chlamydia trachomatis, the most commonly diagnosed sexually transmitted infection in young women. Another cause of pelvic inflammatory disease is gonorrhea. Both male and female factors contribute to the remainder of cases of infertility.

Fertility treatment: The majority of infertility cases (85-90 percent) are treated using fertility drugs to increase ovulation or with surgical procedures to repair the reproductive organs or remove scar tissue from the reproductive tract. In vitro fertilization is used to treat infertility in less than 5 percent of cases. IVF is used when a woman has blocked or deformed fallopian tubes or sometimes when a man has a very low sperm count. This procedure involves removing eggs from the female and fertilizing the eggs outside the woman's body. The fertilized egg is then reinserted in the woman's uterus. The average cost of IVF is over $12,000 and the success rate is between 5 to 30 percent. IVF makes up about 99 percent of artificial reproductive procedures.

Less common procedures include gamete intra-fallopian tube transfer (GIFT) which involves implanting both sperm and ova into the fallopian tube and fertilization is allowed to occur naturally. The success rate of implantation is higher for GIFT than for IVF (Carroll, 2007). Zygote intra-fallopian tube transfer (ZIFT) is another procedure in which sperm and ova are fertilized outside of the woman's body and the fertilized egg or zygote is then implanted in the fallopian tube. This allows the zygote to travel down the fallopian tube and embed in the lining of the uterus naturally. This procedure also has a higher success rate than IVF.

Insurance coverage for infertility is required in fourteen states, but the amount and type of coverage available varies greatly (ASRM, 2000-2007). The majority of couples seeking treatment for infertility pay much of the cost. Consequently, infertility treatment is much more accessible to couples with higher incomes. However, grants and funding sources are available for lower income couples seeking infertility treatment as well.

CC licensed content, Shared previously

- Psyc 200 Lifespan Psychology. **Authored by**: Laura Overstreet. **Located at**: http://opencourselibrary.org/econ-201/. **License**: *CC BY: Attribution*

Public domain content

- woman jogging. **Located at**: http://www.freestockphotos.biz/stockphoto/15312. **License**: *Public Domain: No Known Copyright*

Cognitive Development

Beyond Formal Operational Thought: Post-formal Thought

In our last lesson, we discussed formal operational thought. The hallmark of this type of thinking is the ability to think abstractly or to consider possibilities and ideas about circumstances never directly experienced. Thinking abstractly is only one characteristic of adult thought, however. If you compare a 15 year old with someone in their late 30s, you would probably find that the later considers not only what is possible, but also what is likely. Why the change? The adult has gained experience and understands why possibilities do not always become realities. This difference in adult and adolescent thought can spark arguments between the generations. Here is an example. A student in her late 30s relayed such an argument she was having with her 14 year old son. The son had saved a considerable amount of money and wanted to buy an old car and store it in the garage until he was old enough to drive. He could sit in it; pretend he was driving, clean it up, and show it to his friends. It sounded like a perfect opportunity. The mother, however, had practical objections. The car could just sit for several years without deteriorating. The son would certainly change his mind about the type of car he wanted before he was old enough to drive and they would be stuck with a car that would not run. Having a car nearby would be too much temptation and the son might decide to sneak it out for a quick run around the block, etc.

Postformal thought is practical, realistic and more individualistic. As a person approaches the late 30s, chances are they make decisions out of necessity or because of prior experience and are less influenced by what others think. Of course, this is particularly true in individualistic cultures such as the United States.

Dialectical Thought

In addition to moving toward more practical considerations, thinking in early adulthood may also become more flexible and balanced. Abstract ideas that the adolescent believes in firmly may become standards by which the adult evaluates reality. Adolescents tend to think in dichotomies; ideas are true or false; good or bad; right or wrong and there is no middle ground. However, with experience, the adult comes to recognize that there is some right and some wrong in each position, some good or some bad in a policy or approach, some truth and some falsity in a particular idea. This ability to bring together salient aspects of two opposing viewpoints or positions is referred to as dialectical thought and is considered one of the most advanced aspects of postformal thinking (Basseches, 1984). Such thinking is more realistic because very few positions, ideas, situations, or people are completely right or wrong. So, for example, parents who were considered angels or devils by the adolescent eventually become just people with strengths and weaknesses, endearing qualities and faults to the adult.

Educational Concerns

In 2005, 37 percent of people in the United States between 18 and 24 had some college or an associate degree; about 30 percent of people between 25 and 34 had completed an education at the bachelor's level or higher (U. S. Bureau of the Census, 2005). Of current concern is the relationship between higher education and the workplace. Bok (2005), American educator and Harvard University President, calls for a closer alignment between the goals of educators and the demands of the economy. Companies outsource much of their work, not only to save costs, but to find workers with the skills they need. What is required to do well in today's economy?

Colleges and universities, he argues, need to promote global awareness, critical thinking skills, the ability to communicate, moral reasoning, and responsibility in their students (Bok, 2006). Regional accrediting agencies and state organizations provide similar guidelines for educators. Workers need skills in listening, reading, writing, speaking, global awareness, critical thinking, civility, and computer literacy-all skills that enhance success in the workplace. The U. S. Secretary of Education, Margaret Spellings challenges colleges and universities to demonstrate their effectiveness in providing these skills to students and to work toward increasing America's competitiveness in the global economy (U. S. Department of Education, 2006).

A quality education is more than a credential. Being able to communicate and work well with others is crucial for success. There is some evidence to suggest that most workers who lose their jobs do so because of an inability to work with others, not because they do not know how to do their jobs (Cascio, in Berger 2005). Writing, reading, being able to work with a diverse work team, and having the social skills required to be successful in a career and in society are qualities that go beyond merely earning a credential to compete for a job. Employers must select employees who are not only degreed, but who will be successful in the work environment. Hopefully, students gain these skills as they pursue their degrees. Listen to this story about the lack of rigor in higher education and the problems students face as a result: A Lack Of Rigor Leaves Students 'Adrift' In College.

Psychosocial Development

Gaining Adult Status

Many of the developmental tasks of early adulthood involve becoming part of the adult world and gaining independence. Young adults sometimes complain that they are not treated with respect-especially if they are put in positions of authority over older workers. Consequently, young adults may emphasize their age to gain credibility from those who are even slightly younger. "You're only 23? I'm 27!" a young adult might exclaim. (Note: This kind of statement is much less likely to come from someone in their 40s!).

The focus of early adulthood is often on the future. Many aspects of life are on hold while people go to school, go to work, and prepare for a brighter future. There may be a belief that the hurried life now lived will improve 'as soon as I finish school' or 'as soon as I get promoted' or 'as soon as the children get a little older.' As a result, time may seem to pass rather quickly. The day consists of meeting many demands that these tasks bring. The incentive for working so hard is that it will all result in better future.

Levinson's Theory

In 1978, Daniel Levinson published a book entitled *The Seasons of a Man's Life* in which he presented a theory of development in adulthood. Levinson's work was based on in-depth interviews with 40 men between the ages of 35-45. He later conducted interviews with women as well (1996). According to Levinson, these adults have an image of the future that motivates them. This image is called "the dream" and for the men interviewed, it was a dream of how their career paths would progress and where they would be at midlife. Women held a "split dream"; an image of the future in both work and family life and a concern with the timing and coordination of the two. Dreams are very motivating. Dreams of a home bring excitement to couples as they look, save, and fantasize about how life will be. Dreams of careers motivate students to continue in school as they fantasize about how much their hard work will pay off. Dreams of playgrounds on a summer day inspire would be parents. A dream is perfect and retains that perfection as long as it remains in the future. But as the realization of it moves closer, it may or may not measure up to its image. If it does, all is well. But if it does not, the image must be replaced or modified. And so, in adulthood, plans are made, efforts follow, and plans are reevaluated. This creating and recreating characterizes Levinson's theory.

Levinson's stages are presented below (Levinson, 1978). He suggests that period of transition last about 5 years and periods of "settling down" last about 7 years. The ages presented below are based on life in the middle class about 30 years ago. Think about how these ages and transitions might be different today.

- Early adult transition (17-22): Leaving home, leaving family; making first choices about career and education
- Entering the adult world (22-28): Committing to an occupation, defining goals, finding intimate relationships
- Age 30 transition (28-33): Reevaluating those choices and perhaps making modifications or changing one's attitude toward love and work
- Settling down (33 to 40): Reinvesting in work and family commitments; becoming involved in the community
- Midlife transition (40-45): Reevaluating previous commitments; making dramatic changes if necessary; giving expression to previously ignored talents or aspirations; feeling more of a sense of urgency about life and its meaning
- Entering middle adulthood (45-50): Committing to new choices made and placing one's energies into these commitments

Adulthood, then, is a period of building and rebuilding one's life. Many of the decisions that are made in early adulthood are made before a person has had enough experience to really understand the consequences of such decisions. And, perhaps, many of these initial decisions are made with one goal in mind-to be seen as an adult. As a result, early decisions may be driven more by the expectations of others. For example, imagine someone who chose a career path based on other's advice but now find that the job is not what was expected. The age 30 transition may involve recommitting to the same job, not because it's stimulating, but because it pays well. Settling down may involve settling down with a new set of expectations for that job. As the adult gains status, he or she may be freer to make more independent choices. And sometimes these are very different from those previously made. The midlife transition differs from the age 30 transition in that the person is more aware of how much time has gone by and how much time is left. This brings a sense of urgency and impatience about making changes. The future focus of early adulthood gives way to an emphasis on the present in midlife. (We will explore this in our next lesson.) Overall, Levinson calls our attention to the dynamic nature of adulthood.

Erikson's Theory

Intimacy vs. Isolation

Erikson believed that the main task of early adulthood was to establish intimate relationships. Intimate relationships are more difficult if one is still struggling with identity. Achieving a sense of identity is a life-long process, but there are periods of identity crisis and stability. And having some sense of identify is essential for intimate relationships. In early adulthood, intimacy (or emotional or psychological closeness) comes from friendships and mates.

Friendships as a source of intimacy

In our twenties, intimacy needs may be met in friendships rather than with partners. This is especially true in the United States today as many young adults postpone making long-term commitments to partners either in marriage or in cohabitation. The kinds of friendships shared by women tend to differ from those shared by men (Tannen, 1990). Friendships between men are more likely to involve sharing information, providing solutions, or focusing on activities rather than discussion problems or emotions. Men tend to discuss opinions or factual information or spend time together in an activity of mutual interest. Friendships between women are more likely to focus on sharing weaknesses, emotions, or problems. Women talk about difficulties they are having in other relationships and express their sadness, frustrations, and joys. These differences in approaches lead to problems when men and women come together. She may want to vent about a problem she is having; he may want to provide a solution and move on to some activity. But when he offers a solution, she thinks he does not care!

Friendships between men and women become more difficult because of the unspoken question about whether the friendships will lead to a romantic involvement. It may be acceptable to have opposite-sex friends as an adolescent, but once a person begins dating or marries; such friendships can be considered threatening. Consequently, friendships may diminish once a person has a partner or single friends may be replaced with couple friends.

Partners as a source of intimacy: Dating, Cohabitation, and Mate Selection

Dating

In general, traditional dating among teens and those in their early twenties has been replaced with more varied and flexible ways of getting together. The Friday night date with dinner and a movie that may still be enjoyed by those in their 30s gives way to less formal, more spontaneous meetings that may include several couples or a group of friends. Two people may get to know each other and go somewhere alone. How would you describe a "typical" date? Who calls? Who pays? Who decides where to go? What is the purpose of the date? In general, greater planning is required for people who have additional family and work responsibilities. Teens may simply have to negotiate getting out of the house and carving out time to be with friends.

Cohabitation or Living Together

How prevalent is cohabitation? There are over 5 million heterosexual cohabiting couples in the United States and, an additional 594,000 same-sex couples share households (U. S. Census Bureau, 2006). In 2000, 9 percent of women and 12 percent of men were in cohabiting relationships (Bumpass in Casper & Bianchi, 2002). This number reflects only those couples who were together when census data were collected, however. The number of cohabiting couples in the United States today is over 10 times higher than it was in 1960.

Similar increases have also occurred in other industrialized countries. For example, rates are high in Great Britain, Australia, Sweden, Denmark, and Finland. In fact, more children in Sweden are born to cohabiting couples than to married couples. The lowest rates of cohabitation are in Ireland, Italy, and Japan (Benokraitis, 2005).

How long do cohabiting relationships last?

Cohabitation tends to last longer in European countries than in the United States. Half of cohabiting relationships in the U. S. end within a year; only 10 percent last more than 5 years. These short-term cohabiting relationships are more characteristics of people in their early 20s. Many of these couples eventually marry. Those who cohabit more than five years tend to be older and more committed to the relationship. Cohabitation may be preferable to marriage for a number of reasons. For partners over 65, cohabitation is preferable to marriage for practical reasons. For many of them, marriage would result in a loss of Social Security benefits and consequently is not an option. Others may believe that their relationship is more satisfying because they are not bound by marriage. Consider this explanation from a 62-year old woman who was previously in a long-term, dissatisfying marriage. She and her partner live in New York but spend winters in South Texas at a travel park near the beach. "There are about 20 other couples in this park and we are the only ones who aren't married. They look at us and say, 'I wish we were so in love'. I don't want to be like them." (Author's files.) Or another couple who have been happily cohabiting for over 12 years. Both had previously been in bad marriages that began as long-term, friendly, and satisfying relationships. But after marriage, these relationships became troubled marriages. These happily cohabiting partners stated that they believe that there is something about marriage that "ruins a friendship".

The majority of people who cohabit are between the ages of 25-44. Only about 20 percent of those who cohabit are under age 24. Cohabitation among younger adults tends to be short-lived. Relationships between older adults tend to last longer.

Why do people cohabit?

People cohabit for a variety of reasons. The largest number of couples in the United States engages in premarital cohabitation. These couples are testing the relationship before deciding to marry. About half of these couples eventually get married. The second most common type of cohabitation is dating cohabitation. These partnerships are entered into for fun or convenience and involve less commitment than premarital cohabitation. About half of these partners break up and about one-third eventually marry. Trial marriage is a type of cohabitation in which partners are trying to see what it might be like to be married. They are not testing the other person as a potential mate, necessarily; rather, they are trying to find out how being married might feel and what kinds of adjustments they might have to make. Over half of these couples split up. In the substitute marriage, partners are committed to one another and are not necessarily seeking marriage. Forty percent of these couples continue to cohabit after 5 to 7 years (Bianchi & Casper, 2000). Certainly, there are other reasons people cohabit. Some cohabit out of a feeling of insecurity or to gain freedom from someone else (Ridley, C. Peterman, D. & Avery, A., 1978). And many cohabit because they cannot legally marry.

Same-Sex Couples

Same sex marriage is legal in 21 countries, including the United States. Many other countries either recognize same-sex couples for the purpose of immigration, grant rights for domestic partnerships, or grant common law marriage status to same-sex couples.

Same sex couples struggle with concerns such as the division of household tasks, finances, sex, and friendships as do heterosexual couples. One difference between same sex and heterosexual couples, however, is that same sex couples have to live with the added stress that comes from social disapproval and discrimination. And continued contact with an ex-partner may be more likely among homosexuals and bisexuals because of closeness of the circle of friends and acquaintances.

Mate-Selection

Contemporary young adults in the United States are waiting longer than before to marry. The median age of first marriage is 25 for women and 27 for men. This reflects a dramatic increase in age of first marriage for women, but the age for men is similar to that found in the late 1800s. Marriage is being postponed for college and starting a family often takes place after a woman has completed her education and begun a career. However, the majority of women will eventually marry (Bianchi & Casper, 2000).

Photo Courtesy Salvor Gissurardottir

Social exchange theory suggests that people try to maximize rewards and minimize costs in social relationships. Each person entering the marriage market comes equipped with assets and liabilities or a certain amount of social currency with which to attract a prospective mate. For men, assets might include earning potential and status while for women, assets might include physical attractiveness and youth.

A fair exchange

Customers in the market do not look for a 'good deal', however. Rather, most look for a relationship that is mutually beneficial or equitable. One of the reasons for this is because most a relationship in which one partner has far more assets than the other will result if power disparities and a difference in the level of commitment from each partner. According to Waller's principle of least interest, the partner who has the most to lose without the relationship (or is the most dependent on the relationship) will have the least amount of power and is in danger of being exploited. A greater balance of power, then, may add stability to the relationship.

Homogamy and the filter theory of mate selection: Societies specify through both formal and informal rules who is an appropriate mate. Consequently, mate selection is not completely left to the individual. Rules of endogamy indicate within which groups we should marry. For example, many cultures specify that people marry within their own race, social class, age group, or religion. These rules encourage homogamy or marriage between people who share social characteristics. The majority of marriages in the U. S. are homogamous with respect to race, social class, age and to a lesser extent, religion. Rules of exogamy specify the groups into which one is prohibited from marrying. For example, in most of the United States, people are not allowed to marry someone of the same sex.

According to the filter theory of mate selection (Kerckhoff & Davis, 1962), the pool of eligible partners becomes narrower as it passes through filters used to eliminate members of the pool. One such filter is propinquity or geographic proximity. Mate selection in the United States typically involves meeting eligible partners face to face. Those with whom one does not come into contact are simply not contenders. Race and ethnicity is another filter used to eliminate partners. Although interracial dating has increased in recent years and interracial marriage rates are higher than before, interracial marriage still represents only 5.4 percent of all marriages in the United States. Physical appearance is another feature considered when selecting a mate. Age, social class, and religion are also criteria used to narrow the field of eligibles. Thus, the field of eligibles becomes significantly smaller before those things we are most conscious of such as preferences, values, goals, and interests, are even considered.

Online Relationships

What impact does the internet have on the pool of eligibles? There are hundreds of websites designed to help people meet. Some of these are geared toward helping people find suitable marriage partners and others focus on less committed involvements. Websites focus on specific populations-big beautiful women, Christian motorcyclists, parents without partners, and people over 50, etc. Theoretically, the pool of eligibles is much larger as a result. However, many who visit sites are not interested in marriage; many are already married. And so if a person is looking for a partner online, the pool must be filtered again to eliminate those who are not seeking long-term relationships. While this is true in the traditional marriage market as well, knowing a person's intentions and determining the sincerity of their responses becomes problematic online.

Photo Courtesy Vikram Kharvi

This young man offers his picture and a description of his professional status and stability. While he's looking for employment, his ad might also help him find an eligible partner online.

Online communication differs from face-to-face interaction in a number of ways. In face-to-face meetings, people have many cues upon which to base their first impressions. A person's looks, voice, mannerisms, dress, scent, and surroundings all provide information in face-to-face meetings. But in computer- mediated meetings, written messages are the only cues provided. Fantasy is used to conjure up images of voice, physical appearance, mannerisms, and so forth. The anonymity of online involvement makes it easier to become intimate without fear of interdependence. It is easier to tell one's secrets because there is little fear of loss. One can find a virtual partner who is warm, accepting, and undemanding (Gwinnell, 1998). And exchanges can be focused more on emotional attraction than physical appearance.

When online, people tend to disclose more intimate details about themselves more quickly. A shy person can open up without worrying about whether or not the partner is frowning or looking away. And someone who has been abused may feel safer in virtual relationships. None of the worries of home or work get in the way of the exchange. The partner can be given one's undivided attention, unlike trying to have a conversation on the phone with a houseful of others or at work between duties. Online exchanges take the place of the corner café as a place to relax, have fun, and be you (Brooks, 1997). However, breaking up or disappearing is also easier. A person can simply not respond, or block e-mail.

But what happens if the partners meet face to face? People often complain that pictures they have been provided of the partner are misleading. And once couples begin to think more seriously about the relationship, the reality of family situations, work demands, goals, timing, values, and money all add new dimensions to the mix. Next we will turn our attention to theories of love.
CC licensed content, Shared previously

- Psyc 200 Lifespan Psychology. **Authored by**: Laura Overstreet. **Located at**: http://opencourselibrary.org/econ-201/. **License**: *CC BY: Attribution*
- Map of where same-sex marriage is legal. **Provided by**: Wikipedia. **Located at**: https://en.wikipedia.org/wiki/Same-sex_marriage#/media/File:World_marriage-equality_laws.svg. **License**: *CC BY-SA: Attribution-ShareAlike*

Types of Love

Sternberg's Triangle of Love: Three Components

Sternberg (1988) suggests that there are three main components of love: passion, intimacy, and commitment. Love relationships vary depending on the presence or absence of each of these components. Passion refers to the intense, physical attraction partners feel toward one another. Intimacy involves the ability the share feelings, personal thoughts and psychological closeness with the other. Commitment is the conscious decision to stay together. Passion can be found in the early stages of a relationship, but intimacy takes time to develop because it is based on knowledge of the partner. Once intimacy has been established, partners may resolve to stay in the

relationship. Although many would agree that all three components are important to a relationship, many love relationships do not consist of all three. Let's look at other possibilities.

Liking: In this relationship, intimacy or knowledge of the other and a sense of closeness is present. Passion and commitment, however, are not. Partners feel free to be themselves and disclose personal information. They may feel that the other person knows them well and can be honest with them and let them know if they think the person is wrong. These partners are friends. However, being told that your partner 'thinks of you as a friend' can be a devastating blow if you are attracted to them and seek a romantic involvement.

Infatuation: Perhaps, this is Sternberg's version of "love at first sight". Infatuation consists of an immediate, intense physical attraction to someone. A person who is infatuated finds it hard to think of anything but the other person. Brief encounters are played over and over in one's head; it may be difficult to eat and there may be a rather constant state of arousal. Infatuation is rather short-lived, however, lasting perhaps only a matter of months or as long as a year or so. It tends to be based on chemical attraction and an image of what one thinks the other is all about.

Fatuous Love: However, some people who have a strong physical attraction push for commitment early in the relationship. Passion and commitment are aspects of fatuous love. There is no intimacy and the commitment is premature. Partners rarely talk seriously or share their ideas. They focus on their intense physical attraction and yet one, or both, is also talking of making a lasting commitment. Sometimes this is out of a sense of insecurity and a desire to make sure the partner is locked into the relationship.

Empty Love: This type of love may be found later in a relationship or in a relationship that was formed to meet needs other than intimacy or passion (money, childrearing, status). Here the partners are committed to staying in the relationship (for the children, because of a religious conviction, or because there are no alternatives perhaps), but do not share ideas or feelings with each other and have no physical attraction for one another.

Romantic Love: Intimacy and passion are components of romantic love, but there is no commitment. The partners spend much time with one another and enjoy their closeness but have not made plans to continue 'no matter what'. This may be true because they are not in a position to make such commitments or because they are looking for passion and closeness and are afraid it will die out if they commit to one another and start to focus on other kinds of obligations.

Companionate Love: Intimacy and commitment are the hallmarks of companionate love. Partners love and respect one another and they are committed to staying together. But their physical attraction may have never been strong or may have just died out. This may be interpreted as 'just the way things are' after so much time together or there may be a sense of regret and loss. Nevertheless, partners are good friends committed to one another.

Consummate Love: Intimacy, passion, and commitment are present in consummate love. This is often the ideal type of love. The couple shares passion; the spark has not died, and the closeness is there. They feel like best friends as well as lovers and they are committed to staying together.

Types of Lovers

Lee (1973) offers a theory of love styles or types of lovers derived from an analysis of writings about love through the centuries. As you read these, think about how these styles might become part of the types of love described above.

Pragma is a style of love that emphasizes the practical aspects of love. The pragmatic lover considers compatibility and the sensibility of their choice of partners. This lover will be concerned with goals in life, status, family reputation, attitudes about parenting, career issues and other practical concerns.

Mania is a style of love characterized by volatility, insecurity, and possessiveness. This lover gets highly upset during arguments or breakups, may have trouble sleeping when in love, and feels emotions very intensely.

Agape is an altruistic, selfless love. These partners give of themselves without expecting anything in return. Such a lover places the partner's happiness above their own and is self-sacrificing to benefit the partner.

Eros is an erotic style of loving in which the person feels consumed. Physical chemistry and emotional involvement are important to this type of lover.

Ludus refers to a style of loving that emphasizes the game of seduction and fun. Such a lover stays away from commitment and often has several love interests at the same time. This lover does not self-disclose and in fact may prefer to keep the other guessing. This lover can end a relationship easily.

Storge is a style of love that develops slowly over time. It often begins as a friendship and becomes sexual much later. These partners are likely to remain friends even after the breakup.

Frames of Relationships

A H M

Another useful way to consider relationships is to consider the amount of dependency in the relationship. Davidson (1991) suggests three models. The **A-frame** relationship is one in which the partners lean on one another and are highly dependent on the other for survival. If one partner changes, the other is at risk of 'falling over'. This type of relationship cannot easily accommodate change and the partners are vulnerable should change occur. A breakup could be devastating.

The **H-frame** relationship is one in which the partners live parallel lives. They rarely spend time with one another and tend to have separate lives. What time they do share is usually spent meeting obligations rather than sharing intimacies. This independent type of relationship can end without suffering emotionally.

The **M-frame** relationship is interdependent. Partners have a strong sense of connection but also are able to stand alone without suffering devastation. If this relationship ends, partners will be hurt and saddened, but will still be able to stand alone. This ability comes from a strong sense of self-love. Partners can love each other without losing a sense of self. And each individual has self-respect and confidence that enriches the relationship as well as strengthens the self.

We have been looking at love in the context of many kinds of relationships. In our next lesson, we will focus more specifically on marital relationships. But before we do, we examine the dynamics of falling in and out of love.

The Process of Love and Breaking Up

Reiss (1960) provides a theory of love as process. Based on the wheel theory of love, love relationships begin with the establishment of rapport.

Rapport involves sharing likes, preferences, establishing some common interests. The next step is to begin to disclose more personal information through self-revelation. When one person begins to open up, the social expectation is that the other will follow and also share more personal information so that each has made some risk and trust is built. Sexual intimacy may also become part of the relationship. Gradually, partners begin to disclose even more about themselves and are met with support and acceptance as they build mutual dependency. With time, partners come to rely on each other for need fulfillment. The wheel must continue in order for love to last. It becomes important for partners to continue to establish rapport by discussing the day's events, communicating about their goals and desires, and showing signs of trust. Partners must continue to rely on one another to have certain needs fulfilled. If the wheel turns backward, partners talk less and less, rely less on one another and are less likely to disclose.

Process of Disaffection: Breaking Up

When relationships are new, partners tend to give one another the benefit of the doubt and focus on what they like about one another. Flaws and imperfections do not go unnoticed; rather, they are described as endearing qualities. So, for example, the partner who has a very large nose is described as 'distinguished' or as having a 'striking feature.' This is very exhilarating because features that someone may have previously felt self-conscious about are now accepted or even appreciated. However, once partners begin the process of breaking up, these views are abandoned and questionable qualities are once again flaws and imperfections.

Kersten (1990) provides a look at the dynamics of breaking up. Although this work is primarily about divorce, the dynamics of dissolving any long-term relationship are similar. The beginning phase of breaking up involves seeing imperfections in the relationship but remaining hopeful that things will improve. This improvement will require the partner's cooperation because they are primarily at fault. So, as long as the offending partner makes the necessary changes, and of course the offended partner will provide the advice, support, and guidance required, the relationship will continue. (If you are thinking that this is not going to work-you are right. Attempts to change one's partner are usually doomed to failure. Would you want your partner to try to change you?)

Once it becomes clear that efforts to change are futile, the middle phase is entered. This phase is marked by disappointment. Partners talk less and less, make little eye contact, and grow further apart. One may still try to make contact, but the other is clearly disengaged and is considering the benefits and costs of leaving the relationship.

In the end phase, the decision to leave has been made. The specific details are being worked out. Turning a relationship around is very difficult at this point. Trust has diminished, and thoughts have turned elsewhere. This stage is one of hopelessness.

We will explore marriage, divorce, and cohabitation more fully in our next lesson.
CC licensed content, Shared previously

- Psyc 200 Lifespan Psychology. **Authored by**: Laura Overstreet. **Located at**:

Module 9: Middle Adulthood

Introduction to Middle Adulthood

Introduction

Middle adulthood (or midlife) refers to the period of the lifespan between young adulthood and old age. This period lasts from 20 to 40 years depending on how these stages, ages, and tasks are culturally defined. The most common age definition is from 40 to 65, but there can be a range of up to 10 years (ages 30-75) on either side of these numbers. The mid-thiries or the forties through the late 60s can be our guide. Research on this period of life is relatively new and many aspects of midlife are still being explored. This may be the least studied period of the lifespan. And this is a varied group. We can see considerable differences in individuals within this developmental stage. There is much to learn about this group. In the United States, the large Baby Boom cohort (those born between 1946 and 1964) are now midlife adults and this has led to increased interest in this developmental stage.

This is a relatively new period of life. One hundred years ago, life expectancy in the United States was about 47 years. Life-expectancy has increased globally by about 6 years since 1990 and now stands at 68 years and ranges from 57 years in low-income countries to 80 in high-income countries (World Health Organization, 2011). This number reflects an increase in life expectancy in Africa due to availability of antiretroviral medications to reduce HIV/AIDS, and a decrease in Europe and in countries in the former Soviet Union. Life expectancy in the United States for those born in 2007 is now at 75.9 for white males, 80.8 for white females, 70.0 for black males, and 76.8 for black females (U.S. National Center for Health Statistics, 2010). The U. S. ranks 42nd in the world and has been declining in rank. Children born in the U. S. today may be the first generation to have a shorter life span than their parents. Much of this decline has been attributed to the increase in sedentary lifestyle and obesity. See the Washington Post article, U.S. Deaths Rise by 50,000 in 2005, for more details.

Of course, longevity is not the only consideration. How long can we expect to lead health lives? Healthy life expectancy, or the years one can expect to live in good health, is 67 for males and 71 for females in the United States. It is higher in Japan with a healthy life expectancy of 72 for males and 78 for females. Certainly, living healthier lives is the goal. In the United States, Canada, and other countries where people live well in midlife, there are new concerns are about the aging process, the impact of lifestyle on health, productivity at work, and how to best spend the second half of life.

Developmental Tasks

Lachman (2004) provides a comprehensive overview of the challenges facing midlife adults. These include:

> Losing parents and experiencing associated grief.
> Launching children into their own lives.
> Adjusting to home life without children (often referred to as the empty nest).
> Dealing with adult children who return to live at home (known as boomerang children in the United States).
> Becoming grandparents.
> Preparing for late adulthood.
> Acting as caregivers for aging parents or spouses.

Let's explore these tasks and this stage of life.

REFERENCES:

Anderson, S. A., & Sabatelli, R. M. (2007). Family interaction: A multigenerational developmental perspective. Boston: Pearson/A & B.

Barnett, R. C. (1997). Gender, employment, and psychological well-being: Historical and life course perspectives. In Lachman & James (Eds.), Multiple Paths of Midlife Development (pp. 325-343). Chicago: University of Chicago Press.

Bengstron, V. L. (2001). Families, intergenerational relationships, and kinkeeping in midlife. In N. M. Putney (Author) & M. E. Lachman (Ed.), Handbook of midlife development (pp. 528-579). New York: Wiley.

Berger, K. S. (n.d.). The developing person through the life span. (6th ed.). New York: Worth.

Berk, L. (2007). Development through the life span (4th ed.). Boston: Allyn and Bacon.

Bohannan, P. (1971). Divorce and after. New York: Doubleday.

Bumpass, L. L., & Aquilino, W. S. (1995). A social map of midlife: Family and work over the life course. Prepared for the MacArthur Foundation Research Network on Successful Midlife Development.

Cuber, J. F., & Harroff, P. B. (1965). Sex and the significant Americans: A study of sexual behavior among the affluent. Baltimore: Penguin Books.

Firth, K. (2004). The adaptive value of feeling in control in midlife. In M. E. Lachman (Author) & O. D. Brim, C. D. Ryff, & R. Kessler (Eds.), How healthy are we: A national study of health in midlife. (pp. 320-349). Chicago: University of Chicago Press.

Global Health Observatory: Life expectancy at birth. (Rep.). (2011). Retrieved February 21, 2011, from World Health   Organization   website:

http://www.who.int/gho/mortality_burden_disease/life_tables/situation_trends_life_expectancy/en/index.html

Gottman, J. M., & Silver, N. (1999). The seven principles for making marriage work. New York: Crown.

Hochschild, A. R., & Machung, A. (1989). The second shift: Working parents and the revolution at home. New York, NY: Viking.

Knowles, M. S. (1998). The adult learner: A neglected species. Houston: Gulf Pub., Book Division.

Lachman, M. E. (2004). Development in Midlife. Annual Review of Psychology, 55(1), 305-331. doi: 10.1146/annurev.psych.55.090902.141521

Low Testosterone: MedlinePlus Interactive Health Tutorial from the Patient Education Institute. (n.d.). National Library of Medicine – National Institutes of Health. Retrieved May 07, 2011, from http://www.nlm.nih.gov/medlineplus/tutorials/lowtestosterone/htm/index.htm

Marks, N. F. (1998). Does it hurt to care? Caregiving, work-family conflict, and midlife well-being. Journal of Marriage and the Family, 60(4), 951-966.

McCrae, R. R., & Costa, P. T. (2003). Personality in adulthood: A five-factor theory perspective. New York: Guilford Press.

Menopause: MedlinePlus Medical Encyclopedia. (2007, January 11). National Library of Medicine – National Institutes of Health. Retrieved May 07, 2011, from http://www.nlm.nih.gov/medlineplus/ency/article/000894.htm

Neugarten, B. L. (1968). The awareness of middle aging. In B. L. Neugarten (Ed.), Middle age and aging (pp. 93-98). Chicago: University of Chicago Press.

NIH Research Matters has moved. (2007, January 12). National Institutes of Health (NIH). Retrieved May 07, 2011, from http://www.nih.gov/news/research_matters/january2007/01122007skills.htm

Reid, J. D. (1999). Women's health in midlife. In N. E. Avis (Author) & S. L. Willis (Ed.), Life in the Middle: Psychological and Social Development in Middle Age (pp. 105-147). San Diego, CA: Academic.

Research network on successful midlife development. (2007, February 7). Midlife Research – MIDMAC WebSite. Retrieved May 07, 2011, from http://midmac.med.harvard.edu/research.html

Rossi, A. S. (2004). The menopausal transition and aging process. In How healthy are we: A national study of health in midlife. (pp. 550-575). Chicago: University of Chicago Press.

Schaie, K. W. (2005). Developmental influences on adult intelligence the Seattle longitudinal study. Oxford: Oxford University Press.

Seccombe, K., & Warner, R. L. (2004). Marriages and families: Relationships in social context. Belmont, CA: Wadsworth/Thomson Learning.

Shapiro, S. M. (2006). Goal-free living: How to have the life you want now! Hoboken, NJ: John Wiley & Sons.

Shure, J., & Cahan, V. (1998, September 10). Launch an Exercise Program Today, Say Aging Institute, Senator John Glenn. National Institute on Aging. Retrieved May 07, 2011, from http://www.nia.nih.gov/NewsAndEvents/PressReleases/PR19980910Launch.htm

Stein, J. (1981). Single life: Unmarried adults in social context. New York: St. Martin's Press.

The 2011 Statistical Abstract: Life Expectancy. (n.d.). Census Bureau Home Page. Retrieved May 07, 2011, from http://www.census.gov/compendia/statab/cats/births_deaths_marriages_divorces/life_expectancy.html

United States, National Institute on Aging. (2005, December 20). Sexuality in Later Life. Retrieved February 3, 2007, from http://www.niapublications.org/agepages/sexuality.asp

United States, U.S. National Library of Medicine and the National Institute of Health. (2007, February 1). Erectile Dysfunction Affects 18 Million U. S. Men. Retrieved February 3, 2007, from http://www.nim.nih.gov/medlineplus/news/fullstory_44724.htm

Willis, S. L., & Schaie, K. W. (1999). Intellectual functioning in midlife. In S. L. Willis & J. D. Reid (Eds.), Life in the Middle: Psychological and Social Development in Middle Age (pp. 233-247). San Diego: Academic.
CC licensed content, Shared previously

- Psyc 200 Lifespan Psychology. **Authored by**: Laura Overstreet. **Located at**: http://opencourselibrary.org/econ-201/. **License**: *CC BY: Attribution*

Physical Development

There are few biologically based physical changes in midlife other than changes in vision, more joint pain, and weight gain (Lachman, 2004). Vision is affected by age. As we age, the lens of the eye gets larger but the eye loses some of the flexibility required to adjust to visual stimuli. Middle aged adults often have trouble seeing up close as a result. Night vision is also affected as the pupil loses some of its ability to open and close to accommodate drastic changes in light. Autoimmune disease

such as rheumatoid arthritis often starts in the 50s. Weight gain, sometimes referred to as the middle-aged spread, or the accumulation of fat in the abdomen is one of the common complaints of midlife adults. Men tend to gain fat on their upper abdomen and back while women tend to gain more fat on their waist and upper arms. Many adults are surprised at this weight gain because their diets have not changed. However, the metabolism slows during midlife by about one-third (Berger, 2005). Consequently, midlife adults have to increase their level of exercise, eat less, and watch their nutrition to maintain their earlier physique.

Hearing loss is experienced by about 14 percent of midlife adults (Gratton & Vasquez in Berk, 2007) as a result of being exposed to high levels of noise. Men may experience some hearing loss by 30 and women by 50. High frequency sounds are the first affected by such hearing loss. This loss accumulates after years of being exposed to intense noise levels. Men are more likely to work in noisy occupations. Hearing loss is also exacerbated by cigarette smoking, high blood pressure, and stroke. Most hearing loss could be prevented by guarding against being exposed to extremely noisy environments. (There is new concern over hearing loss in early adulthood with the widespread use of headphones for IPods and other similar devices.)

Most of the changes that occur in midlife can be easily compensated for (by buying glasses, exercising, and watching what one eats, for example.) And most midlife adults experience general good health. However, the percentage of adults who have a disability increases through midlife; while 7 percent of people in their early 40s have a disability, the rate jumps to 30 percent by the early 60s. This increase is highest among those of lower socioeconomic status (Bumpass and Aquilino, 1995).

What can we conclude from this information? Again, lifestyle has a strong impact on the health status of midlife adults. Smoking tobacco, drinking alcohol, poor diet, stress, physical inactivity, and chronic disease such as diabetes or arthritis reduce overall health. It becomes important for midlife adults to take preventative measures to enhance physical well-being. Those midlife adults who have a strong sense of mastery and control over their lives, who engage in challenging physical and mental activity, who engage in weight bearing exercise, monitor their nutrition, and make use of social resources are most likely to enjoy a plateau of good health through these years (Lachman, 2004).

The Climacteric

One biologically based change that occurs during midlife is the climacteric. During midlife, men may experience a reduction in their ability to reproduce. Women, however, lose their ability to reproduce once they reach menopause.

Menopause for women: Menopause refers to a period of transition in which a woman's ovaries stop releasing eggs and the level of estrogen and progesterone production decreases. After menopause, a woman's menstruation ceases (U. S. National Library of Medicine and National Institute of Health [NLM/NIH], 2007).

Changes typically occur between the mid 40s and mid 50s. The median age range for a women to have her last menstrual period is 50-52, but ages vary. A woman may first begin to notice that her periods are more or less frequent than before. These changes in menstruation may last from 1 to 3 years. After a year without menstruation, a woman is considered menopausal and no longer capable of reproduction. (Keep in mind that some women, however, may experience another period even after going for a year without one.) The loss of estrogen also affects vaginal lubrication which diminishes and becomes more watery. The vaginal wall also becomes thinner, and less elastic.

Menopause is not seen as universally distressing (Lachman, 2004). Changes in hormone levels are associated with hot flashes and sweats in some women, but women vary in the extent to which these are experienced. Depression, irritability, and weight gain are not menopausal (Avis, 1999; Rossi, 2004). Depression and mood swings are more common during menopause in women who have prior histories of these conditions rather than those who have not. And the incidence of depression and mood swings is not greater among menopausal women than non-menopausal women.

Cultural influences seem to also play a role in the way menopause is experienced. Numerous international students enrolled in my class have expressed their disbelief when we discuss menopause. For example, after listing the symptoms of menopause, a woman from Kenya or Nigeria might respond, "We do not have this in my country or if we do, it is not a big deal" to which some U. S. students reply, "I want to go there!" Indeed, there are cultural variations in the experience of menopausal symptoms. Hot flashes are experienced by 75 percent of women in Western cultures, but by less than 20 percent of women in Japan (Obermeyer in Berk, 2007).

Women in the United States respond differently to menopause depending upon the expectations they have for themselves and their lives. White, career-oriented women, African-American, and Mexican-American women overall tend to think of menopause as a liberating experience. Nevertheless, there has been a popular tendency to erroneously attribute frustrations and irritations expressed by women of menopausal age to menopause and thereby not take her concerns seriously. Fortunately, many practitioners in the United States today are normalizing rather than pathologizing menopause.

Concerns about the effects of hormone replacement has changed the frequency with which estrogen replacement and hormone replacement therapies have been prescribed for menopausal women. Estrogen replacement therapy was once commonly used to treat menopausal symptoms. But more recently, hormone replacement therapy has been associated with breast cancer, stroke, and the development of blood clots (NLM/NIH, 2007). Most women do not have symptoms severe enough to warrant estrogen or hormone replacement therapy. But if so, they can be treated with lower doses of estrogen and monitored with more frequent breast and pelvic exams. There are also some other ways to reduce symptoms. These include avoiding caffeine and alcohol, eating soy, remaining sexually active, practicing relaxation techniques, and using water-based lubricants during intercourse.

Andropause for men: Do males experience a climacteric? They do not lose their ability to reproduce as they age, although they do tend to produce lower levels of testosterone and fewer sperm. However, men are capable of reproduction throughout life. It is natural for sex drive to diminish slightly as men age, but a lack of sex drive may be a result of extremely low levels of testosterone. About 5 million men experience low levels of testosterone that results in symptoms such as: a loss of interest in sex, loss of body hair, difficulty achieving or maintaining erection, loss of muscle mass, and breast enlargement. Low testosterone levels may be due to glandular disease such as testicular cancer. Testosterone levels can be tested and if they are low, men can be treated with testosterone replacement therapy. This can increase sex drive, muscle mass, and beard growth. However, long term HRT for men can increase the risk of prostate cancer (The Patient Education Institute, 2005).

The Climacteric and Sexuality

Sexuality is an important part of people's lives at any age. Midlife adults tend to have sex lives that are very similar to that of younger adulthood. And many women feel freer and less inhibited sexually as they age. However, a woman may notice less vaginal lubrication during arousal and men may experience changes in their erections from time to time. This is particularly true for men after age 65. As discussed in the previous paragraph, men who experience consistent problems are likely to have medical conditions (such as diabetes or heart disease) that impact sexual functioning (National Institute on Aging, 2005).

Couples continue to enjoy physical intimacy and may engage in more foreplay, oral sex, and other forms of sexual expression rather than focusing as much on sexual intercourse. Risk of pregnancy continues until a woman has been without menstruation for at least 12 months, however, and couples should continue to use contraception. People continue to be at risk of contracting sexually transmitted infections such as genital herpes, chlamydia, and genital warts. And 10 percent of new cases of AIDS in the United States are of people 50 and older. Practicing safe sex is important at any age. Hopefully, when partners understand how aging affects sexual expression, they will be less likely to misinterpret these changes as a lack of sexual interest or displeasure in the partner and more able to continue to have satisfying and safe sexual relationships.

Exercise, Nutrition, and Health

The impact of exercise: Exercise is a powerful way to combat the changes we associate with aging. Exercise builds muscle, increases metabolism, helps control blood sugar, increases bone density, and relieves stress. Unfortunately, fewer than half of midlife adults exercise and only about 20 percent exercise frequently and strenuously enough to achieve health benefits. Many stop exercising soon after they begin an exercise program-particularly those who are very overweight. The best exercise programs are those that are engaged in regularly-regardless of the activity. But a well-rounded program that is easy to follow includes walking and weight training. Having a safe, enjoyable place to walk can make the difference in whether or not someone walks regularly. Weight lifting and stretching exercises at home can also be part of an effective program. Exercise is particularly helpful in reducing stress in midlife. Walking, jogging, cycling, or swimming can release the tension caused by stressors. And learning relaxation techniques can have healthful benefits. Exercise can be thought of as preventative health care; promoting exercise for the 78 million "baby boomers" may be one of the best ways to reduce health care costs and improve quality of life (Shure & Cahan, 1998).

Nutritional concerns: Aging brings about a reduction in the number of calories a person requires. Many Americans respond to weight gain by dieting. However, eating less does not typically mean eating right and people often suffer vitamin and mineral deficiencies as a result. Very often, physicians will recommend vitamin supplements to their middle aged patients.

The new food pyramid: The ideal diet is one low in fat, sugar, high in fiber, low in sodium, and cholesterol. In 2005, the Food Pyramid, a set of nutritional guidelines established by the U. S. Government was updated to accommodate new information on nutrition and to provide people with guidelines based on age, sex, and activity levels.

The ideal diet is also one low in sodium (less than 2300 mg per day). Sodium causes fluid retention which may in turn exacerbate high blood pressure. The ideal diet is also low in cholesterol (less than 300 mg per day). The ideal diet is also one high in fiber. Fiber is thought to reduce the risk of certain cancers and heart disease. Finally, an ideal diet is low in sugar. Sugar is not only a problem for diabetics; it is also a problem for most people. Sugar satisfies the appetite but provides no protein, vitamins or minerals. It provides empty calories. High starch diets are also a problem because starch is converted to sugar in the body. A 1-2 ounce serving of red wine (or grape juice) can have beneficial effects as well. Red wine can increase "good cholesterol" or HDLs (high density lipoproteins) in the blood and provides antioxidants important to combating aging.
CC licensed content, Shared previously

- Psyc 200 Lifespan Psychology. **Authored by**: Laura Overstreet. **Located at**: http://opencourselibrary.org/econ-201/. **License**: *CC BY: Attribution*
- **Authored by**: Ed Yourdan. **Located at**:

Cognitive Development

Plasticity of Intelligence

Prior research on cognition and aging has been focused on comparing young and old adults and assuming that midlife adults fall somewhere in between. But some abilities may decrease while others improve during midlife. The concept of plasticity means that intelligence can be shaped by experience. Intelligence is influenced by culture, social contexts, and personal choices as much as by heredity and age. In fact, there is new evidence that mental exercise or training can have lasting benefits (National Institutes of Health, 2007). We explore aspects of midlife intelligence below.

Formal Operational and Post-formal Intelligence

Remember formal operational thought? Formal operational thought involves being able to think abstractly; however, this ability does not apply to all situations or subjects. Formal operational thought is influenced by experience and education. Some adults lead patterned, orderly, lives in which they are not challenged to think abstractly about their world. Many adults do not receive any formal education and are not taught to think abstractly about situations they have never experienced. Nor are they exposed to conceptual tools used to formally analyze hypothetical situations. Those who do think abstractly, in fact, may be able to do so more easily in some subjects than others. For example, English majors may be able to think abstractly about literature, but be unable to use abstract reasoning in physics or chemistry. Abstract reasoning in a particular field requires a knowledge base that we might not have in all areas. So our ability to think abstractly depends to a large extent on our experiences.

Post-formal thought continues: As discussed previously, adults tend to think in more practical terms than do adolescents. Although they may be able to use abstract reasoning when they approach a situation and consider possibilities, they are more likely to think practically about what is likely to occur.

Increases and Decreases

Tacit knowledge (Hedlund, Antonakis, and Sternberg, 2001) increases with age. Tacit knowledge is pragmatic or practical and learned through experience rather than explicitly taught. It might be thought of as "know-how" or "professional instinct." It is referred to as tacit because it cannot be codified or written down. It does not involve academic knowledge, rather it involves being able to use skills and to problem-solve in practical ways. Tacit knowledge can be understood in the workplace and by blue collar workers such as carpenters, chefs, and hair dressers. These occupations and cognitive skills are the subject of the book, *The Mind at Work, by Mike Rose.* Read an interview with Rose HERE.

Verbal memory, spatial skills, inductive reasoning (generalizing from particular examples), and vocabulary increase with age as well (Willis and Shaie, 1999). You may have heard that wisdom comes with age. However, wisdom may be more of a function of personality than cognition. Those who exhibit wisdom in midlife, may have made wiser choices at younger ages as well.

The mechanics of cognition such as working memory and speed of processing gradually decline with age but can be easily compensated for through the use of higher order cognitive skills such as forming strategies to enhance memory or summarizing and comparing ideas rather than relying on rote memorization (Lachman, 2004). Further, the declines mentioned above may diminish as new generations, equipped with higher levels of education, begin to enter midlife.

Learning in Older Adults

Midlife adults in the United States often find themselves in classrooms. Whether they enroll in school to sharpen particular skills, to retool and reenter the workplace, or to pursue interests that have previously been neglected, these students tend to approach learning differently than do younger college students (Knowles, Horton, & Swanson, 1998).

An 18 year-old college student may focus more on rote memorization in studying for tests. They may be able to memorize information more quickly than an older student, but not have as thorough a grasp on the meaning of that information. Older students may take a bit longer to learn material, but are less likely to forget it quickly. Adult learners tend to look for relevance and meaning when learning information. Older adults have the hardest time learning material that is meaningless or unfamiliar. They are more likely to ask themselves, "What does this mean?" or "Why is this important?" when being introduced to information or when trying to concepts or facts. Older adults are more task-oriented learners and want to organize their activity around problem-solving. They see the instructor as a resource person rather than the "expert" and appreciate having their life experience recognized and incorporated into the material being covered.

This type of learning is more easily accomplished if adequate time is allowed for mastering the material. Keeping distractions at a minimum and studying when rested and energetic enhances adult learning. **Androgogy** is a type of teaching that considers the needs of adults (versus pedagogy which was originally geared toward teaching children).

Gaining Expertise: The Novice and the Expert

When we work extensively in an area, we may gain expertise. Some areas of expertise develop after about 10 years of working in a field. Some gain expertise after a shorter period of time. Consider the study skills of a seasoned student versus a new student or a new nurse versus an experienced nurse. One of the major differences is that the new one operates as a novice while the seasoned student or nurse performs more like an expert. An expert has a different approach to learning and problem-solving than does a novice or someone new to a field. While a novice tends to rely on formal procedures or guidelines, the expert relies more on intuition and is more flexible in solving problems. a novice's performance tends to be more conscious and methodical than an experts. An expert tends to perform actions in a more automatic fashion. An expert cook, for example, may be able to prepare a difficult recipe but not really describe how they did it. The novice cook might rigidly adhere to the recipe, hanging on every word and measurement. The expert also has better strategies for tackling problems than does a novice.

Psychosocial Development

Midlife crisis?

Remember Levinson's theory from our last lesson? Levinson found that the men he interviewed sometimes had difficulty reconciling the "dream" they held about the future with the reality they now experience. "What do I really get from and give to my wife, children, friends, work, community-and self?" a man might ask (Levinson, 1978, p. 192). Tasks of the midlife transition include **1) ending early adulthood; 2) reassessing life in the present and making modifications if needed; and 3) reconciling "polarities" or contradictions in ones sense of self**. Perhaps, early adulthood ends when a person no longer seeks adult status-but feels like a full adult in the eyes of others. This 'permission' may lead to different choices in life; choices that are made for self-fulfillment instead of social acceptance. While people in their early 20s may emphasize how old they are (to gain respect, to be viewed as experienced), by the time people reach their 40s, they tend to emphasize how young they are. (Few 40 year olds cut each other down for being so young: "You're only 43? I'm 48!!")

This new perspective on time brings about a new sense of urgency to life. The person becomes focused more on the present than the future or the past. The person grows impatient at being in the "waiting room of life" postponing doing the things they have always wanted to do. Now is the time. If it's ever going to happen, it better happen now. A previous focus on the future gives way to an emphasis on the present. Neugarten (1968) notes that in midlife, people no longer think of their lives in terms of how long they have lived. Rather, life is thought of in terms of how many years are left. If an adult is not satisfied at midlife, there is a new sense of urgency to start to make changes now.

Changes may involve ending a relationship or modifying one's expectations of a partner. These modifications are easier than changing the self (Levinson, 1978). Midlife is a period of transition in which one holds earlier images of the self while forming new ideas about the self of the future. A greater awareness of aging accompanies feelings of youth. And harm that may have been done previously in relationships haunts new dreams of contributing to the well-being of others. These polarities are the quieter struggles that continue after outward signs of "crisis" have gone away.

Levinson characterized midlife as a time of developmental crisis. However, research suggests that most people in the United States today do not experience a midlife crisis and that, in fact, many women find midlife a freeing, satisfying period. Results of a 10 year study conducted by the MacArthur Foundation Research Network on Successful Midlife Development, based on telephone interviews with over 3,000 midlife adults suggest that the years between 40 and 60 are ones marked by a sense of well-being. Only 23 percent of their participants reported experiencing a midlife crisis. The crisis tended to occur among the highly educated and was triggered by a major life event rather than out of a fear of aging (Research Network on Successful Midlife Development, accessed 2007). Maybe only the more affluent and educated have the luxury (or burden) of such self-examination. Nevertheless, sales of products designed to make one feel younger and "over the hill" birthday parties with black balloons and banners abound.

Goal-Free Living

One of the reasons the men in Levinson's study became concerned about their life was because it had not followed the course they had envisioned. Shapiro (2006) offers an alternative to linear thinking about the future and career paths. Many plan their futures by using a map. They have a sense of where they are and where they want to be and form strategies to get from point A to point B. While this seems perfectly logical, Shapiro suggests that following a map closes one to opportunities for the future and provides a standard by which all actual events may fall short. Life, then, is evaluated by how closely actual life events have followed the map. If so, all is well. If not, a feeling of frustration and failure creeps in. Shapiro suggests using a compass rather than a map as one's guide. A compass indicates a direction, but does not provide a destination. So, a person who lives "goal free" has direction and areas of interest that guide decision-making, but does not know the outcome. (Many of us do not know the outcome-even when we follow a map!) This approach opens a person up to possibilities that often occur by chance and frees one from being stressed or devastated if a preset destination is not reached by a certain time. And more importantly, goal-free (or compass-guided living) focuses a person's attention on the process of the journey and helps them appreciate all of their experiences along the way. What do you think? How many of your plans were mapped out previously? Could you be happy knowing that you do not know where you will be 5 years from now?

A clear sense of self, identity, and control can be important for meeting the challenges of midlife (Lachman and Firth, 2004). Consider this story of overcoming gender identity at midlife.

Finding Identity at Midlife: The Story of Erika

The late 40s brought about dramatic change in Erika's life. Erika is a transsexual who began the process of transitioning from male to female at about age 48. Since about age 8, Erika (then Richard) felt that he was more feminine than masculine. An impromptu game of "dress up" with a girl who lived in the neighborhood left Richard feeling a sense of connection and 'rightness' he had not before experienced. Through the years, dressing up and wearing make-up provided comfort and relief as well as the anxiety of possibly being discovered. Richard married and pursued a career in the military and later as a geologist, two very masculine careers, but all the while felt out of place in a masculine world.

Through the years, discomfort gave rise to depression and thoughts of suicide. "I felt like some sick, weird person." Not knowing what was wrong and not having anyone to talk to was very difficult. Erika finally found out what was wrong after searching the internet. First, she looked up "transvestite". "Is that what I am?" she wondered. But these descriptions did not apply. Finally, she learned about gender identity disorder, marked by a feeling of discomfort and disconnection between one's sense of self and biological gender. Eventually, Richard got the courage to tell his wife. Her response was, "you're killing my husband", to which he replied, "He would have died anyway." The couple separated after 24 years of marriage. After several months, however, the couple got back together. "We were just too good of friends to break up." But her wife did not want to see it, initially. "I would get dressed in the garage or dress like a man from the waist up and then stop behind a grocery store and finish changing before I got to my destination."

Erika found a psychologist in the phone book and began treatment under the Harry Benjamin standard of care. This care requires that an individual be identified as transsexual by two psychologists, and lives completely as a member of the other sex for one year before beginning surgical and hormonal treatments. Erika's surgery cost about $30,000. Hormone therapy and electrolysis cost far more.

Now in their 30th year together, Erika and wife they live under the same roof, but no longer share a bedroom. Erika now has full status through the state and government as a female. And her wife, is a warm, accepting, roommate. "The day that she yelled from her bedroom, 'do you have any pantyhose' was an important one." And seeing her lipstick on the rim of a wine glass created a feeling of congruence for Erika. Erika could now be Erika.

Erikson's Theory

According to Erikson, midlife adults face the crisis of generativity vs. stagnation. This involves looking at one's life while asking the question, "Am I doing anything worthwhile? Is anyone going to know that I was here? What am I contributing to others?" If not, a feeling of being stuck or stagnated may result. This discomfort can motivate a person to redirect energies into more meaningful activities. It is important to make revisions here so that in later life, one may feel a sense of pride and accomplishment and feel content with the choices that have been made.

Productivity at home

Family relationships

Younger and older adults tend to experience more spouse-related stress than do midlife adults. Midlife adults often have overload stressors such as having too many demands placed on them by children or due to financial concerns. Parents adjust to launching their children into lives of their own during this time. Some parents who feel uncomfortable about their children leaving home may actually precipitate a crisis to keep it from happening or push their child out too soon (Anderson and Sabatelli, 2007). But even welcomed and anticipated departure can still require adjustment on the part of the parents as they get used to their empty nest.

Adult children typically maintain frequent contact with their parents if for no other reason, for money and advice. Attitudes toward one's parents may become more accepting and forgiving as parents are seen in a more objective way-as people with good points and bad. And, as adults, children can continue to be subjected to criticism, ridicule, and abuse at the hand of parents. How long are we "adult children"? For as long as our parents are living, we continue in the role of son or daughter. (I had a neighbor in her nineties who would tell me her "boys" were coming to see her this weekend. Her boys were in their 70s-but they were still her boys!) But after ones parents are gone, the adult is no longer a child; as one 40 year old man explained after the death of his father, "I'll never be a kid again." And adult children, known as boomerang kids, may return home to live temporarily after divorces or if they lose employment.

Being a midlife child sometimes involves **kinkeeping**; organizing events and communication in order to maintain family ties. Kinkeepers are often midlife daughters (they are the person who tells you what food to bring to a gathering or makes arrangement for a family reunion), but kinkeepers can be midlife sons as well.

Caregiving of a disabled child, spouse, or other family member is part of the lives of some midlife adults. Overall, one major source of stress is that of trying to balance caregiving with meeting the demands of work away from home. Caregiving can have both positive and negative consequences that depend in part on the gender of the caregiver and the person receiving the care. Men and women express greater distress when caring for a spouse than when caring for other family members. Men who care are providing care for a spouse are more likely to experience greater hostility but also more personal growth than non-caregiving males. Men who are caring for disabled children express having more positive relationships with others. Women experience more positive relationships with others and greater purpose in life when caring for parents either in or outside of their home. But women who are caring for disabled children may experience poorer health and greater distress as a result (Marks, 1998).
CC licensed content, Shared previously

- Psyc 200 Lifespan Psychology. **Authored by**: Laura Overstreet. **Located at**: http://opencourselibrary.org/econ-201/. **License**: *CC BY: Attribution*

Relationships

Intimate Relationships

Single or Spouse-free? The number of adults who remain single has increased dramatically in the last 30 years. We have more people who never marry, more widows and more divorcees driving up the number of singles. Singles represent about 25 percent of American households. Singlehood has become a more acceptable lifestyle than it was in the past and many singles are very happy with their status. Whether or not a single person is happy depends on the circumstances of their remaining single.

Stein's Typology of Singles

Many of the research findings about singles reveal that they are not all alike. Happiness with one's status depends on whether the person is single by choice and whether the situation is permanent. Let's look at Stein's (1981) four categories of singles for a better understanding of this.

Voluntary temporary singles: These are younger people who have never been married and divorced people who are postponing marriage and remarriage. They may be more involved in careers or getting an education or just wanting to have fun without making a commitment to any one person. They are not quite ready for that kind of relationship. These people tend to report being very happy with their single status.

Voluntary permanent singles: These individuals do not want to marry and aren't intending to marry. This might include cohabiting couples who don't want to marry, priests, nuns, or others who are not considering marriage. Again, this group is typically single by choice and understandably more contented with this decision.

Involuntary temporary: These are people who are actively seeking mates. They hope to marry or remarry and may be involved in going on blind dates, seeking a partner on the internet or placing "getting personal" aids in search of a mate. They tend to be more anxious about being single.

Involuntary permanent: These are older divorced, widowed, or never-married people who wanted to marry but have not found a mate and are coming to accept singlehood as a probable permanent situation. Some are bitter about not having married while others are more accepting of how their life has developed.

Marriage: It has been said that marriage can be the greatest source of happiness or pain in one's life, depending on the relationship. Those who are in marriages can experience deeper happiness and pain than those who are unattached. All marriages are not alike and the same marriage between two people may change through the years. Below we will look at how satisfaction with marriage is affected by the life cycle and two ways to characterizing marriages.

Marital satisfaction & the life cycle: Marital satisfaction has peaks and valleys during the course of the life cycle. Rates of happiness are highest in the years prior to the birth of the first child. It hits a low point with the coming of children. Relationships become more traditional and there are more financial hardships and stress in living. Then it begins to improve when children leave home. Children bring new expectations to the marital relationship. Two people, who are comfortable with their roles as partners, may find the added parental duties and expectations more challenging to meet. Some couples elect not to have children in order to have more time and resources for the marriage. These child-free couples are happy keeping their time and attention on their partners, careers, and interests.

Types of Marriages

Intrinsic and Utilitarian Marriages: One way marriages vary is with regard to the reason the partners are married. Some marriages have intrinsic value: the partners are together because they enjoy, love and value one another. Marriage is not thought of as a means to another end-is an end in itself. These partners look for someone they are drawn to and with whom they feel a close and intense relationship. These partners find the relationship personally rewarding. Other marriages called utilitarian marriages are unions entered primarily for practical reasons. The partners see one another as a means to an end. The marriage brings financial security, children, social approval, housekeeping, political favor, a good car, a great house, and so on. These partners do not focus on intimacy. These marriages may be chosen more out of default. ("She was there when it was time to get married so here we are.") Marriages entered for practical reasons are more common throughout history and throughout the world.

Intrinsic marriages are a relatively recent phenomenon arising out of the 20th century focus on romantic love as a basis for marriage and increased independence of the partners. Marriage today is viewed as less necessary for economic survival. In general, utilitarian marriages tend to be more stable than intrinsic ones. In an intrinsic marriage, if the love or passion cools, there is nothing else to keep the partners together. In utilitarian marriages, there may be numerous ties to one another (children, property, and status). However, intrinsic marriages may be more romantically satisfying. Are most marriages intrinsic or utilitarian?

In reality, marriages fall somewhere in between these two extremes. Now let's look at another typology of marriage. As you read these types, think of whether these are more utilitarian or more intrinsic.

Cuber and Harroff

This classic typology of marriages is based on interviews with 437 highly educated, upper-middle class people, and ages 35 to 55 (Cuber & Haroff, 1965). All were financially successful and emotionally adjusted. From their interviews, the researchers found five major types of marriages. Some of these are more intrinsic and some more utilitarian. (One of the merits of this model is that it calls attention to the variation we find in marriages.)

1) **Conflict-habituated marriages**: In these marriages, there is considerable tension and unresolved conflict. Spouses habitually quarrel, nag, and bring up the past. As a rule, both spouses acknowledge their incompatibility and recognize the atmosphere of tension as normal. The subject of the argument hardly seems important, and partners do not resolve or expect to resolve their differences. 'Of course we don't settle any of the issues. It's sort of a matter of principle not to. Because somebody would have to give in and lose face for the next encounter', explained a member of a 25 year long conflict-habituated marriage. The conflict between them is "controlled" meaning it doesn't escalate. And it may be main way the partners interact with one another.

2) **Devitalized relationships**: These marriages are characterized as being empty, apathetic relationships which once had something more. Usually couples have been married several years, and over the course of time, the relationship has lost it's zest, intimacy, and meaning. Once deeply in love, they recall spending a great deal of time enjoying sex, and having a close emotional relationship in the past. But now they spend

little time together, enjoy sex together less, and no longer share many interests and activities. Most of their time is "duty time" together spent entertaining, planning and sharing activities with their children, and participating in community responsibilities and functions. Once their marriage was intrinsic, but now has become utilitarian.

Cuber and Haroff found these to be common among their respondents. Couples accepted this and tried to be "mature" about it. Some attributed it to being in middle-age; as a normal part of growing older. Others were resentful, bitter about it and others were ambivalent. Many felt it was appropriate for spouses who have been married for several years and these marriages were stable.

3) **Passive-congenial**: These utilitarian marriages emphasize qualities in the partners rather than emotional closeness. These upper-middle class couples tended to emphasize civic and professional responsibilities and the importance of property, children, and reputation. Among working class people the focus might be on the need for security or hopes for children. Unlike devitalized marriages, passive-congenial partners never expected the marriage to be emotionally intense. Instead, they stress the "sensibility" of their decision to marry. There is little conflict, but that does not mean there are no unspoken frustrations. There is little intimacy but the partner's fail each other's need for casual companionship. Passive-congenial marriages are less likely to end in divorce than unions in which partners have high expectations for emotional intensity. But if the marriage fails to fill practical needs, such as economic support or professional advancement, the partners may decide to divorce. Or, if one partner discovers they want more intimacy, they may leave.

4) **Vital**: These intrinsic marriages are created out of a desire for being together for the sake of enjoying one another. Vital partners retain their separate identities, but really enjoy sharing activities. They do have conflict, but it is likely to center on real issues rather than on "who said what first" or old grievances. They try to settle disagreements quickly so they can resume the relationship that means so much to them. There are few long-term areas of tension. Sex is important and pleasurable. Cuber and Haroff found these marriages to be in the minority.

5) **Total marriage**: These are also intrinsic. They are like vital marriages but the marriage encompasses even more areas of the partner's lives. Spouses may share work life, friends and leisure activities, as well as home life. They may organize their lives to make it possible to be alone together for long periods. These relationships are emotionally intense. Total marriages were also rare. They may also be at risk for rapid disintegration if the marital quality changes. These partners tend to want such intensity and be dissatisfied with anything less. These marriages also foster a mutual dependency that makes it hard for the remaining partner to adjust in case of death or divorce.

Marital Communication

Advice on how to improve one's marriage is centuries old. One of today's experts on marital communication is John Gottman. Gottman (1999) differs from many marriage counselors in his belief that having a good marriage does not depend on compatibility. Rather, the way that partners communicate to one another is crucial. At the University of Washington in Seattle, Gottman has measures the physiological responses of thousands of couples as they discuss issues of disagreement. Fidgeting in one's chair, leaning closer to or further away from the partner while speaking, increases in respiration and heart rate are all recorded and analyzed along with videotaped recordings of the partners' exchanges. Gottman believes he can accurately predict whether or not a couple will stay together by analyzing their communication. In marriages destined to fail, partners engage in the "marriage killers": contempt, criticism, defensiveness, and stonewalling. Each of these undermines the politeness and respect that healthy marriages require. And stonewalling, or shutting someone out, is the strongest sign that a relationship is destined to fail. Listen to *Act One: What Really Happens in Marriage* to hear Gottman talk about his work.

Divorce

We have examined divorce from the standpoint of its impact on children. And, in our last lesson, we looked at the "process of disaffection." One way to understand divorce is to look at the types of divorces people experience when a relationship ends. Bohannon (1971) describes six "stations of divorce". The first is the emotional divorce. This involves a lot of mini-divorces in which partners make alienating remarks to one another. Partners become disengaged from one another and emotionally withdrawn. Some couples divorce emotionally, but never legally.

The **economic divorce** involves the division of property and debt, determining whether alimony will be paid, and determining if a spouse who provided support while their partner was in school or other lengthy training that increased their earning potential will be entitled to future earnings. Sometimes custody battles are motivated by economic concerns.

The **legal divorce** involves court proceedings and negotiations that legally dissolve the partners' marital ties to one another. This is when society views a couple as divorced and may be a process that is somewhat anticlimactic. The actual time spent in the courtroom may be brief and the final culmination of much of what has occurred in the other stations of divorce.

The **coparental divorce** is experienced by those couples who have children together. Determining custody and visitation are part of this station of divorce. This can be the most difficult station of divorce.

The **community divorce** is perhaps given the least attention when thinking of divorce. This involves severing ties with neighbors, coworkers, friends, and relatives following divorce. When family and friends choose sides in a break-up, relationships are lost. Divorced adults may find that they are no longer included in events and ties are no longer maintained. A person begins to get used to their single status. This may initially involve a sense of anxiety about the future.

The **psychic divorce** takes the longest to complete. This involves grieving, becoming more objective about one's role in the break up, and feeling whole again as a single person. This transition may take 5 years or more. Many people never complete this because they remarry before getting to this point.

Remarriage

Rates of remarriage: Half of all marriages are remarriages for at least one partner. But remarriage rates have declined slightly in the past few years. Cohabitation is the main way couples prepare for remarriage, but even when living together, many important issues are still not discussed. Issues concerning money, ex-spouses, children, visitation, future plans, previous difficulties in marriage, etc. can all pose problems later in the relationship. And few couples engage in premarital counseling or other structured efforts to cover this ground before entering marriage again.

Happiness in remarriage: Reviews are mixed as to how happy remarriages are. Some say that they have found the right partner and have learned from mistakes. But the divorce rates for remarriages are higher than for first marriages. This is especially true in stepfamilies for reasons which we have already discussed. People who have remarried tend to divorce more quickly than do first marriages. This may be due to the fact that they have fewer constraints on staying married (are more financially or psychologically independent).

Factors effecting remarriage: The chances of remarrying depend on a number of things. First, it depends on the availability of partners. As time goes by, there are more available women than men in the marriage pool. Consequently, men are more likely than women to remarry. This lack of available partners is experienced by all women, but especially by African-American women where the ratio of women to men is quite high. Women are more likely to have children living with them, and this diminishes the chance of remarriage as well. And marriage is more attractive for males than females (Seccombe & Warner, 2004). Men tend to remarry sooner (3 years after divorce on average vs. 5 years on average for women).

Many women do not remarry because they do not want to remarry. Traditionally, marriage has provided more benefits to men than to women. Women typically have to make more adjustments in work (accommodating work life to meet family demands or the approval of the husband) and at home (taking more responsibility for household duties). Further, men's physical desirability is not as influenced by aging as is women's. The cultural emphasis on youth and physical beauty for women does not apply for men.

Education increases men's likelihood of remarrying but may reduce the likelihood for women. Part of this is due to the expectation (almost an unspoken rule) referred to as the "marriage gradient". This rule suggests among couples, the man is supposed to have more education than the woman. Today, there are more women with higher levels of education than before and women with higher levels are less likely to find partners matching this expectation. Being happily single requires being economically self-sufficient and being psychologically independent. Women in this situation may find remarriage much less attractive.

How Do Children Influence Recoupling/Repartnering?

Children lower the probability of remarriage, especially for women. One of the reasons for this is because women with children have less time and fewer resources for dating. Dating is difficult for a woman who has to find a babysitter, pay for a babysitter, and 'come home on time' if she is concerned about what her children think about her relationships. There is more guilt experienced about going out and finding the time and location for sexual intimacy can be problematic. Men may shy away from the responsibility of children or may find it difficult to get along with a girlfriend's children. And parents may find it difficult to date someone who wants to change the relationship they have with their children. Sometimes, she may feel pulled in two directions as the children and the man in her life all seek attention and engage in power struggles to get it. Some women decide that it is easier to be single than to experience such divisions. (This can also be true for men whose dates try to establish their importance over the importance of the children.) Children usually remain central to a single parent's life.

Courtship in Remarriage

Courtships are shorter in remarriage than in first marriages. When couples are "dating", there is less going out and more time spent in activities at home or with the children. So the couple gets less time together to focus on their relationship. Anxiety or memories of past relationships can get in the way. As one Talmudic scholar suggests "when a divorced man marries a divorced woman, four go to bed." (Secombe & Warner, 2004).

Remarried couples tend to have more realistic expectations for marriage, but also tend to be less willing to stay in unhappy situations. And re-divorce is more likely, especially when children are involved.

CC licensed content, Shared previously

- Psyc 200 Lifespan Psychology. **Authored by**: Laura Overstreet. **Located at**: http://opencourselibrary.org/econ-201/. **License**: *CC BY: Attribution*

Public domain content

- smiling couple. **Authored by**: Bill Branson. **Located at**: http://www.freestockphotos.biz/stockphoto/17066. **License**: *Public Domain: No Known Copyright*

Work and Personality

Productivity at Work

We have already discussed expertise as part of our look at cognitive development in midlife. A person may be at their peak of performance at work during this time. Connections between work units, companies, culture, and operations may be appreciated for the first time and with that, a midlife worker may be able to contribute to an organization in new, more comprehensive ways. Midlife may also be the peak time for earning and spending to meet the demands of launching children or caring for aging parents.

Work and midlife includes many scenarios. Some experience stable careers while others experience lay-offs and find themselves back in school to gain new skills for reemployment. Others experience discrimination due to age or find it difficult to gain employment because of the higher salary demands compared with younger, less experienced workers (Barnett, 1997). Many people over 50 seek meaning as well as income in careers entered into in midlife known as "encore careers" www.encore.org/). Some midlife adults anticipate retirement, while others may be postponing it for financial reasons. Listen to this story of *Encore Careers in the lives of Baby Boomers.*

https://www.youtube.com/watch?v=UMIFOSrzmNM

The workplace today is one in which many people from various walks of life come together. Work schedules are more flexible and varied, and more work independently from home or anywhere there is an internet connection. The midlife worker must be flexible, stay current with technology, and be capable of working within a global community. And the midlife mind seeks meaningful work.

Personality in Midlife

Does the personality change in midlife? Think about your parents or other adults you've known for some time. Did their personalities change when they reached midlife? Or were they pretty much the same? Some theorists maintain that personality becomes more stable as we reach middle adulthood. Other suggest that with age comes the addition of new personality traits-one's we may not have felt comfortable showing when we were younger.

Midlife is viewed as a time of increased stability especially if compared with early adulthood or adolescence. A person's tendency toward extraversion, agreeableness, neuroticism, conscientiousness, and openness, the Big Five personality traits, is more consistent (McCrae & Costa, 2003). Midlife adults become more agreeable, but decline in openness and neuroticism.

However, midlife is also viewed as a time of change. Carl Jung believed that our personality actually matures as we get older. A healthy personality is one that is balanced. People suffer tension and anxiety when they fail to express all of their qualities. Jung believed that each of us possess a "shadow side". For example, those who are typically introverted also have an extroverted side that rarely finds expression unless we are relaxed and uninhibited. Each of us has both a masculine and feminine side but in younger years, we feel societal pressure to give expression only to one. As we get older, we may become freer to express all of our traits as the situation arises. We find gender convergence in older adults. Men become more interested in intimacy and family ties. Women may become more assertive. This gender convergence is also affected by changes in society's expectations for males and females. With each new generation we find that the roles of men and women are less stereotypic and this allows for change as well.

Again, a sense of mastery and control over one's life can help midlife adults meet the challenges of this time of life (Lachman and Firth, 2004).

Conclusion

Midlife is a period of transition. It is also a time of productivity and expertise; a time of putting things together. Midlife is perhaps the least studied period of life. The story of midlife will continue to unfold as more attention is given to it as a part of the lifespan.
CC licensed content, Shared previously

- Psyc 200 Lifespan Psychology. **Authored by**: Laura Overstreet. **Located at**: http://opencourselibrary.org/econ-201/. **License**: *CC BY: Attribution*

Assignment 4

Choose two of the following three options and write a 2 page double-spaced response:

1. Find examples in the media of at least 3 of Cuber and Harroff's types of marriages. Describe these.

2. Write an instruction manual for people in midlife or late adulthood to enhance optimal aging.

3. Imagine that you are training others to work with people who are terminally ill or in grief. Advise your group about how to work most effectively with those populations.

CC licensed content, Shared previously

Module 10: Late Adulthood

Introduction to Late Adulthood

Learning Objectives

Objectives: At the end of this lesson, you will be able to

- Differentiate between impaired, normal, and optimal aging.
- Report numbers of people in late adulthood age categories in the United States.
- Discuss changes in the age structure of society in the U. S. and globally.
- Report life expectancies in the United States based on gender, race, and ethnicity.
- Explain the reasons for changes in life expectancies.
- Identify examples of ageism.
- Compare primary and secondary aging.
- Report on the leading sources of secondary aging.
- Describe changes in the senses in late adulthood.
- Discuss the impact of aging on the sensory register, working memory, and long-term memory.
- Describe theories of aging.
- Define Hayflick Limit.
- Evaluate previous ideas about aging and cognition based on new research.
- Describe abnormal memory loss due to Alzheimer's disease, delirium, and dementia.
- Differentiate between organic and nonorganic causes of dementia.
- Describe Erikson's psychosocial stage for late adulthood.
- Contrast disengagement, activity, and continuity theories of aging.
- Describe ways in which people are productive in late adulthood.
- Describe grandparenting styles.
- Compare marriage, divorce, being single, and widowhood in late adulthood.
- Report rates at which people in late adulthood require long-term care.
- Examine caregiving for dependent older adults.
- Define socio-emotional selectivity theory.
- Classify types of elder abuse.

Defining Late Adulthood: Age or Quality of Life?

Photo Courtesy Overstreet

We are considered in late adulthood from the time we reach our mid-sixties until death. In this lesson, we will learn how many people are in late adulthood, how that number is expected to change, and how life changes and continues to be the same as before in late adulthood. About 13 percent of the U. S. population or 38.9 million Americans are 65 and older (U. S. Census Bureau, 2011). This number is expected to grow to 88.5 million by the year 2050 at which time people over 65 will make up 20 percent of the population. This group varies considerably and is divided into categories of 65 plus, 85 plus, and centenarians for comparison by the census. Developmentalists, however, divide this population in to categories based on health and social well-being. Optimal aging refers to those who enjoy better health and social well-being than average. Normal aging refers to those who seem to have the same health and social concerns as most of those in the population. However, there is still much being done to understand exactly what normal aging means. Impaired aging refers to those who experience poor health and dependence to a greater extent than would be considered normal. Aging successfully involves making adjustments as needed in order to continue living as independently and actively as possible. This is referred to as selective optimization with compensation and means, for example, that a person who can no longer drive, is able to find alternative transportation. Or a person who is compensating for having less energy, learns how to reorganize the daily routine to avoid over-exertion. Perhaps nurses and other allied health professionals working with this population will begin to focus more on helping patients remain independent than on simply treating illnesses. Promoting health and independence are important for successful aging.

Age Categories: 65 to 74

These 18.3 million Americans tend to report greater health and social well-being than older adults. Having good or excellent health is reported by 41 percent of this age group (Center for Disease Control, 2004). Their lives are more similar to those of midlife adults than those who are 85 and older. This group is less likely to require long-term care, to be dependent or to be poor, and more likely to be married, working for pleasure rather than income, and living independently. About 65 percent of men and 50 percent of women between the ages of 65-69 continue to work full-time (He et al., 2005). Physical activity tends to decrease with age, despite the dramatic health benefits enjoyed by those who exercise. People with more education and income are more likely to continue being physically active. And males are more likely to engage in physical activity than are females. The majority of the young-old continue to live independently. Only about 3 percent of those 65-74 need help with daily living skills as compared with about 22.9 percent of people over 85. (Another way to consider think of this is that 97 percent of people between 65-74 and 77 percent of people over 85 do not require assistance!) This age group is less likely to experience heart disease, cancer, or stroke than the old, but nearly as likely to experience depression (U. S. Census, 2005).

75 to 84

This age group is more likely to experience limitations on physical activity due to chronic disease such as arthritis, heart conditions, hypertension (especially for women), and hearing or visual impairments. Rates of death due to heart disease, cancer, and cerebral vascular disease are double that experienced by people 65-74. Poverty rates are 3 percent higher (12 percent) than for those between 65 and 74. However, the majority of these 12.9 million Americans live independently or with relatives. Widowhood is more common in this group-especially among women.

85 plus

The number of people 85 and older is 34 times greater than in 1900 and now includes 5.7 million Americans. This group is more likely to require long-term care and to be in nursing homes. However, of the 38.9 million American over 65, only 1.6 million require nursing home care. Sixty-eight percent live with relatives and 27 percent live alone (He et al., 2005; U. S. Census Bureau, 2011).

Centenarians

There are 104,754 people over 100 years of aging living in the United States. This number is expected to increase to 601,000 by the year 2050 (U. S. Census Bureau, 2011). The majority is between ages 100 and 104 and eighty percent are women. Out of almost 7 billion people on the planet, about 25 are over 110. Most live in Japan, a few live the in United States and three live in France (National Institutes of Health, 2006). These "super-Centenarians" have led varied lives and probably do not give us any single answers about living longer. Jeanne Clement smoked until she was 117. She lived to be 122. She also ate a diet rich in olive oil and rode a bicycle until she was 100. Her family had a history of longevity. Pitskhelauri (in Berger, 2005) suggests that moderate diet, continued work and activity, inclusion in family and community life, and exercise and relaxation are important ingredients for long life.

The "Graying" of America and the globe:

This trend toward an increasingly aged population has been referred to as the "graying of America." However, populations are aging in most other countries of the world. (One exception to this is in sub-Saharan Africa where mortality rates are high due to HIV/AIDS) (He et al., 2005). There are 520 million people over 65 worldwide. This number is expected to increase to 1.53 billion by 2050 (from 8 percent to 17 percent of the global population.) Currently, four countries, Germany, Italy, Japan, and Monaco, have 20 percent of their population over 65. China has the highest number of people over 65 at 112 million (U. S. Census Bureau, 2011).

As the population ages, concerns grow about who will provide for those requiring long-term care. In 2000, there were about 10 people 85 and older for every 100 persons between ages 50 and 64. These midlife adults are the most likely care providers for their aging parents. The number of old requiring support from their children is expected to more than double by the year 2040 (He et al., 2005). These families will certainly need external physical, emotional, and financial support in meeting this challenge.

REFERENCES:

Berger, K. S. (2005). The developing person through the life span (6th ed.). New York: Worth.

Berk, L. (2007). Development through the life span (4th ed.). Boston: Allyn and Bacon.

Brehm, S. S., Miller, R., Perlman, D., & Campbell, S. (2002). Intimate relationships. (3rd ed.). Boston: McGraw-Hill Higher Education.

Busse, E. W. (1969). Theories of aging. In E. W. Busse & E. Pfeiffer (Eds.), Behavior and adaptation in late life. (pp. 11-31).

Cahill, S., South, K., & Spade, J. (n.d.). Outing age: Public policy issues affecting gay, lesbian, bisexual and transgender elders | National Gay and Lesbian Task Force. National Gay and Lesbian Task Force | Building LGBT Political Power from the Ground up. Retrieved May 07, 2011, from http://www.thetaskforce.org/reports_and_research/outing_age

Carroll, J. (2007). Sexuality now: Embracing diversity (2nd ed.). Belmont, CA: Wadsworth.

Carstenson, L. L., Fung, H. H., & Charles, S. T. (2003). Socioemotional selectivity theory and the regulation of emotion in the second half of life. Motivation and Emotion, 27, 103-123.

Chapman, D. P., Williams, S. M., Strine, T. W., Anda, R. F., & Moore, M. J. (2006, February 18). Preventing Chronic Disease: April 2006: 05_0167. Centers for Disease Control and Prevention. Retrieved May 07, 2011, from http://www.cdc.gov/pcd/issues/2006/apr/05_0167.htm

Cherlin, A. J., & Furstenberg, F. F. (1986). The new American grandparent: A place in the family, a life apart. New York: Basic Books.

Chevan, A. (1996). As cheaply as one: Cohabitation in the older population. Journal of Marriage and the Family, 58, 656-667.

Demographic Data on Aging. (n.d.). National Institute on Aging. Retrieved May 07, 2011, from http://www.nia.nih.gov/ResearchInformation/ExtramuralPrograms/BehavioralAndSocialResearch/DemographicAgi ng.htm

Dollemore, D. (2006, August 29). Publications. National Institute on Aging. Retrieved May 07, 2011, from http://www.nia.nih.gov/HealthInformation/Publications?AgingUndertheMicroscope/

Erikson, E. H. (1980). Identity and the life cycle. New York: Norton.

He, W., Sengupta, M., Velkoff, V., & DeBarros, K. (n.d.). U. S. Census Bureau, Current Popluation Reports, P23-209, 65+ in the United States: 2005 (United States, U. S. Census Bureau). Retrieved May 7, 2011, from http://www.census.gov/prod/1/pop/p23-190/p23-190.html

Kwong, T., & Ryan, E. (1999). Intergenerational communication: The survey interview as a social exchange. In S. See (Author) & N. Schwarz, D. C. Parker, B. Knauer, & Sudman (Eds.), Cognition, aging, and self reports. Philadelphia: Psychology Press.

Meegan, S. P., & Berg, C. A. (2002). Contexts, functions, forms, and processes of collaborative everyday problem solving in older adulthood. International Journal of Behavioral Development, 26(1), 6-15. doi: 10.1080/01650250143000283

National Center for Health Statistics: Health, United States, 2010: With special feature on death and dying. (n.d.). Centers for Disease Control and Prevention. Retrieved May 07, 2011, from http://www.cdc.gov/nchs/hus.htm

National Institute on Aging, Baltimore Longitudinal Study of Aging Home Page. (n.d.). National Institute on Aging – Intramural Research Program. Retrieved May 07, 2011, from http://www.grc.nia.nih.gov/branches/blsa/blsa.htm

Newsroom: Facts for Features & Special Editions: Facts for Features: Older Americans Month: May 2010. (2011, February 22). Census Bureau Home Page. Retrieved May 07, 2011, from http://www.census.gov/newsroom/releases/archives/facts_for_features_special_editions/cb10-ff06.html

Overstreet, L. (2006). Unhappy birthday: Stereotypes in late adulthood. Unpublished manuscript, Texas Woman's University.

Strough, J., Hicks, P. J., Swenson, L. M., Cheng, S., & Barnes, K. A. (2003). Collaborative everyday problem solving: Interpersonal relationships and problem dimensions. International Journal of Aging and Human Development, 56, 43-66.

Tennstedt, S., Morris, J., Unverzagt, F., Rebok, G., Willis, S., Ball, K., & Marsiske, M. (n.d.). ACTIVE: Advanced Cognitive Training for Independent and Vital Elderly Clinical Trial | Clinical Trials Search.org. Clinical Trials Database and Worldwide Listings | ClinicalTrialsSearch.org. Retrieved May 07, 2011, from http://www.clinicaltrialssearch.org/active-advanced-cognitive-training-for-independent-and-vital-elderly-nct002985 58.html

Umberson, D., Williams, K., Powers, D., Hui, L., & Needham, B. (2006). You make me sick: Marital quality and health over the life course. Journal of Health and Social Behavior, 47(1), 1-16.

United States, National Center for Health Statistics. (2002). National Vital Statistics Report, 50(16). Retrieved May 7, 2011, from http://www.cdc.gov/nchs/data/dvs/LCWK1_2000.pdf

United States, National Institute on Aging. (n.d.). Alzheimer's Disease, Education, and Referral Center. Update January 21, 2011. Retrieved February 17, 2011, from http://www.nia.nih.gov/Alzheimers/Publications/ADProgress2009/Introduction

Uscher, J. (2006, January). How to make a world of difference-without leaving home. AARP The Magazine – Feel Great. Save Money. Have Fun. Retrieved May 07, 2011, from http://www.aarpmagazine.org/lifestyle/virtual_volunteering.html

Weitz, R. (2007). The sociology of health, illness, and health care : A critical approach. Wadsworth Publishing.
CC licensed content, Shared previously

- Psyc 200 Lifespan Psychology. **Authored by**: Laura Overstreet. **Located at**:
  http://opencourselibrary.org/econ-201/. **License**: *CC BY: Attribution*

Physical Development

Life Expectancy and Quality of Life

One way to prepare for the future is to find ways to improve quality of life. Life expectancy in 1900 was about 47 years. Today, life expectancy for all races is 77.9 (75.4 for males and 80.4 for females.) For whites, life expectancy is 75.9 for males and 80.8 for females. For black males, life expectancy is 70 and is 76.8 for black females (U. S. Census Bureau, 2011). Historic racism or years of living under oppressive prejudice and discrimination can increase the incidence of stress-related illness and contribute to a lower life expectancy. The United States ranks 17th among other countries for its life expectancy for women and 19th for men. Japanese women and Swedish men have the longest life expectancies (He et al., 2005).

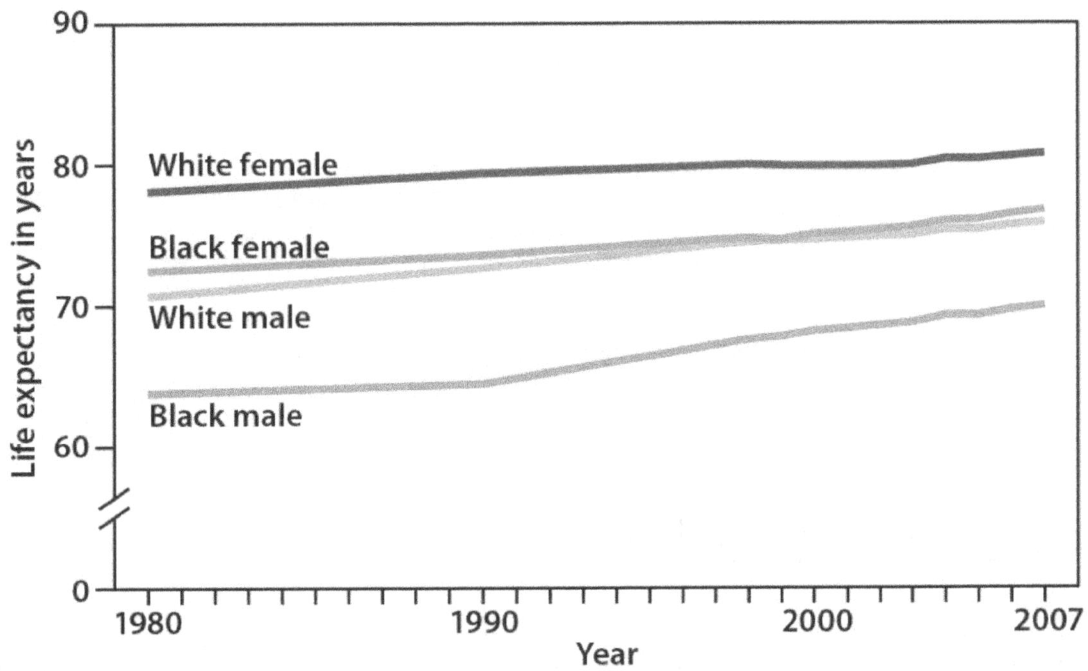

SOURCE: CDC/NCHS, *Health, United States, 2010*, Figure 1. Data from the National Vital Statistics System.

Increased life expectancy brings concern over the health and independence of those living longer. Greater attention is now being given to the number of years a person can expect to live without disability which is referred to as active life expectancy. When this distinction is made, we see that although women live longer than men, they are more at risk of living with disability (Weitz, 2007). What factors contribute to poorer health? Marriage has been linked to longevity, but spending years in a stressful marriage can increase the risk of illness. This negative effect is experienced more by women than men and seems accumulates through the years. Its impact on health may not occur until a woman reaches 70 or older (Umberson, Williams, et. al., 2006). Sexism can also create chronic stress. The stress experienced by women as they work outside the home as well as care for family members can also ultimately have a negative impact on health. Poorer health in women is further attributed to an increase in rates of smoking by women in recent years (He et als, 2005).

The shorter life expectancy for men in general, is attributed to greater stress, poorer attention to health, more involvement in dangerous occupations, and higher rates of death due to accidents, homicide, and suicide. Social support can increase longevity. For men, life expectancy and health seems to improve with marriage. Spouses are less likely to engage in risky health practices and wives are more likely to monitor their husband's diet and health regimes. But men who live in stressful marriages can also experience poorer health as a result.

Key players in improving the quality of life among older adults will be those adults. By exercising, reducing stress, stopping smoking, limiting use of alcohol, and consuming more fruits and vegetables, older adults can expect to live longer and more active lives. (He et. als, 2005). Stress reduction both in late adulthood and earlier in life is also crucial. The reduction of societal stressors can promote active life expectancy. In the last 40 years, smoking rates have decreased, but obesity has increased, and physical activity has only modestly increased.

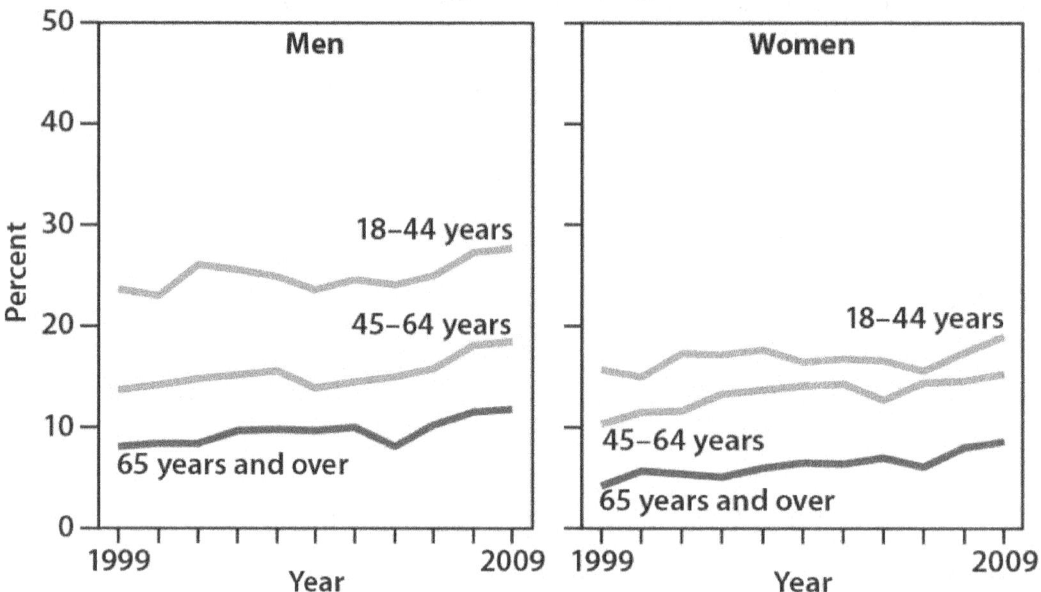

NOTE: *Activities that meet the 2008 federal guidelines available at: http://www.health.gov/paguidelines/default.aspx.
SOURCE: CDC/NCHS, *Health, United States, 2010*, Figure 12. Data from the National Health Interview Survey.

Attitudes about Aging

Stereotypes about people of in late adulthood lead many to assume that aging automatically brings poor health and mental decline. These stereotypes are reflected in everyday conversations, the media and even in greeting cards (Overstreet, 2006). The following examples serve to illustrate.

1) Grandpa, fishing pole in one hand, pipe in the other, sits on the ground and completes a story being told to his grandson with ". . . and that, Jimmy, is the tale of my very first colonoscopy." The message inside the card reads, "Welcome to the gross personal story years." (Shoebox, A Division of Hallmark Cards.)

2) An older woman in a barber shop cuts the hair of an older, dozing man. "So, what do you say today, Earl?" she asks. The inside message reads, "Welcome to the age where pretty much anyplace is a good place for a nap." (Shoebox, A Division of Hallmark Cards.)

3) A crotchety old man with wire glasses, a crumpled hat, and a bow tie grimaces and the card reads, "Another year older? You're at the age where you should start eatin' right, exercisin', and takin' vitamins . . ." The inside reads, "Of course you're also at the age where you can ignore advice by actin like you

can't hear it." (Hallmark Cards, Inc.)

Of course, these cards are made because they are popular. Age is not revered in the United States, and so laughing about getting older is one way to get relief. The attitudes are examples of ageism, prejudice based on age. Stereotypes such as these can lead to a self-fulfilling prophecy in which beliefs about one's ability results in actions that make it come true. A positive, optimistic outlook about aging and the impact one can have on improving health is essential to health and longevity. Removing societal stereotypes about aging and helping older adults reject those notions of aging is another way to promote health and active life expectancy among the old.

Primary and Secondary Aging

Healthcare providers need to be aware of which aspects of aging are reversible and which ones are inevitable. By keeping this distinction in mind, caregivers may be more objective and accurate when diagnosing and treating older patients. And a positive attitude can go a long way toward motivating patients to stick with a health regime. Unfortunately, stereotypes can lead to misdiagnosis. For example, it is estimated that about 10 percent of older patients diagnosed with dementia are actually depressed or suffering from some other psychological illness (Berger, 2005). The failure to recognize and treat psychological problems in older patients may be one consequence of such stereotypes.

Primary aging refers to the inevitable changes associated with aging (Busse, 1969). These changes include changes in the skin and hair, height and weight, hearing loss, and eye disease. However, some of these changes can be reduced by limiting exposure to the sun, eating a nutritious diet, and exercising.

Skin and hair change as we age. The skin becomes drier, thinner, and less elastic as we age. Scars and imperfections become more noticeable as fewer cells grow underneath the surface of the skin. Exposure to the sun, or photoaging, accelerates these changes. Graying hair is inevitable. And hair loss all over the body becomes more prevalent.

Height and weight vary with age. Older people are more than an inch shorter than they were during early adulthood (Masoro in Berger, 2005). This is thought to be due to a settling of the vertebrae and a lack of muscle strength in the back. Older people weigh less than they did in mid-life. Bones lose density and can become brittle. This is especially prevalent in women. However, weight training can help increase bone density after just a few weeks of training.

Muscle loss occurs in late adulthood and is most noticeable in men as they lose muscle mass. Maintaining strong leg and heart muscles is important for independence. Weight-lifting, walking, swimming, or engaging in other cardiovascular exercises can help strengthen the muscles and prevent atrophy.

Visual Problems: The majority of people over 65 have some difficulty with vision, but most is easily corrected with prescriptive lenses. Three percent of those 65 to 74 and 8 percent of those 75 and older have hearing or vision limitations that hinder activity. The most common causes of vision loss or impairment are glaucoma, cataracts, age-related macular degeneration, and diabetic retinopathy (He et al., 2005).

Hearing Loss is experienced by 30 percent of people age 70 and older. Almost half of people over 85 have some hearing loss (He et al., 2005). Among those who are in nursing homes, rates are higher. Older adults are more likely to seek help with vision impairment than with hearing loss, perhaps due to the stereotype that older people who have difficulty hearing are also less mentally alert. Being unable to hear causes people to withdraw from conversation and others to ignore them or shout. Unfortunately, shouting is usually high pitched and can be harder to hear than lower tones. The speaker may also begin to use a patronizing form of 'baby talk' known as **elderspeak** (See et al., 1999). This language reflects the stereotypes of older adults as being dependent, demented, and childlike. Image others speaking to you in that way. How would you feel? I am reminded of a man dying at home and a hospice worker, on shift for the first time, comes to his bedside and shouts, "Hi, baby. Want me to rub your little feet?" His response was an indignant look of disapproval.

Hearing loss is more prevalent in men than women. And it is experienced by more white, non-Hispanics than by Black men and women. Smoking, middle ear infections, and exposure to loud noises increase hearing loss.

In summary, primary aging can be compensated for through exercise, corrective lenses, nutrition, and hearing aids. And, more importantly, by reducing stereotypes about aging, people of age can maintain self-respect, recognize their own strengths, and count on receiving the respect and social inclusion they deserve.

Secondary Aging

Secondary aging refers to changes that are caused by illness or disease. These illnesses reduce independence, impact quality of life, affect family members and other caregivers, and bring financial burden. Some of the most prevalent illnesses that cause impairment are discussed below.

Arthritis: This is the leading cause of disability in older adults. Arthritis results in swelling of the joints and connective tissue that limits mobility. Arthritis is more common among women than men and increases with age. About 19.3 percent of people over 75 are disabled with arthritis; 11.4 percent of people between 65 and 74 experience this disability.

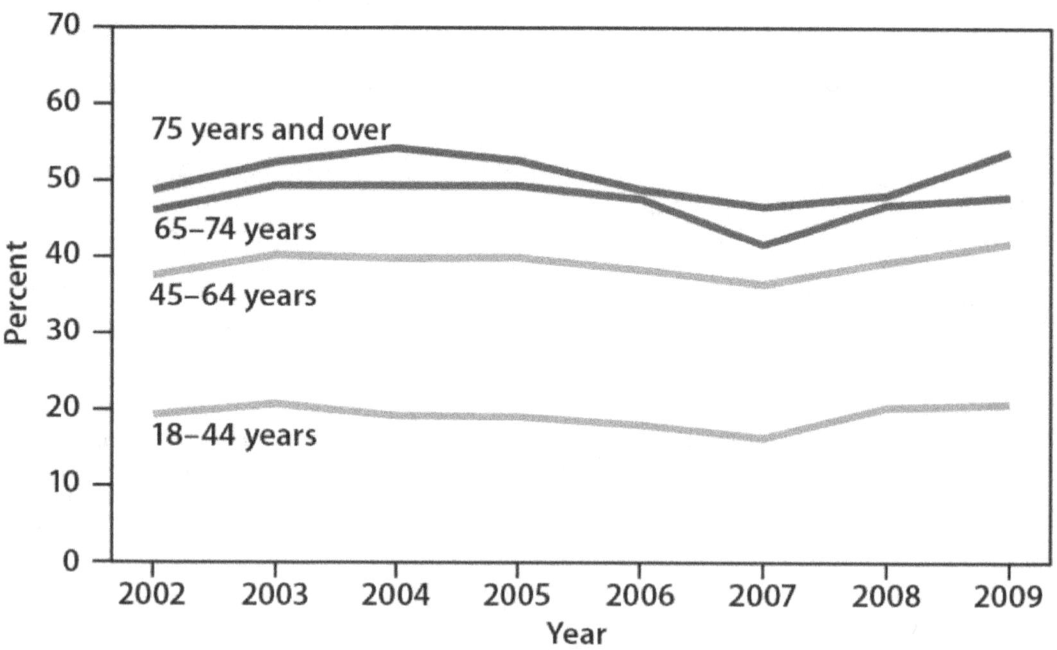

SOURCE: CDC/NCHS, *Health, United States, 2010*, Figure 7. Data from the National Health Interview Survey.

Hypertension: Hypertension or high blood pressure and associated heart disease and circulatory conditions increase with age. Hypertension disables 11.1 percent of 65 to 74 year olds and 17.1 percent of people over 75. Rates are higher among women and Blacks. Rates are highest for women over 75.

Heart Disease and Stroke: Coronary disease and stroke are higher among older men than women. The incidence of stroke is lower than that of coronary disease.

Diabetes: In 2008, 27 percent of those 65 and older had diabetes. Rates are higher among Mexican origin individuals and Blacks than non-Hispanic whites. The treatment for diabetes includes dietary changes, increasing physical activity, weight loss for those who are overweight, and medication (National Institute on Aging, 2011).

Diabetes prevalence

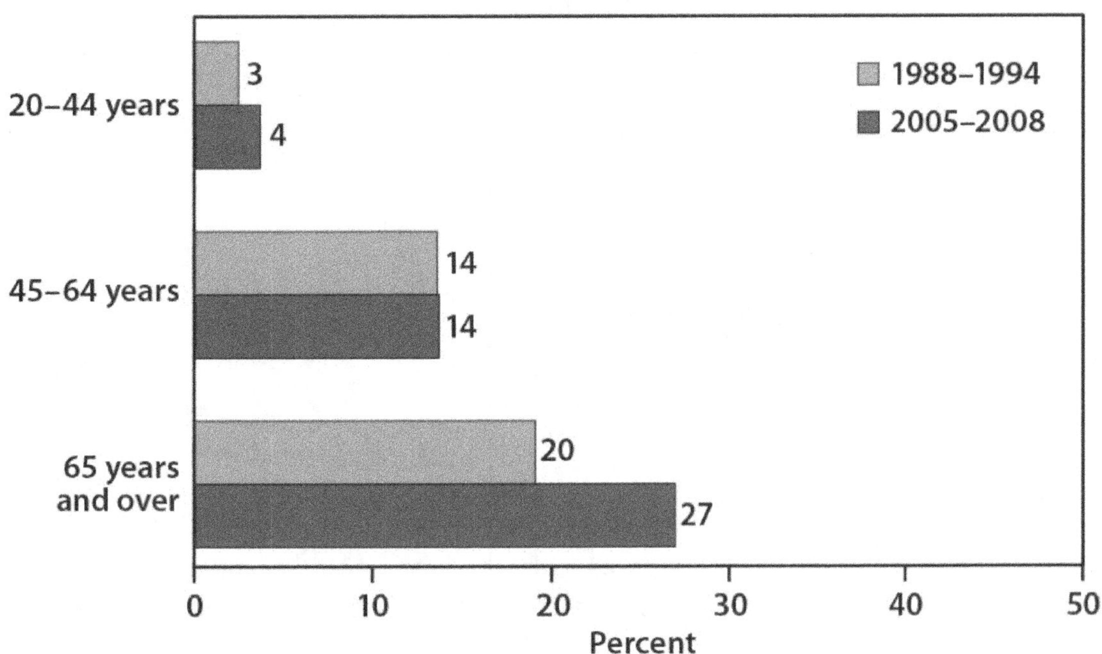

SOURCE: CDC/NCHS, *Health, United States, 2010*, Figure 5. Data from the National Health and Nutrition Examination Survey.

Cancer: Men over 75 have the highest rates of cancer at 28 percent. Women 65 and older have rates of 17 percent. Rates for older non-Hispanic Whites are twice as high as for Hispanics and non-Hispanic Blacks. The most common types of cancer found in men are prostate and lung cancer. Breast and lung cancer are the most common forms in women.

Respondent-reported lifetime cancer prevalence

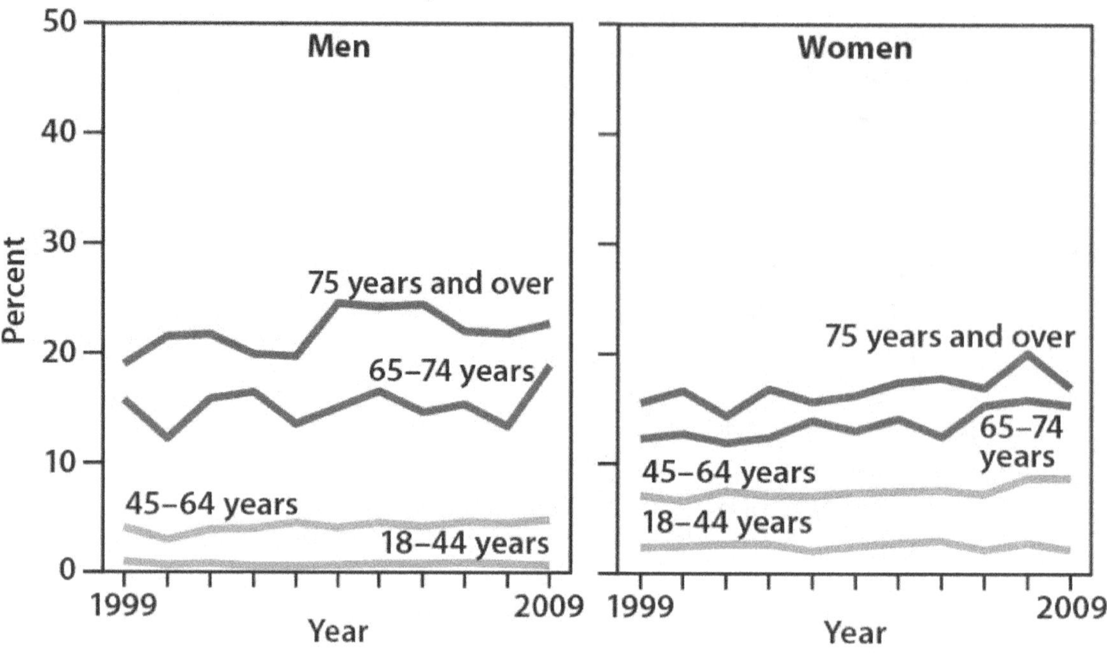

SOURCE: CDC/NCHS, *Health, United States, 2010*, Figure 4. Data from the National Health Interview Survey.

Osteoporosis: Osteoporosis increases with age as bones become brittle and lose minerals. Bone loss is four times more likely in women than in men and becomes even more prevalent in women 85 and older. Whites suffer osteoporosis more than do non-Hispanic Blacks.

Alzheimer's disease: Between 2.4 and 5.1 million people in the United States suffer with Alzheimer's disease (AD) (National Institute on Aging, 2011). This disease is not becomes more prevalent with age, but is not inevitable. This typically appears after age 60 but develops slowly for years before it's appearance. Social support, and aerobic exercise can reduce the risk of Alzheimer's disease. As the large cohort of Baby Boomers begins turning 65 in 2011, the number of cases of Alzheimer's disease is expected to increase dramatically. Where will these people receive care? Seventy percent of AD patients are cared for in the home. Such care can be emotionally, financially, and physically stressful. Most AD patients live 8 to 10 years with the disease and long-term care costs an average of $174,000 per patient (He et al., 2005).

Normal Aging

The Baltimore Longitudinal Study on Aging (2006) began in 1958 and has traced the aging process in 1,400 people from age 20 to 90. Researchers from the BLSA have found that the aging process varies significantly from individual to individual and from one organ system to another. Kidney function may deteriorate earlier in some individuals. Bone strength declines more rapidly in others. Much of this is determined by genetics, lifestyle, and disease. However, some generalizations about the aging process have been found:

- Heart muscles thicken with age
- Arteries become less flexible
- Lung capacity diminishes
- Brain cells lose some functioning but new neurons can also be produced
- Kidneys become less efficient in removing waste from the blood
- The bladder loses its ability to store urine
- Body fat stabilizes and then declines

- Muscle mass is lost without exercise
- Bone mineral is lost. Weight bearing exercise slows this down.

Theories of Aging

Why do we age?

There are a number of attempts to explain why we age and many factors that contribute to aging. Genetics, diet, lifestyle, activity, and exposure to pollutants all play a role in the aging process.

Cell Life

Cells divide a limited number of times and then stop. This phenomenon, known as the Hayflick limit, is evidenced in cells studied in test tubes which divide about 50 times before becoming senescent. Senescent cells do not die. They simply stop replicating. Senescent cells can help limit the growth of other cells which may reduce risk of developing tumors when younger, but can alter genes later in life and result in promoting the growth of tumors as we age (Dollemore, 2006). Limited cell growth is attributed to telomeres which are the tips of the protective coating around chromosomes. Each time cells replicate, the telomere is shortened. Eventually, loss of telomere length is thought to create damage to chromosomes and produce cell senescence.

Biochemistry and Aging

Free Radical Theory: As we metabolize oxygen, mitochondria in the cells convert oxygen to adenosine triphosphate (ATP) which provides energy to the cell. Unpaired electrons are a by product of this process and these unstable electrons cause cellular damage as they find other electrons with which to bond. These free radicals have some benefits and are used by the immune system to destroy bacteria. However, cellular damage accumulates and eventually reduces functioning of organs and systems. Many food products and vitamin supplements are promoted as age-reducing. Antioxidant drugs have been shown to increase the longevity in nematodes (small worms), but the ability to slow the aging process by introducing antioxidants in the diet is still controversial.

Protein Crosslinking: This theory focuses on the role blood sugar, or glucose, plays in the aging of cells. Glucose molecules attach themselves to proteins and form chains or crosslinks. These crosslinks reduce the flexibility of tissue and tissue become stiff and loses functioning. The circulatory system becomes less efficient as the tissue of the heart, arteries and lungs lose flexibility. And joints grow stiff as glucose combines with collegen. (To conduct your own demonstration of this process, take a piece of meat and place it in a hot skillet. The outer surface of the meat will caramelize and the tissue will become stiff and hard.)

DNA Damage: As we live, DNA is damaged by environmental factors such as toxic agents, pollutants, and sun exposure (Dollemore, 2006). This results in deletions of genetic material, and mutations in the DNA that is duplicated in new cells. The accumulation of these errors results in reduced functioning in cells and tissues.

Decline in the Immune System: As we age, B-lymphocytes and T-lymphocytes become less active. These cells are crucial to our immune system as they secrete antibodies and directly attack infected cells. The thymus, where T-cells are manufactured, shrinks as we age. This reduces our body's ability to fight infection Berger, 2005).
CC licensed content, Shared previously

- Psyc 200 Lifespan Psychology. **Authored by**: Laura Overstreet. **Located at**: http://opencourselibrary.org/econ-201/. **License**: *CC BY: Attribution*

Cognitive Development

How does aging affect memory?

The Sensory Register

Aging may create small decrements in the sensitivity of the sensory register. And, to the extent that a person has a more difficult time hearing or seeing, that information will not be stored in memory. This is an important point, because many older people assume that if they cannot remember something, it is because their memory is poor. In fact, it may be that the information was never seen or heard.

The Working Memory

Older people have more difficulty using memory strategies to recall details (Berk, 2007). As we age, the working memory loses some of its capacity. This makes it more difficult to concentrate on more than one thing at a time or to keep remember details of an event. However, people compensate for this by writing down information and avoiding situations where there is too much going on at once to focus on a particular cognitive task.

The Long-Term Memory

This type of memory involves the storage of information for long periods of time. Retrieving such information depends on how well it was learned in the first place rather than how long it has been stored. If information is stored effectively, an older person may remember facts, events, names and other types of information stored in long-term memory throughout life. The memory of adults of all ages seems to be similar when they are asked to recall names of teachers or classmates. And older adults remember more about their early adulthood and adolescence than about middle adulthood (Berk, 2007). Older adults retain semantic memory or the ability to remember vocabulary.

Younger adults rely more on mental rehearsal strategies to store and retrieve information. Older adults focus rely more on external cues such as familiarity and context to recall information (Berk, 2007). And they are more likely to report the main idea of a story rather than all of the details (Jepson & Labouvie-Vief, in Berk, 2007).

A positive attitude about being able to learn and remember plays an important role in memory. When people are under stress (perhaps feeling stressed about memory loss), they have a more difficult time taking in information because they are preoccupied with anxieties. Many of the laboratory memory tests require compare the performance of older and younger adults on timed memory tests in which older adults do not perform as well. However, few real life situations require speedy responses to memory tasks. Older adults rely on more meaningful cues to remember facts and events without any impairment to everyday living.

New Research on Aging and Cognition

Can the brain be trained in order to build cognitive reserve to reduce the effects of normal aging? ACTIVE (Advanced Cognitive Training for Independent and Vital Elderly), a study conducted between 1999 and 2001 in which 2,802 individuals age 65 to 94, suggests that the answer is "yes". These participants (26 percent who were African-American) received 10 group training sessions and 4 follow up sessions to work on tasks of memory, reasoning, and speed of processing. These mental workouts improved cognitive functioning even 5 years later. Many of the participants believed that this improvement could be seen in everyday tasks as well (Tennstedt, Morris, et al, 2006). Learning new things, engaging in activities that are considered challenging, and being physically active at any age may build a reserve to minimize the effects of primary aging of the brain.

Wisdom

Wisdom is the ability to use common sense and good judgment in making decisions. A wise person is insightful and has knowledge that can be used to overcome obstacles in living. Does aging bring wisdom? While living longer brings experience, it does not always bring wisdom. Those who have had experience helping others resolve problems in living and those who have served in leadership positions seem to have more wisdom. So it is age combined with a certain type of experience that brings wisdom. However, older adults do have greater emotional wisdom or the ability to empathize with and understand others.

Problem Solving

Problem solving tasks that require processing non-meaningful information quickly (a kind of task that might be part of a laboratory experiment on mental processes) declines with age. However, real life challenges facing older adults do not rely on speed of processing or making choices on one's own. Older adults are able to make resolve everyday problems by relying on input from others such as family and friends. And they are less likely than younger adults to delay making decisions on important matters such as medical care (Strough et al., 2003; Meegan & Berg, 2002).

Abnormal Loss of Cognitive Functioning During Late Adulthood

Dementia refers to severely impaired judgment, memory or problem-solving ability. It can occur before old age and is not an inevitable development even among the very old. Dementia can be caused by numerous diseases and circumstances, all of which result in similar general symptoms of impaired judgment, etc. Alzheimer's disease is the most common form of dementia and is incurable. But there are also nonorganic causes of dementia that can be prevented. Malnutrition, alcoholism, depression, and mixing medications can result in symptoms of dementia. If these causes are properly identified, they can be treated. Cerebral vascular disease can also reduce cognitive functioning.

Delirium is a sudden experience of confusion experienced by some older adults. Read the article and listen to the story, Treating Delirium: An Often Missed Diagnosis, for more information on treating delirium and the possible links between delirium and Alzheimer's Disease.

Psychosocial Development

Integrity vs. Despair

How do people cope with old age? Erikson (1980) believed that late adulthood is a time for making sense out of one's life, finding meaning to one's existence, and adjusting to inevitable death. He called this stage integrity vs. despair. Imagine being able to look back on life with the sense that if you had a chance to do it over again; you would probably make many of the same choices. Of course, life does not typically involve perfect choices. But a sense of contentment and acceptance, understanding and tolerance of others are important features of integrity. Bitterness and resentments in relationships and life events can bring a sense of despair at the end of life.

Disengagement vs. Activity

Disengagement theory (Cummings & Henry, 1961) suggests that during late adulthood, the individual and society mutually withdraw. Older people become more isolated from others and less concerned or involved with life in general. This once popular theory is now criticized as being ageist and used in order to justify treating older adults as second class citizens. **Activity theory** suggests that people are barred form meaningful experiences as they age. But older adults continue to want to remain active and work toward replacing opportunities lost with new ones. **Continuity theory** suggests that as people age, they continue to view the self in much the same way as they did when they were younger. Their approach to problems, goals, and situations is much the same as it was before. They are the same individuals, but simply in older bodies. Consequently, older adults continue to maintain their identity even as they give up previous roles. For example, a retired Coast Guard commander attends reunions with shipmates, stays interested in new technology for home use, is meticulous in the jobs he does for friends or at church, and displays mementos of life on the ship. He is able to maintain a sense of self as a result. We do not give up who we are as we age. Hopefully, we are able to share these aspects of our identity with others throughout life. Focusing on what a person can do and pursuing those interests and activities is one way to optimize and maintain self-identity.

Generativity in Late Adulthood

People in late adulthood continue to be productive in many ways. These include work, education, volunteering, family life, and intimate relationships.

Productivity in Work

Some continue to be productive in work. Mandatory retirement is now illegal in the United States. However, we find that many do choose retirement by age 65 and most leave work by choice. Those who do leave by choice adjust to retirement more easily. Chances are, they have prepared for a smoother transition by gradually giving more attention to an avocation or interest as they approach retirement. And they are more likely to be financially ready to retire. Those who must

leave abruptly for health reasons or because of layoffs or downsizing have a more difficult time adjusting to their new circumstances. Men, especially, can find unexpected retirement difficult. Women may feel less of an identify loss after retirement because much of their identity may have come from family roles as well. But women tend to have poorer retirement funds accumulated from work and if they take their retirement funds in a lump sum (be that from their own or from a deceased husband's funds), are more at risk of outliving those funds. Women need better financial retirement planning.

Sixteen percent of adults over 65 were in the labor force in 2008 (U. S. Census Bureau 2011). Globally, 6.2 percent are in the labor force and this number is expected to reach 10.1 million by 2016. Many adults 65 and older continue to work either full-time or part-time either for income or pleasure or both. In 2003, 39 percent of full-time workers over 55 were women over the age of 70; 53 percent were men over 70. This increase in numbers of older adults is likely to mean that more will continue to part of the workforce in years to come. (He et al., article, U. S. Census, 2005).

Education

Twenty percent of people over 65 have a bachelors or higher degree. And over 7 million people over 65 take adult education courses (U. S. Census Bureau, 2011). Lifelong learning through continuing education programs on college campuses or programs known as "Elderhostels" which allow older adults to travel abroad, live on campus and study provide enriching experiences. Academic courses as well as practical skills such as computer classes, foreign languages, budgeting, and holistic medicines are among the courses offered. Older adults who have higher levels of education are more likely to take continuing education. But offering more educational experiences to a diverse group of older adults, including those who are institutionalized in nursing homes can bring enhance the quality of life.

Volunteering: Face-to-face and Virtually

About 40 percent of older adults are involved in some type of structured, face-to-face, volunteer work. But many older adults, about 60 percent, engage in a sort of informal type of volunteerism helping out neighbors or friends rather than working in an organization (Berger, 2005). They may help a friend by taking them somewhere or shopping for them, etc. Some do participate in organized volunteer programs but interestingly enough, those who do tend to work part-time as well. Those who retire and do not work are less likely to feel that they have a contribution to make. (It's as if when one gets used to staying at home, their confidence to go out into the world diminishes.) And those who have recently retired are more likely to volunteer than those over 75 years of age.

New opportunities exist for older adults to serve as virtual volunteers by dialoguing online with others from around their world and sharing their support, interests, and expertise. According to an article from AARP (American Association of Retired Persons), virtual volunteerism has increased from 3,000 in 1998 to over 40,000 participants in 2005. These volunteer opportunities range from helping teens with their writing to communicating with 'neighbors' in villages of developing countries. Virtual volunteering is available to those who cannot engage in face-to-face interactions and opens up a new world of possibilities and ways to connect, maintain identity, and be productive (Uscher, 2006).

Religious Activities

People tend to become more involved in prayer and religious activities as they age as well. This provides a social network as well as a belief system that combats the fear of death. It provides a focus for volunteerism and other activities as well. For example, one elderly woman prides herself on knitting prayer shawls that are given to those who are sick. Another serves on the alter guild and is responsible for keeping robes and linens clean and ready for communion.

Political Activism

The elderly are very politically active. They have high rates of voting and engage in letter writing to congress on issues that not only affect them, but on a wide range of domestic and foreign concerns. In the 2008 election, 70 percent of people 65 and older voted. This group tied with 45-65 year olds as having the highest voter turnout (U. S. Census Bureau, 2011).
CC licensed content, Shared previously

- Psyc 200 Lifespan Psychology. **Authored by**: Laura Overstreet. **Located at**: http://opencourselibrary.org/econ-201/. **License**: *CC BY: Attribution*

Relationships

Grandparenting

Grandparenting typically begins in midlife rather than late adulthood, but because people are living longer, they can anticipate being grandparents for longer periods of time. Cherlin and Furstenberg (1986) describe three styles of grandparents:

1. Remote: These grandparents rarely see their grandchildren. Usually they live far away from the grandchildren, but may also have a distant relationship. Contact is typically made on special occasions such as holidays or birthdays. Thirty percent of the grandparents studied by Cherlin and Furstenberg were remote.

2. Companionate Grandparents: Fifty-five percent of grandparents studied were described as "companionate". These grandparents do things with the grandchild but have little authority or control over them. They prefer to spend time with them without interfering in parenting. They are more like friends to their grandchildren.

3. Involved Grandparents: Fifteen percent of grandparents were described as "involved". These grandparents take a very active role in their grandchild's life. They children might even live with the grandparent. The involved grandparent is one who has frequent contact with and authority over the grandchild.

An increasing number of grandparents are raising grandchildren today. Issues such as custody, visitation, and continued contact between grandparents and grandchildren after parental divorce are contemporary concerns.

Marriage and Divorce

Fifty-six percent of people over 65 are married. The majority of older men and just over 40 percent of older women are married (He et al., 2005). Seven percent of older men and 9 percent of older women are divorced and about 4 percent of older adults have never married. Many married couples feel their marriage has improved with time and the emotional intensity and level of conflict that might have been experienced earlier, has declined. This is not to say that bad marriages become good ones over the years, but that those marriages that were very conflict-ridden may no longer be together, and that many of the disagreement couples might have had earlier in their marriages may no longer be concerns. Children have grown and the division of labor in the home has probably been established. Men tend to report being satisfied with marriage more than do women. Women are more likely to complain about caring for a spouse who is ill or accommodating a retired husband and planning activities. Older couples continue to engage in sexual activity, but with less focus on intercourse and more on cuddling, caressing, and oral sex (Carroll, 2007).

Divorce after long-term marriage does occur, but is not very common. However, with the number of older adults on the rise, the divorce rate is likely to increase. A longer life expectancy and the expectation of happiness cause some older couples to begin a new life after divorce after 65. Consider Betty who divorced after 40 years of marriage. Her marriage had never been ideal but she stuck with it hoping things would improve and because she didn't want to hurt her husband's reputation (he was in a job in which divorce was frowned upon). But she always hoped for more freedom and happiness in life and once her family obligations were no longer as great (the children and grandchildren were on their own), she and her husband divorced. She characterized this as an act of love in that both she and her ex-husband were able to pursue their dreams in later life (Author's notes). Older adults who have been divorce since midlife tend to have settled into comfortable lives and, if they have raised children, to be proud of their accomplishments as single parents.

Widowhood

Twenty-nine percent of people over 65 are widowed (U. S. Census Bureau, 2011). The death of a spouse is one of life's most disruptive experiences. It is especially hard on men who lose their wives. Often widowers do not have a network of friends or family members to fall back on and may have difficulty expressing their emotions to facilitate grief. Also, they may have been very dependent on their mates for routine tasks such as cooking, cleaning, etc. In addition, they typically expect to precede their wives in death and by losing a wife, have to adjust to something unexpected. However, if a man can adjust, he will find that he is in great demand, should he decide to remarry.

Widows may have less difficulty because they do have a social network and can take care of their own daily needs. They may have more difficulty financially if their husband's have handled all the finances in the past. They are much less likely to remarry because many do not wish to and because there are fewer men available. At 65, there are 73 men to every 100 women. The sex ratio becomes even further imbalanced at 85 with 48 men to every 100 women (U. S. Census Bureau, 2011).

Loneliness or solitude? Loneliness is a discrepancy between the social contact a person has and the contacts a person wants (Brehm et al., 2002). It can result from social or emotional isolation. Women tend to experience loneliness as a result of social isolation; men from emotional isolation. Loneliness can be accompanied by a lack of self-worth, impatience, desperation, and depression. This can lead to suicide, particularly in older, white, men who have the highest suicide rates of any age group, higher than Blacks, and higher than for females. Rates of suicide continue to climb and peaks in males after age 85 (National Center for Health Statistics, CDC, 2002).

Being alone does not always result in loneliness. For some, it means solitude. Solitude involves gaining self-awareness, taking care of the self, being comfortable alone, and pursuing one's interests (Brehm et al., 2002). Winnie, aged 80, describes her life alone as comfortable and meaningful. "I'm up early to take care of my 3 year old great-granddaughter who stays with me. We play and have lunch and later her mother comes after her. I love to sing and sing all the time. I sing in the choir. . . I enjoy my mornings at the kitchen table with my coffee. And me and Coco (her dog) enjoy sitting in the sun." (Author's notes).

Single, Cohabiting, and Remarried Older Adults

About 4 percent of adults never marry. Many have long-term relationships, however. The never married tend to be very involved in family and care giving and do not appear to be particularly unhappy during late adulthood, especially if they have a healthy network of friends. Friendships tend to be an important influence in life satisfaction during late adulthood. Friends may be more influential than family members for many older adults. According to socioemotional selectivity theory, older adults become more selective in their friendships than when they were younger (Carstensen, Fung, & Charles, 2003). Friendships are not formed in order to enhance status or careers, and may be based purely on a sense of connection or the enjoyment of being together. Most elderly people have at least one close friend. These friends may provide emotional as well as physical support. Being able to talk with friends and rely on others is very important during this stage of life.

About 4 percent of older couples chose cohabitation over marriage (Chevan, 1996). As discussed in our lesson on early adulthood, these couples may prefer cohabitation for financial reasons, may be same-sex couples who cannot legally marry, or couples who do not want to marry because of previous dissatisfaction with marital relationships. There are between 1 and 3 million gay and lesbian older adults in America today and numbers will continue to increase (Cahill et al., 2000). These older adults have concerns over health insurance, being able to share living quarters in nursing homes and assisted living residences where staff members tend not to be accepting of homosexuality and bisexuality. SAGE (Senior Action in a Gay Environment) is an advocacy group working on remedying these concerns. Same-sex couples who have endured prejudice and discrimination through the years and can rely upon one another continue to have support through late adulthood. Those who are institutionalized, however, may find it harder to live together.

Couples, who remarry after midlife, tend to be happier in their marriages than in first marriage. These partners are likely to be more financially independent, have children who are grown, and enjoy a greater emotional wisdom that comes with experience.

Residence

Older adults do not typically relocate far from their previous places of residence during late adulthood. A minority lives in planned retirement communities that require residents to be of a certain age. However, many older adults live in age-segregated neighborhoods that have become segregated as original inhabitants have aged and children have moved on. A major concern in future city planning and development will be whether older adults wish to live in age integrated or age segregated communities.

Older Adults, Caregiving, and Long-Term Care

We previously noted the number of older adults who require long-term care and noted that the number increases with age. Most (70 percent) of older adults who require care receive that care in the home. Most are cared for by their spouse, or by a daughter or daughter-in-law. However, those who are not cared for at home are institutionalized. In 2008, 1.6 million out of the total 38.9 million Americans age 65 and older were nursing home residents (U. S. Census Bureau, 2011). Among 65-74, 11 per 1,000 adults aged 65 and older were in nursing homes. That number increases to 182 per 1,000 after age 85. More residents are women than men, and more are Black than white. As the population of those over 85 continues to increase, more will require nursing home care. Meeting the psychological and social as well as physical needs of nursing home residents is a growing concern. Rather than focusing primarily on food, hygiene, and medication, quality of life within these facilities is important. Residents of nursing homes are sometimes stripped of their identity as their personal possessions and reminders of their life are taken away. A rigid routine in which the residents have little voice can be alienating to an older adult. Routines that encourage passivity and dependence can be damaging to self-esteem and lead to further deterioration of health. Greater attention needs to be given to promoting successful aging within institutions.

Elderly Abuse

Nursing homes have been publicized as places where older adults are at risk of abuse. Abuse and neglect of nursing home residents is more often found in facilities that are run down and understaffed. However, older adults are more frequently abused by family members. The most commonly reported types of abuse are financial abuse and neglect. Victims are usually very frail and impaired and perpetrators are usually dependent on the victims for support. Prosecuting a family member who has financially abused a parent is very difficult. The victim may be reluctant to press charges and the court dockets are often very full resulting in long waits before a case is heard. Granny dumping or the practice of family members abandoning older family members with severe disabilities in emergency rooms is a growing problem. An estimated 100,000 and 200,000 are dumped each year (Tanne in Berk, 2007).

Conclusion

Greater understanding of the needs of older adults and more resources with which to provide for these needs are necessary to promote healthy aging in our growing population of older adults. We are coming to recognize the strengths of late adulthood and to move beyond the stereotypes of aging. This new appreciation of the value of older adults promises to lay the groundwork for a new approach to this period of life.
CC licensed content, Shared previously

- Psyc 200 Lifespan Psychology. **Authored by**: Laura Overstreet. **Located at**: http://opencourselibrary.org/econ-201/. **License**: *CC BY: Attribution*
- image of elderly couple. **Authored by**: Candida Performa. **Located at**: https://en.wikipedia.org/wiki/Remarriage#/media/File:It%27s_all_about_love.jpg. **License**: *CC BY: Attribution*

Module 11: Death and Dying

Introduction to Death and Dying

"Everything has to die," he told her during a telephone conversation.

"I want you to know how much I have enjoyed being with you, having you as my friend, and confidant and what a good father you have been to me. Thank you so much." she told him.

"You are entirely welcome." he replied.

He had known for years that smoking will eventually kill him. But he never expected that lung cancer would take his life so quickly or be so painful. A diagnosis in late summer was followed with radiation and chemotherapy during which time there were moments of hope interspersed with discussions about where his wife might want to live after his death and whether or not he would have a blood count adequate to let him precede with his next treatment. Hope and despair exist side by side. After a few months, depression and quiet sadness preoccupied him although he was always willing to relieve others by reporting that he 'felt a little better' if they asked. He returned home in January after one of his many hospital stays and soon grew worse. Back in the hospital, he was told of possible treatment options to delay his death. He asked his family members what they wanted him to do and then announced that he wanted to go home. He was ready to die. He returned home. Sitting in his favorite chair and being fed his favorite food gave way to lying in the hospital bed in his room and rejecting all food. Eyes closed and no longer talking, he surprised everyone by joining in and singing "Happy birthday" to his wife, son, and daughter-in-law who all had birthdays close together. A pearl necklace he had purchased 2 months earlier in case he died before his wife's birthday was retrieved and she told him how proud she would be as she wore it. He kissed her once and then again as she said goodbye. He died a few days later (Author's notes).

Photo Courtesy Robert Paul Young

A dying process that allows an individual to make choices about treatment, to say goodbyes and to take care of final arrangements is what many people hope for. Such a death might be considered a "good death." But of course, many deaths do not occur in this way. Not all deaths include such a dialogue with family members or being able to die in familiar surroundings. People die suddenly and alone. People leave home and never return. Children precede parents in death; wives precede husbands, and the homeless are bereaved by strangers.

In this lesson, we look at death and dying, grief and bereavement. We explore palliative care and hospice. And we explore funeral rites and the right to die.

REFERENCES:

Almost one million dying receive hospice care last year: New record. (2004). Senior Journal, (November 3, 2004). Retrieved from http://www.seniorjournal.com/NEWS/Eldercare/4-11-03HospiceMonth.htm

Attorney General vs. State of Oregon, Ruling of Supreme Court of the United States, § No. 04-623 (2007).

Berger, K. S. (2005). The developing person through the life span (6th ed.). New York: Worth.

End of Life Issues and Care — Brochure. (n.d.). American Psychological Association (APA). Retrieved May 07, 2011, from http://www.apa.org/topics/death/end-of-life.aspx

Kübler-Ross, E. (1969). On death and dying. [New York]: Macmillan.

Kübler-Ross, E. (1975). Death; The final stage of growth. Englewood Cliffs, N. J.: Prentice-Hall.

Kübler-Ross, E., & Kessler, D. (n.d.). On grief and grieving. New York: Schribner.

Living with grief: Diverstiy and end of life care. (2009). Hospital Foundation of America.

NCHS Pressroom – 2003 Fact Sheet – Hospice Care in the United States. (2003, August 21). Centers for Disease Control and Prevention. Retrieved May 07, 2011, from http://www.cdc.gov/nchs/pressroom/03facts/hospicecare.htm

Pattison, E. M. (1977). The experience of dying. Englewood Cliffs, N. J.: Prentice-Hall.

Stein, W. R. (2005, October 05). GONZALES V. OREGON. LII | Legal Information Institute at Cornell Law School. Retrieved May 07, 2011, from http://www.law.cornell.edu/supct/html/04-623.ZS.html

Survivor's Fact Sheet. (n.d.). American Association of Suicidology. Retrieved January 12, 2007, from http://www.suicidology.org/associations/1045/files/SurvivorsFactSheet.pdf

United States, Center for Disease Control. (2006, June 26). National Vital Statistics Reports, 54(19). Retrieved February 24, 2007, from http://www.cdc.gov/nchs/data/nvsr/nvsr54/nvsr54_19.pdf

United States, National Institute on Health. (2007, January 7). Hospitals Embrace the Hospice Model. Retrieved February 25, 2007, from http://www.nlm.nih.gov/medlineplus/news/fullstory_43523.html

Weitz, R. (2007). The sociology of health, illness, and health care: A critical approach (4th ed.). Belmont, CA: Thomson/Wadsworth.

WHO | What is the deadliest disease in the world? (n.d.). Retrieved May 07, 2011, from http://www.who.int/features/qa/18/en/
CC licensed content, Shared previously

Most Common Causes of Death

The United States

In 1900, the most common causes of death were infectious diseases which brought death quickly. Today, the most common causes of death are chronic diseases in which a slow and steady decline in health ultimately results in death. How might this impact the way we think of death, how we grieve, and the amount of control a person has over his or her own dying process?

The leading causes of death and number of deaths per category in 2004 in the United States are listed below. (National Vital Statistics Reports, Center for Disease Control, 2006).

- Heart Disease (654,092)
- Malignant neoplasms (cancer) (550,270)
- Cerebrovascular disease (stroke) (150,147)
- Chronic lower respiratory disease (123,884)
- Accidents (123,884)
- Diabetes Mellitus (106.694)
- Alzheimer's Disease (72,815)
- Influenza and Pneumonia (65,829)
- Nephritis (61,472)
- Septicemia (42,762)
- Suicide (33,464)
- Chronic Liver Disease (31,647)
- Hypertension and hypertensive renal disease (26,549)
- Parkinson's disease (22,953)
- Pneumonitis (18,018)

These numbers reflect a change in Alzheimer's disease which moved up from the 8th leading cause of death to the 7th and influenza and pneumonia moved down in rank from 7th to 8th.

Deadliest Diseases Worldwide

The top 12 deadliest diseases in the world are listed below along with the estimated number of deaths per cause. These figures are for 2002 and do not reflect deaths due to violence or suicide (World Health Organization, World Health Report, 2004). Notice the higher rates of death due to HIV/AIDS, perinatal conditions and diarrheal conditions than is found in the United States. Deaths of infants, young children, young mothers, and men and women in adolescence, young adulthood and midlife are more common. Many of these deaths are due to preventable causes. Ideas about the swiftness and unpredictable nature of death are certainly greater when living under such circumstances.

Heart disease (7.2 million)
Cerebrovascular disease (5.5 million)
Lower respiratory infections (3.9 million)
HIV/AIDS (2.8 million)
Chronic obstructive pulmonary (2.7 million)
Perinatal conditions (2.5 million)

Diarrheal diseases (1.8 million)
Tuberculosis (1.6 million)
Malaria (1.3 million)
Trachea, bronchus, lung cancers (1.2 million)
Road traffic accidents (1.2 million)
Diabetes mellitus (1 million)

A Comparison of Death by Age in the United States:

A comparison of the causes of death in the United States in the year 2007 for people in late adulthood and among all ages is given below. Notice that 29 percent of all deaths were of people ages 85 and older and that rates of death due to heart disease had declined since 1997, although heart disease is still the leading cause of death.

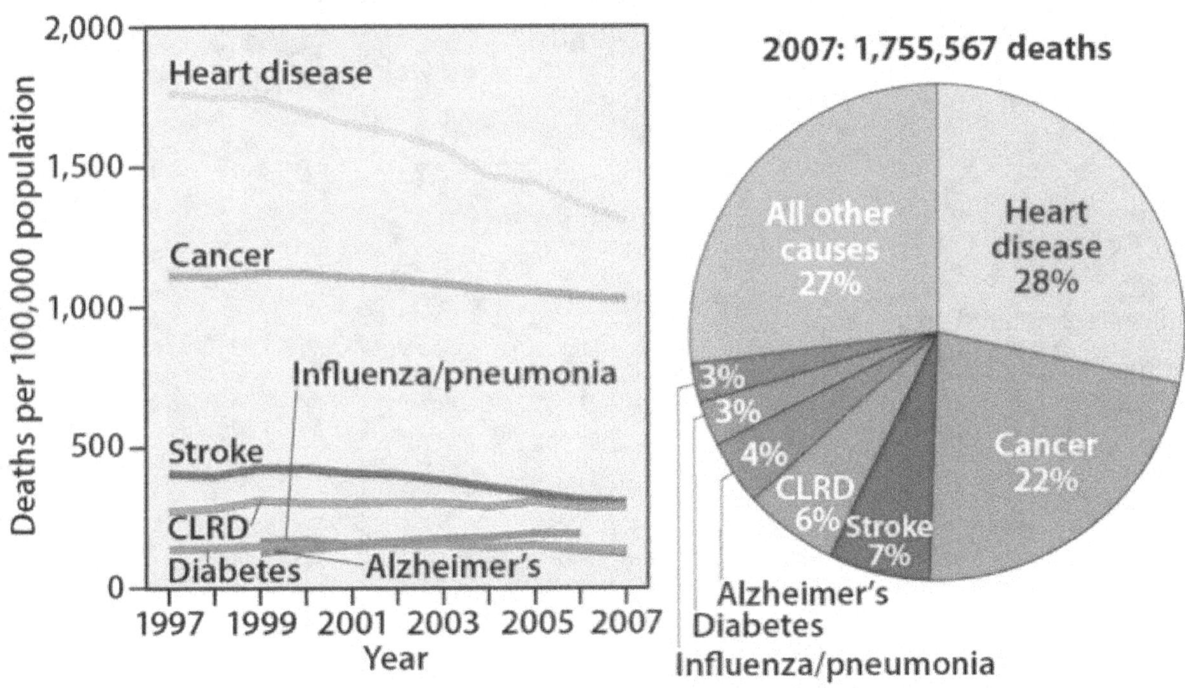

Deaths for all ages, 2007

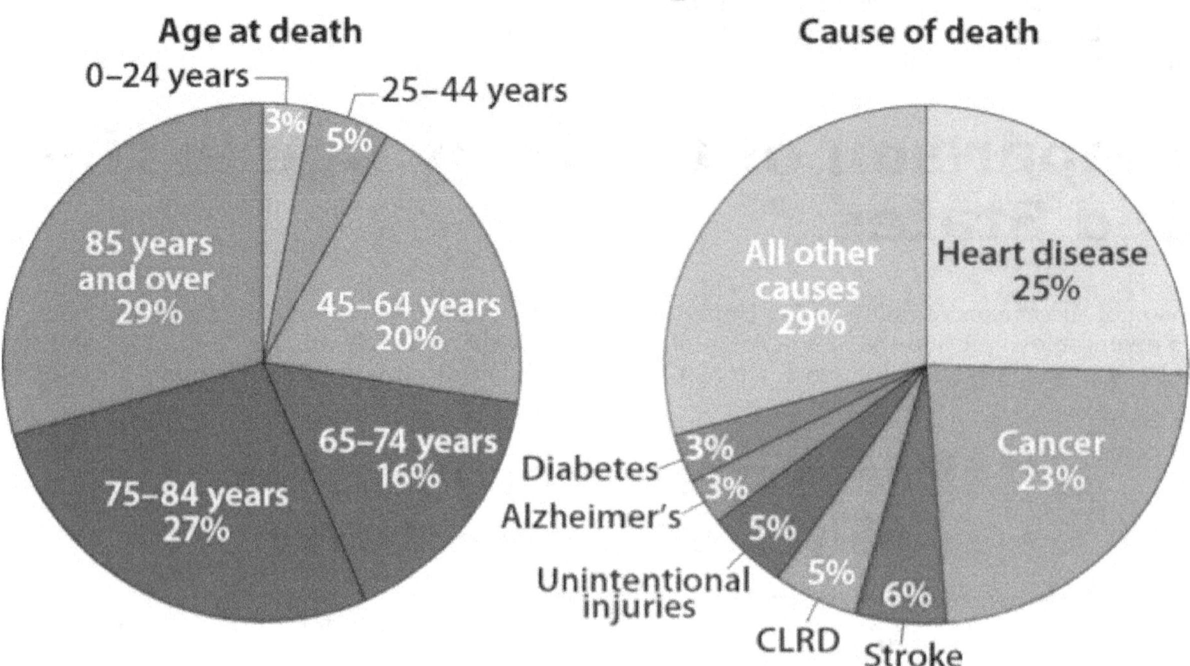

CC licensed content, Shared previously

- Psyc 200 Lifespan Psychology. **Authored by**: Laura Overstreet. **Located at**: http://opencourselibrary.org/econ-201/. **License**: *CC BY: Attribution*

The Process of Dying

Aspects of Death

One way to understand death and dying is to look more closely at physical death, psychological death, and social death. These deaths do not occur simultaneously. Rather, a person's physiological, social, and psychic death can occur at different times (Pattison, 1977).

Physiological death occurs when the vital organs no longer function. The digestive and respiratory systems begin to shut down during the gradual process of dying. A dying person no longer wants to eat as digestion slows and the digestive track loses moisture and chewing, swallowing, and elimination become painful processes. Circulation slows and mottling or the pooling of blood may be noticeable on the underside of the body appearing much like bruising. Breathing becomes more sporadic and shallow and may make a rattling sound as air travels through mucus filled passageways. The person often sleeps more and more and may talk less although continues to hear. The kinds of symptoms noted prior to death in patients under hospice care (care focused on helping patients die as comfortably as possible) is noted below.

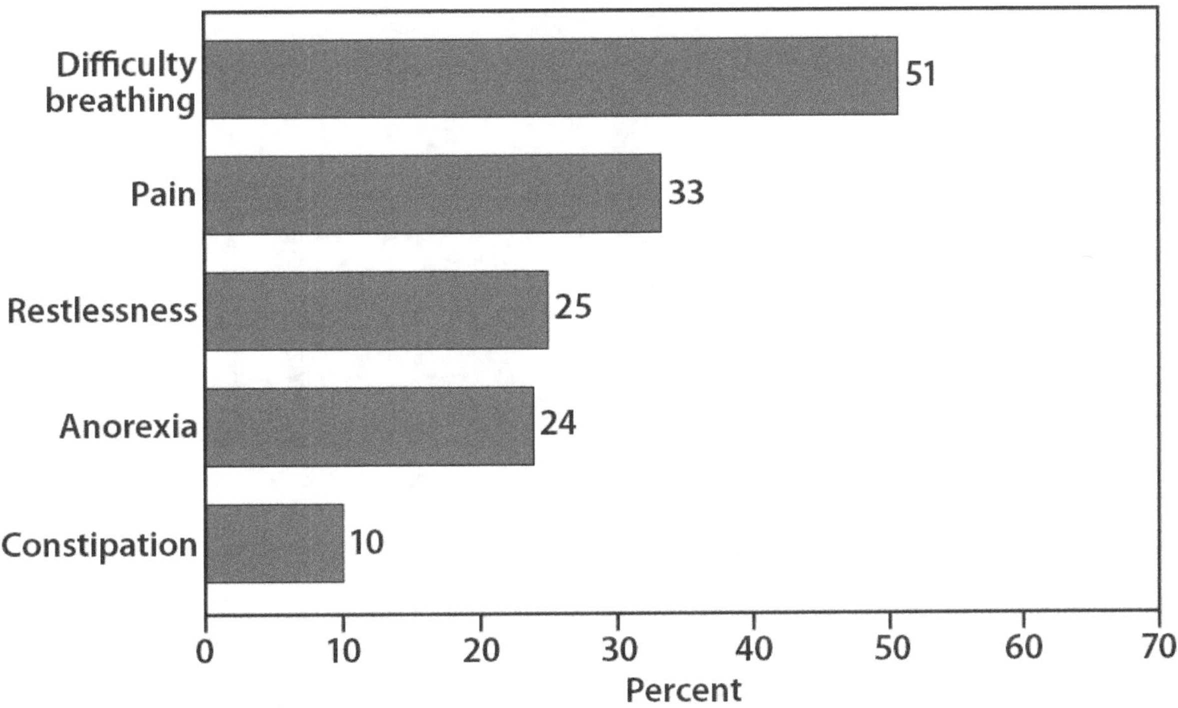

SOURCE: CDC/NCHS, *Health, United States, 2010*, Figure 40. Data from the National Home and Hospice Care Survey.

When a person no longer has brain activity, they are clinically dead. Physiological death may take 72 or fewer hours.

Social death begins much earlier than physiological death. Social death occurs when others begin to withdraw from someone who is terminally ill or has been diagnosed with a terminal illness. Those diagnosed with conditions such as AIDS or cancer may find that friends, family members, and even health care professionals begin to say less and visit less frequently. Meaningful discussions may be replaced with comments about the weather or other topics of light conversation. Doctors may spend less time with patients after their prognosis becomes poor. Why do others begin to withdraw? Friends and family members may feel that they do not know what to say or that they can offer no solutions to relieve suffering. They withdraw to protect themselves against feeling inadequate or from having to face the reality of death. Health professionals, trained to heal, may also feel inadequate and uncomfortable facing decline and death. A patient who is dying may be referred to as "circling the drain" meaning that they are approaching death. People in nursing homes may live as socially dead for years with no one visiting or calling. Social support is important for quality of life and those who experience social death are deprived from the benefits that come from loving interaction with others.

Psychic death occurs when the dying person begins to accept death and to withdraw from others and regress into the self. This can take place long before physiological death (or even social death if others are still supporting and visiting the dying person) and can even bring physiological death closer. People have some control over the timing of their death and can hold on until after important occasions or die quickly after having lost someone important to them. They can give up their will to live.
CC licensed content, Shared previously

Five Stages of Loss

Kubler-Ross (1969, 1975) describes five stages of loss experienced by someone who faces the news of their impending death. These "stages" are not really stages that a person goes through in order or only once; nor are they stages that occur with the same intensity. Indeed, the process of death is influenced by a person's life experiences, the timing of their death in relation to life events, the predictability of their death based on health or illness, their belief system, and their assessment of the quality of their own life. Nevertheless, these stages help us to understand and recognize some of what a dying person experiences psychologically. And by understanding, we are more equipped to support that person as they die.

Denial is often the first reaction to overwhelming, unimaginable news. Denial, or disbelief or shock, protects us by allowing such news to enter slowly and to give us time to come to grips with what is taking place. The person who receives positive test results for life-threatening conditions may question the results, seek second opinions, or may simply feel a sense of disbelief psychologically even though they know that the results are true.

Anger also provides us with protection in that being angry energizes us to fight against something and gives structure to a situation that may be thrusting us into the unknown. It is much easier to be angry than to be sad or in pain or depressed. It helps us to temporarily believe that we have a sense of control over our future and to feel that we have at least expressed our rage about how unfair life can be. Anger can be focused on a person, a health care provider, at God, or at the world in general. And it can be expressed over issues that have nothing to do with our death; consequently, being in this stage of loss is not always obvious.

Bargaining involves trying to think of what could be done to turn the situation around. Living better, devoting self to a cause, being a better friend, parent, or spouse, are all agreements one might willingly commit to if doing so would lengthen life. Asking to just live long enough to witness a family event or finish a task are examples of bargaining.

Depression is sadness and sadness is appropriate for such an event. Feeling the full weight of loss, crying, and losing interest in the outside world is an important part of the process of dying. This depression makes others feel very uncomfortable and family members may try to console their loved one. Sometimes hospice care may include the use of antidepressants to reduce depression during this stage.

Acceptance involves learning how to carry on and to incorporate this aspect of the life span into daily existence. Reaching acceptance does not in any way imply that people who are dying are happy about it or content with it. It means that they are facing it and continuing to make arrangements and to say what they wish to say to others. Some terminally ill people find that they live life more fully than ever before after they come to this stage.

We no longer think that there is a "right way" to experience the loss. People move through a variety of stages with different frequency and in various ways.

Palliative Care and Hospice

Kubler-Ross's work was introduced at a period in which the **hospice movement** began in the United States. This movement focused attention on caring for the dying. **Palliative care** focuses on providing comfort and relief from physical and emotional pain to patients throughout their illness even while being treated (NIH, 2007). Palliative care is part of hospice programs. Hospice involves caring for dying patients by helping them be as free from pain as possible, providing them with assistance to complete wills and other arrangements for their survivors, giving them social support through the psychological stages of loss, and helping family members cope with the dying process, grief, and bereavement. In order to enter hospice, a patient must be diagnosed as terminally ill with an anticipated death within 6 months. Most hospice care does not include medical treatment of disease or resuscitation although some programs administer curative care as well. The patient is allowed to go through the dying process without invasive treatments. Family members, who have agreed to put their loved one on hospice, may become anxious when the patient begins to experience the death. They may believe that feeding or breathing tubes will sustain life and want to change their decision. Hospice workers try to inform the family of what to expect and reassure them that much of what they see is a normal part of the dying process.

The early hospices established were independently operated and dedicated to giving patients as much control over their own death process as possible. Today, there are more than 4,000 hospice programs and over 1,000 of them are offered through hospitals. Hospice care was given to over 1 million patients in 2004 (NIH, 2007; Senior Journal, 2007). Although hospice care has become more widespread, these new programs are subjected to more rigorous insurance guidelines that dictate the types and amounts of medications used, length of stay, and types of patients who are eligible to receive hospice care (Weitz, 2007). Thus, more patients are being served, but providers have less control over the services they provide, and lengths of stay are more limited. Patients receive palliative care in hospitals and in their homes.

The majority of patients on hospice are cancer patients and typically do not enter hospice until the last few weeks prior to death. The average length of stay is less than 30 days and many patients are on hospice for less than a week (National Center for Health Statistics, 2003). Medications are rubbed into the skin or given in drop form under the tongue to relieve the discomfort of swallowing pills or receiving injections. A hospice care team includes a chaplain as well as nurses and grief counselors to assist spiritual needs in addition to physical ones. When hospice is administered at home, family members may also be part, and sometimes the biggest part, of the care team. Certainly, being in familiar surroundings is preferable to dying in an unfamiliar place. But about 60 to 70 percent of people die in hospitals and another 16 percent die in institutions such as nursing homes (APA Online, 2001). Most hospice programs serve people over 65; few programs are available for terminally ill children (Wolfe et al., in Berger, 2005).

Primary admission diagnosis of discharged hospice care patients

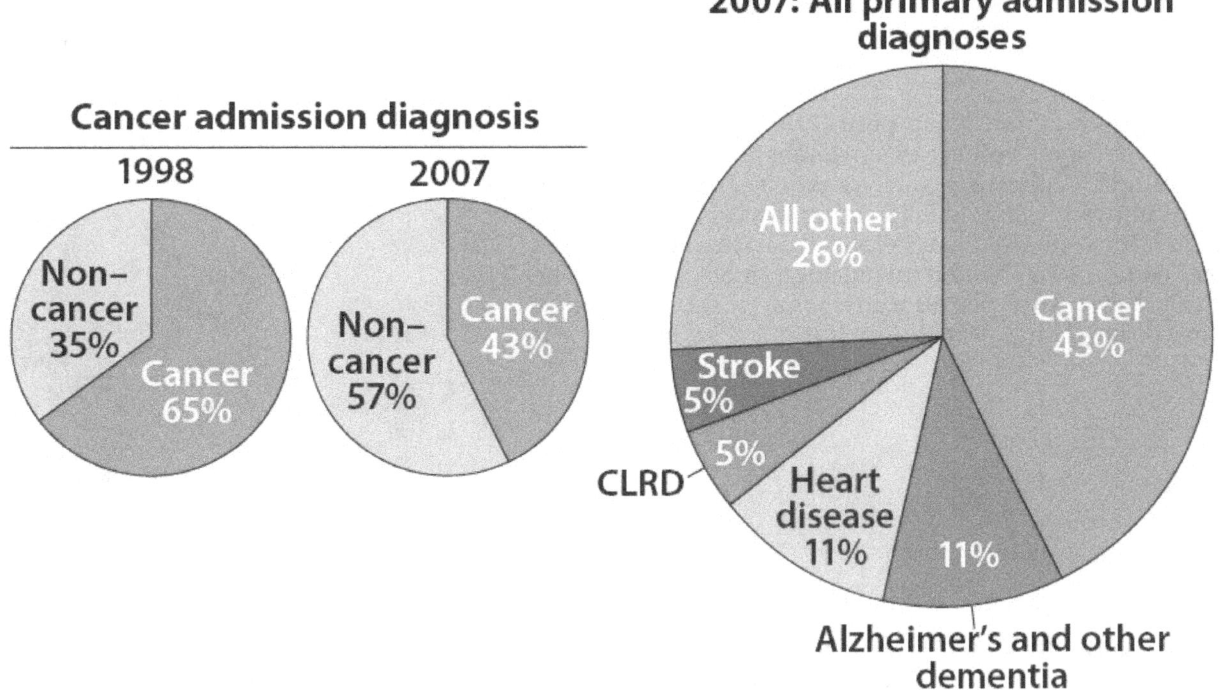

NOTE: CLRD is chronic lower respiratory diseases.
SOURCE: CDC/NCHS, *Health, United States, 2010*, Figure 38. Data from the National Home and Hospice Care Survey.

Dame Cicely Saunders founded the hospice movement in Great Britain and described the kinds of pain experienced by those who are dying and their families. These 7 Pains include emotional include physical pain, spiritual pain, intellectual pain, emotional pain, interpersonal pain, financial pain and bureaucratic pain. Hospice care focuses on alleviating physical pain and providing spiritual guidance. Those suffering from Alzheimer's also experience intellectual pain and frustration as they lose their ability to remember and recognize others. Depression, anger, and frustration are elements of emotional pain, and family members can have tensions that a social worker or clergy member may be able to help resolve. Many patients are concerned with the financial burden their care will create for family members. And bureaucratic pain is also suffered while trying to submit bills and get information about health care benefits or to complete requirements for other legal matters. All of these concerns can be addressed by hospice care teams. Learn more about Saunders in the link provided at the end of this lesson.

The Hospice Foundation of America notes that not all racial and ethnic groups feel the same way about hospice care. African-American families may believe that medical treatment should be pursued on behalf of an ill relative as long as possible and that only God can decide when a person dies. Chinese-American families may feel very uncomfortable discussing issues of death or being near the deceased family member's body. The view that hospice care should always be used is not held by everyone and health care providers need to be sensitive to the wishes and beliefs of those they serve (Hospital Foundation of America, 2009).
CC licensed content, Shared previously

- Psyc 200 Lifespan Psychology. **Authored by**: Laura Overstreet. **Located at**: http://opencourselibrary.org/econ-201/. **License**: *CC BY: Attribution*

Euthanasia

Euthanasia, or helping a person fulfill their wish to die, can happen in two ways: voluntary euthanasia and physician-assisted suicide. Voluntary euthanasia refers to helping someone fulfill their wish to die by acting in such a way to help that person's life end. This can be passive euthanasia such as no longer feeding someone or giving them food. Or it can be active euthanasia such as administering a lethal dose of medication to someone who wishes to die.

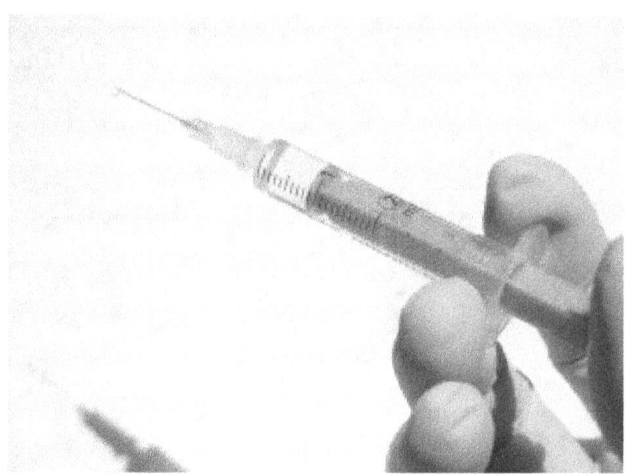

Physician-Assisted Suicide: Physician-assisted suicide occurs when a physician prescribes the means by which a person can end his or her own life. Physician-assisted suicide is legal in Oregon, the Netherlands, Switzerland, and Belgium. The Oregon Death with Dignity Act of 1997 grants physicians this right. Physician-assisted suicides, however, are rare.

A growing number of the population support physician-assisted suicide. In 2000, a ruling of the U. S. Supreme Court upheld the right of states to determine their laws on physician-assisted suicide despite efforts to limit physicians' ability to prescribe barbiturates and opiates for their patients requesting the means to end their lives. The position of the Supreme Court is that the debate concerning the morals and ethics surrounding the right to die is one that should be continued (Stein, 2000). As an increasing number of the population enters late adulthood, the emphasis on giving patients an active voice in determining certain aspects of their own death is likely.

Bereavement and Grief

Bereavement refers to outward expressions of grief. Mourning and funeral rites are expressions of loss that reflect personal and cultural beliefs about the meaning of death and the afterlife. When asked what type of funeral they would like to have, students responded in a variety of ways; each expressing both their personal beliefs and values and those of their culture.

I would like the service to be at a Baptist church, preferably my Uncle Ike's small church. The service should be a celebration of life . . .I would like there to be hymns sung by my family members, including my favorite one, "It is Well With my Soul". . .At the end, I would like the message of salvation to be given to the attendees and an alter call for anyone who would like to give their life to Christ. . .

I want a very inexpensive funeral-the bare minimum, only one vase of flowers, no viewing of the remains and no long period of mourning from my remaining family . . . funeral expenses are extremely overpriced and out of hand. . .

When I die, I would want my family members, friends, and other relatives to dress my body as it is usually done in my country, Ghana. Lay my dressed body in an open space in my house at the night prior to the funeral ceremony for my loved ones to walk around my body and mourn for me. . .

I would like to be buried right away after I die because I don't want my family and friends to see my dead body and to be scared.

In my family we have always had the traditional ceremony-coffin, grave, tombstone, etc. But I have considered cremation and still ponder which method is more favorable. Unlike cremation, when you are 'buried' somewhere and family members have to make a special trip to visit, cremation is a little more personal because you can still be in the home with your loved ones . . .

I would like to have some of my favorite songs played . . .I will have a list made ahead of time. I want a peaceful and joyful ceremony and I want my family and close friends to gather to support one another. At the end of the celebration, I want everyone to go to the Thirsty Whale for a beer and Spang's for pizza!

When I die, I want to be cremated . . . I want it the way we do it in our culture. I want to have a three day funeral and on the 4th day, it would be my burial/cremation day . . .I want everyone to wear white instead of black, which means they already let go of me. I also want to have a mass on my cremation day.

When I die, I would like to have a befitting burial ceremony as it is done in my Igbo customs. I chose this kind of funeral ceremony because that is what every average person wishes to have.

I want to be cremated . . . I want all attendees wearing their favorite color and I would like the song "Riders on the Storm" to be played . . .I truly hope all the attendees will appreciate the bass. At the end of this simple, short service, attendees will be given multi-colored helium filled balloons . . . released to signify my release from this earth. . .They will be invited back to the house for ice cream cones, cheese popcorn and a wide variety of other treats and much, much, much rock music . . .

I want to be cremated when I die. To me, it's not just my culture to do so but it's more peaceful to put my remains or ashes to the world. Let it free and not stuck in a casket.

Ceremonies provide survivors a sense of closure after a loss. These rites and ceremonies send the message that the death is real and allow friends and loved ones to express their love and duty to those who die. Under circumstances in which a person has been lost and presumed dead or when family members were unable to attend a funeral, there can continue to be a lack of closure that makes it difficult to grieve and to learn to live with loss. And although many people are still in shock when they attend funerals, the ceremony still provides a marker of the beginning of a new period of one's life as a survivor.

Grief is the psychological, physical, and emotional experience of loss. The five stages of loss are experienced by those who are in grief (Kubler-Ross & Kessler, 2005). Grief reactions vary depending on whether a loss was anticipated or unexpected, (parents do not expect to lose their children, for example), and whether or not it occurred suddenly or after a long illness, and whether or not the survivor feels responsible for the death. Struggling with the question of responsibility is particularly felt by those who lose a loved one to suicide. There are numerous survivors for every suicide resulting in 4.5 million survivors of suicide in the United States (American Association of Suicidology, 2007). These survivors may torment themselves with endless "what ifs" in order to make sense of the loss and reduce feelings of guilt. And family members may also hold one another responsible for the loss. The same may be true for any sudden or unexpected death making conflict an added dimension to grief. Much of this laying of responsibility is an effort to think that we have some control over these losses; the assumption being that if we do not repeat the same mistakes, we can control what happens in our life.

Anticipatory grief occurs when a death is expected and survivors have time to prepare to some extent before the loss. Anticipatory grief can include the same denial, anger, bargaining, depression, and acceptance experienced in loss. This can make adjustment after a loss somewhat easier, although the stages of loss will be experienced again after the death (Kubler-Ross & Kessler, 2005). A death after a long-term, painful illness may bring family members a sense of relief that the suffering is over. The exhausting process of caring for someone who is ill is over. **Disenfranchised grief** may be experienced by those who have to hide the circumstances of their loss or whose grief goes unrecognized by others. Loss of an ex-spouse, lover, or pet may be examples of disenfranchised grief.

Yet grief continues as long as there is a loss. It has been said that intense grief lasts about two years or less, but grief is felt throughout life. One loss triggers the feelings that surround another. People grieve with varied intensity throughout the remainder of their lives. It does not end. But it eventually becomes something that a person has learned to live with. As long as we experience loss, we experience grief (Kubler-Ross & Kessler, 2005).

There are layers of grief. Initial denial, marked by shock and disbelief in the weeks following a loss may become an expectation that the loved one will walk in the door. And anger directed toward those who could not save our loved one's life, may become anger that life did not turn out as we expected. There is no right way to grieve. A bereavement counselor expressed it well by saying that grief touches us on the shoulder from time to time throughout life.

Grief and mixed emotions go hand in hand. A sense of relief is accompanied by regrets and periods of reminiscing about our loved ones are interspersed with feeling haunted by them in death. Our outward expressions of loss are also sometimes contradictory. We want to move on but at the same time are saddened by going through a loved one's possessions and giving them away. We may no longer feel sexual arousal or we may want sex to feel connected and alive. We need others to befriend us but may get angry at their attempts to console us. These contradictions are normal and we need to allow ourselves and others to grieve in their own time and in their own ways.

The "death-denying, grief-dismissing world" is the modern world (Kubler-Ross & Kessler, 2005, p. 205). We are asked to grieve privately, quickly, and to medicate our suffering. Employers grant us 3 to 5 days for bereavement, if our loss is that of an immediate family member. And such leaves are sometimes limited to no more than one per year. Yet grief takes much longer and the bereaved are seldom ready to perform well on the job. Obviously life does have to continue. But Kubler-Ross and Kessler suggest that contemporary American society would do well to acknowledge and make more caring accommodations to those who are in grief. Listen to this story about Kubler-Ross and her life and work in the link below.

Conclusion

Death and grief are topics that are being given greater consideration. This trend should continue as the population "grays" and our awareness of natural disaster and war, both in the United States and throughout the world grows. Viewing death as an integral part of the lifespan will benefit those who are ill, those who are bereaved, and all of us as friends, caregivers, partners, family members and humans in a global society.